HUMAN CHOICE AND COMPUTERS

HUMAN CHOICE AND COMPUTERS

Proceedings of the IFIP Conference on
Human Choice and Computers
Vienna, April 1-5, 1974

Edited by

ENID MUMFORD

Manchester Business School, Manchester

and

HAROLD SACKMAN

The Rand Corporation, Santa Monica, California

1975

NORTH-HOLLAND PUBLISHING COMPANY – AMSTERDAM • OXFORD
AMERICAN ELSEVIER PUBLISHING COMPANY, INC. – NEW YORK

Library of Congress Catalog Card Number: 74-24343
North-Holland ISBN: 0 7204 2826 2
American Elsevier ISBN: 0 444 10774 6

Published by:
North-Holland Publishing Company – Amsterdam
North-Holland Publishing Company, Ltd. – Oxford

Sole distributors for the U.S.A. and Canada:
American Elsevier Publishing Company, Inc.
52 Vanderbilt Avenue
New York, N.Y. 10017

Printed in The Netherlands

PREFACE

This book is aimed at a broad audience. In addition to the computer/information scientists, social scientists, trade union professionals, and management scientists represented at the original conference, these proceedings are designed for professionals in other fields, for the student concerned with computers and society, and for the computer user in the broad sense of the term. In the limit, the eventual set of computer users will incorporate all levels of society as suggested by several papers in this volume. The language is basically non-technical and is generally suited for the educated layman. The original conference and this book have been constructed to appeal to a broad international audience.

The plan for the conference and the selection of papers was motivated by the belief that all levels of society should take stock of the growing use of computers in all walks of life and decide what it wants to do with computers for the benefits of everyone. Society should deliberately lead and direct the application of computers in the image of its most cherished values and ideals rather than be the unwitting victim of the vagaries of technology and the fluctuations of the market-place. Toward this end, the issue is deliberate human choice and continuing social accountability in determining the role of computers in social affairs.

The most difficult problem during the conference preparations was to find competent individuals who could bridge the gap between the human and the technical side of the computer and who were willing to serve on the Programme Committee, present a paper, or simply participate.

It very soon became apparent that the Programme Committee and speakers could only provide the initial trigger for the conference – the success would predominantly depend on the participants: their interaction and contribution. Therefore a major part of the available time was set aside for discussions in small groups consisting of representatives of the different fields of interest. These small group discussions proved very valuable and the summaries form an integral part of the results of this conference.

The organization of these proceedings reflects key areas of human choice that were highlighted in the conference. The four theme papers set the pace by considering philosophical, scientific, and applied challenges in human choice with computers. They collectively establish a framework for the conference and the proceedings with special emphasis on the interface between computers and the worker in the industrial setting.

The next group of chapters is concerned with management choice broadly considered. This covers various aspects of management science and system design, including analyses of man-computer behaviours, humanizing the system development process, the analysis of humanistic management in the computer milieu, and the differential handling of various classes of open and restricted information in large, computerized systems.

The next cluster of chapters focusses on choices open to trade unions with respect to growing computerization. Theoretical and applied aspects are reviewed, including reports on British and German trade union experiences with computer issues. These chapters address the challenge of the growing imbalance between management and labor in the use of computers.

The next portion of the book surveys the possibilities of democratic choice. The democracy theme is examined from the viewpoint of industrial democracy, community decision-making and with respect to competing political philosophies. The relation of privacy issues to democratic process is analyzed with respect to the conflicting requirements between society's need to know and the individuals need to withhold certain classes of information.

The next group of chapters covers a broad area of social choice. It ranges over the prospective roles of people and computers in increasingly computerized societies, to comparative analyses of different national approaches to various aspects of the computer/privacy issue, to the impact of multinational computers on the international scene.

The final chapter represents a synthesis of the results of the working groups of the conference as interpreted by the co-editors. It reviews basic agreements, disagreements and recommendations generated by the papers, the conference, and its aftermath.

The editors owe a special debt to Fred Margulies and Gerhard Chroust for facilitating liaison with the authors and publishers before and after the conference, and for numerous helpful observations and suggestions in the organization and content of this book. The international Programme Committee for the conference was instrumental in screening and selecting the diversified and balanced set of authors and topics that made the conference and this book possible. We are grateful to Prof. H. Zemanek, past president of IFIP, who provided the original inspiration for the conference, and who provided experienced guidance to the editors throughout all phases of this book. We are indeed indebted to the Austrian government which generously provided the funds and the stimulating intellectual setting in Vienna to support the conference and this book, and to the numerous members of the Austrian Organizing Committee. Our greatest obligation is to the contributing authors from many different countries who have given so much of their time and talent to help society to help itself in deciding how to apply computers to human affairs.

CONTENTS

THEME PAPERS:
ISSUES OF HUMAN CHOICE

E. Mumford and H. Sackman, eds., Human Choice and Computers
North-Holland Publishing Company (1975)

THE HUMAN BEING AND THE AUTOMATON
Selected Aspects of a Philosophy of Information Processing

HEINZ ZEMANEK

President of IFIP, Vienna, Austria

1. Introduction: The basic alternative

Twenty five years ago, Mr. Edmund C. Berkeley wrote a popular book on electronic computers with the title *Giant Brains or Machines that Think* (Berkeley, 49). This title had quite an impact on the cybernetic discussion of the nature of the computer and of the nature of man confronted with science and technology: is man a machine that thinks? Because if so, then the computer will soon outdate and outgrow its creator, the human being.

More than 100 years earlier, in 1843, the Viennese University Professor Joseph Petzval defined *pure mathematics* as *the perfection of a big and powerful thinking machine (Denkmaschine)* (Petzval, 1843). Since he had no computer for his portrait lense, his programmed thinking machines were soldiers, artillery mathematicians of the Austrian army. In Petzval's sense, the term *thinking machine* is acceptable, but *Giant Brains or Machines that Think* is not acceptable as a definition of the computer. The microphone is not an ear, the camera is not an eye – why should the computer be a brain? Computers do the machine version of thinking and that is a very special version of thinking. But Mr. Berkeley's book title indicates a tension of basic character and a field of fascinating problems. No machine before the computer has come as close to the human being and no machine before has invited so urgently a study of the nature of man and machine. The conference during this week is devoted to this field of problems – not to the philosophical issues, but to a series of practical questions: what is the interface between this most man-like machine and man? How should it be designed? What is the relationship between the technical information processing structures and the natural information processing streams? What is the impact of the interweaving of natural and technical information systems on man and society? Since the conference as such will deal with the practical problems, it makes sense to treat a few philosophical aspects in this opening paper.

Of course, man and machine were put in comparison and in contrast long before the computer was invented. Homer did as a poet, when he described artificial metallic servant girls, able to learn and to perform mechanic arts, and J.O. de la Mettrie did as a philosopher of the 18th century, when he wrote his book *L'homme machine* – to mention just two examples.

But the computer has added the explicit new dimension of information and requires a new view of the man–machine relation. Furthermore, in our decade, the general opinion on technology is turning more critical and it may become even more so in the future. My paper will try to combine a set of selected aspects with a modern view of man and machine, of the human being and the automaton.

1.1. The real and the scientific desk

The desk from which I am speaking in fact consists of two desks. Desk No. 1 is the desk which I hold with my hands and on which I have put my manuscript. Desk No. 2 is the desk which appears when I apply my knowledge of science and technology. If I look at this desk as an engineer, I will first consider its geometric shape, the blue-print of its design: drawings, consisting of lines and measures, with an indication somewhere in the corner of what kind of wood and what kind of paint to apply. If I look on it as a physicist, the geometric shape will disappear; I will think of an ensemble of several classes of molecules which are composed of atoms which are composed of even smaller particles. These elements I now imagine in simple geometric shapes, but their combination is far from the simple geometric shape of the blue-print. My mind will imagine little balls and tiny balls rotating around the little balls in elliptic orbits. The next step of scientific refinement will introduce probability theory and make the little and the tiny balls disappear; matter and energy, then, become crude simplifications of very sophisticated fields of probability distributions. It is very good that I still hold desk No. 1 in my hands, because I am no longer sure that I could hold desk No. 2, the result of my scientific view. Of course, I would be embarrassed if somebody were to ask me to write down all the equations which define desk No. 2, because frankly I do not know how to do this. But, in fact, when I now turn over my manuscript, I am not concerned with desk No. 2 and its equations. And this is what the scientist and what even the non-scientist of the 20th century do continuously: they apply certain levels of scientific analysis to some of their actions, but they disregard science in many practical actions and they disregard daily life in their scientific or quasi-scientific general views. A kind of double thinking existed long before George Orwell's "1984" (Orwell, 49). Orwell had only to amplify and exaggerate the truth a little. The computer, always ahead even of science fiction, will intensify this double thinking, but the computer will also bring it into the open. In work, the binary clarity of the computer requires the biblic yes for yes and no for no and does not tolerate double thinking. However, in many applications the computer operates across the two levels No. 2 and No. 1 and suffers if this distinction is disregarded.

In my paper, I will use the difference between level No. 1 and No. 2 in order to make the problems more visible, and I will refer in each case to a *next variation of the basic distinction*.

1.2. The real and the scientific earth

In order to show how universal this distinction is I will take our good old earth as the object of the next variation – the earth on which I am standing here, on which I drive my car and on which they have built my house. It is very familiar to me and I should be in a position to assume that I know the basic facts about it from my experience, from my sensory input. But here comes physics and tells me that I am wrong, that earth is not flat and not at rest. It is, as my physical knowledge says, a giant sphere which rotates and, moreover, it is but a small grain of no particular distinction in an unbelievably giant universe. However, when I stand here, when I drive my car, when I walk into my house, I do not care for the earth of physics. As a matter of fact, my naive earth, the earth No. 1, is for me the perfect case of stillness and, say, down in the Burgenland, where I see no mountains, it is also the perfect case of flatness. Earth No. 2, the physical earth, appears only when my mind enters the field of astronomy. Looking at the situation in this way, the choice between a geocentric and heliocentric image of the world is not a mere question of symmetric coordinate transformation from the apparent impression to reality, it implies moreover a change in the meaning of the word stillness. What is stillness if not the one of this earth? The double thinking of physics goes deep into basic notions, it destroys the natural framework of reference and requires a sophisticated interpretation of terms which remain, at the same time, in use with their original natural meaning. How can one be sure never to confuse every-day objects and scientific objects, the natural and the scientific level? And again: the computer aggravates the situation, because as a rule the computer treats scientific – mostly mathematical – relationships between physical objects, but the human interpretation before and after information processing, full of confidence about the perfection of the electronic tool, often relates input and output information to the natural meaning.

1.3. The real and the scientific human being

The biggest and worst confusion is created when the average man of today looks almost-scientifically on the average man. Our next variation of the basic distinction, therefore, shall be the consideration of the human being – which is neither the biggest nor the smallest of the objects that science can study, but by far the most difficult. There is an approximate measure for this difficulty. Information theory suggests that for this purpose we should study a complete description of the human body – and, of course, a perfect description is meant. The most primitive approach is to subdivide the space of the body into little cubes, small enough for one cell to contain no more than one atom or even no more than one electron. This results in a very long description, and in this form the information density in bits per cubic meter would almost be the same for the human body as for the Milky Way. However, such a description, long as it may be, would tell us very little about both objects. What we need for some understanding is a systems description giving the structure and the transition functions, all the streams of material, energy and information. If we were able to produce such a description, then it would become obvious that the human being has, by several orders of magnitude, more bits per cubic meter than any other object in the universe.

The scientific problem with the human being is that we can estimate how long a complete and perfect description of his body would be, but we are far from writing such a description. And while earlier decades could flatter themselves that they were coming close to it, today we are no longer certain that our new insights do not increase the length of the text faster than we are able to write it down. And even if we were making good progress towards an excellent systems description of the human body – the genetic code can be seen as a hopeful beginning – such a description would only increase the discrepancy between the human being No. 1, which we see and know, and the human being No. 2, the result of our application of scientific knowledge. The abstract description, the set of equations and strange symbol chains which science can deliver will be in hopeless contrast to the live man with whom we shake hands.

Considering a biological object instead of a table not only introduces a larger quantity and a complicated hierarchy of information, it also requires the introduction of other qualities. The living being is not made by a carpenter from simple and clean components like boards and screws and it does not have the stable constitution of a table. The human being is the result of an automatic production process called natural growth, and the resulting product has a systems character in many respects: it has lines for the transportation of air and food and blood, and it has a nervous network for the storage, transportation and processing of information. No two human beings are equal and no states of the same human being are equal. "Do not ask me about the nonsense I said yesterday" is a frank description of this flow of states through which a human being runs from birth to death. For a good systems description of a human being we could not ignore the history of the individual nor the history of his ancestors back into the darkness of pre-historic origins. The hypothesis that so-called simple physical laws govern every event in the body *may* be the correct theory, but it tells us nothing about the body as a system. And, in fact, not only in the present state of physical science but also in the foreseeable future the systems description of man will have to be highly imprecise, far from perfection. Once I coined a very simple sentence to illustrate this: what could the lover gain from the switching diagram of his fiancée?

It could be argued that this is an unfair remark. But any operation of the computer is in fact a man–machine-system and it cannot be made clear enough that this means a cooperation between a structure where the switching diagram is everything, and a structure where the switching diagram is not available and if it were it would mean nothing.

Any computer operation is a twofold man–machine-system. First, there is the operational interface, the level where the programmer and the operator talk to the machine which in turn talks back to the operator and the user of the output. Secondly, there is the systems level interface where computer system and application system are planned and installed and interconnected with the environment as a whole.

To both man–machine-systems we can again apply our basic distinction and see them either as an object of type No. 2, as an object of modern science and technology in which equations and switching diagrams define everything, or as an object of type No. 1, the real life systems with their unknowns of human magnitude and smallness, with features in which reality deviates from what it should be if it is to conform to scientific or technological theory.

It is, of course, the real life system which is the economic and social reality, in which decisions cannot be based on equations and switching diagrams. Science is always good for answering scientific questions – it is rarely good for answering non-scientific questions. The computer, in other words, does not remove the burden of choice, of making decisions from us, the choice between the human and the formal parts as well as the many alternatives between scientifically unknown possibilities.

2. Human choice

Human Choice has become a sociological term which will be explained by much more competent speakers during this conference. At this moment, I can afford to use the term in a simple way. Does the human being have a freedom of choice? Indeed, while we often are a victim, a mere function of the state of affairs, physical restrictions, of decisions we have once made, it is still true that the human being is distinguished from any other known object in the universe by the manner in which he can come to certain decisions, and make certain choices. The computer comes close to this in its simulation, but I will show that it does so in a very restricted sense only. There may be people who will want to challenge this statement in principle – but even those will have to admit that it is true today.

2.1. Human thinking and logical thinking

We come to the next variation of the basic distinction: the distinction between human and physical and logical thinking. We should never forget that disciplined scientific thinking has not been the original task of the brain which has always been and remains in the sharpest thinker, primarily a coordinating and control center for the body functions. To survive comes before thinking – only gradually thinking contributed to survival and it takes considerable development before society can afford purely thinking professions like programmers.

I have spoken of a desk No. 1 and a desk No. 2, but, of course, I do not suggest that there are indeed two different objects. The distinction is a result of our thinking and is rooted in two kinds of human thinking – natural and scientific. We have a choice of applying one or the other and the two objects are a consequence of our decision. Natural thinking is intuitive, operating on direct sensory inputs and on those universals which our mind seems to generate automatically. Note that scientific universals are not generated automatically; they require a long development process full of trial and error. Scientific thinking is logical and mathematical, a selection process which establishes lines of perfect deductive conclusions. This process in itself is highly intuitive. The finding of a new logical proof, a scientific discovery or an engineering creation are a mixture of logical derivations and extremely illogical, hardly repeatable and rarely conscious human behavior. The creative person usually cannot explain how he arrived at the result, because he does not know. All theorizing about the possible simulation of this mixture is far from realization. There is no artificial intelligence – this term is misleading. What can be simulated is what has been transformed into conscious reflection, and that is the more trivial part of intelligence. The history of cybernetics and artificial intelligence is a perfect proof of this statement.

It does not make sense to deny that logic and mathematics are inhuman where they are rigid – that is in their formal nature. Therefore, physics and the physical sciences are also inhuman where they are rigid. All attempts to resolve human problems by physical sciences, by science and by scientists, therefore, deserve a high measure of suspicion and constant critical review – exactly what the philosopher Sir Karl Popper proposes and requests in his book *The Logic of Scientific Discovery* (Popper, 59). We shall come back to such philosophical questions in Section 2.2.

The basic choice we have in our behavior between machine-like and human acting appears in many forms. The machine-like way can be based on a simple chain of built-in and conditioned reflexes, it can be based on some accepted or self-made set of rules, but it can also be on a rational level: in terms of numbers, of geometrical shapes, in terms of laws of nature. When we act beyond the fixed rules, when we break out of the reflex behavior, when we deal with the exceptions rather than with the rules, then we are master of the rules and not their slave.

There is only a small step from the human and creative non-machine-like acting to catastrophe and chaos, but catastrophe and chaos can also be reached by stubborn observation of rules which have lost their meaning or which were wrong from the very beginning. History shows many examples. Non-machine-like behavior must not disregard proper rules and their logical consequences. We may be free to make a choice, but then we are bound by its logical consequences. And we must constantly be on the watch: are the pre-assumptions and are the conditions for the establishment of the rules we follow still valid? Have our terms conserved their meaning? There is only a narrow path between too much confidence and too little trust.

Around the computer, the situation is particularly difficult. It would be so comfortable to resolve human problems in the same spirit in which the computer has been built and installed: rational and emotionless. But it is well-known that programmers – the first people of whom we think – are not always very rational and emotionless. On the contrary, they are a class of artists and being a boss of programmers requires faculties far beyond logic.

2.2. The human computer and the electronic computer

Programmers give us a demonstration of an important capability of the human being, namely the ability to act on two levels, on the human level and on the logical level. This capability is a prerequisite of the technological progress of the last 200 years. The behavior of any machine must be preconceived by a human brain before it can be technically implemented. This is, of course, also true for the computer and indeed the term *computer* may just as well refer to a human being as to a machine. Mathematics and bookkeeping had developed a pattern of strictly conforming to rules long before the first calculating machines were conceived.

If the computer could do nothing but bookkeeping and solving equations, the situation would be much easier. But the computer can do much more, as I will show. The computer processes all kinds of information which then is used for decisions on both the technical and the human level; the computer can be looped into flows of information and decisions which are predominantly on the human level – but unlike the human computer, the electronic computer cannot switch its thinking from the logical to the human level and nobody watches what happens during the high speed process – the programmer trusts that he has foreseen everything, that his programs are used and interpreted exactly as he has conceived them. That is not only optimism, it simply is not so.

This conference will treat many problems which occur in the cooperation between man and machine, and there are many more which must be left for future conferences. The computer creates by its existence and by the growing number of applications, a world of human decisions and choices which did not exist before; they deserve attention and study, investigation and publicity.

From its nature as technical invention, the computer as such supports *machine-like* behavior and disables or weakens *non-machine-like* behavior. The human faculty of behaving like a machine aggravates the situation. Already in the period of primitive machines it was not always the machine which served man – there was the human being who served the machine in order to attain a certain goal. If this goal is being set without due consideration of the people involved, severe damage can be caused. From the weaver's loom to our days, working people have suffered under machines and under goals made possible by machines.

But *machine-like* behavior is not restricted to the industrial environment. Administration can become a hierarchy of rule-performers, not as reliable as an electronic computer, but equally blind for the non-programmed reality, blind for exceptions, for the human dimension. Electronic computers as background tools for such an organization may become terrible instruments. The human aspect in contrast to blind and mechanical performance is important in any administration, it is twice as important in today's giant computer-assisted administration.

Many more examples of this contrast could be described, many other similar problems could be listed. This conference will deal for a week with them and I can restrict this introduction to a sketch of the basic ideas. But I would like to insert one more variation of the basic distinction and to apply a little consideration to a particular abstract object: to the scientific conference and to our conference in particular.

2.3. The formal and human part of a conference

During the 25 years of my international professional life I have been associated with more than 80 conferences and congresses and I can today easily see them as objects to which our basic distinction applies. Each event of this sort has two facets, a formal one and a human one.

As a formal object, the conference is reflected by its official programme with sessions opening and closing at well-defined times, with appointed session chairmen and formally chosen speakers, with meaningful session names and paper titles.

Most of the papers are once more subject to our basic distinction, because they have a formal part of equations and programs and an informal part in natural language, introducing, interconnecting and interpreting the formal sections. This informal part is so essential that even in programming languages the notion of the comment has been introduced, an informal explanation to the program, neglected however by the compiler.

But important as the papers and the whole formal side of a conference may be, its informal, its human aspects are even more important. Any science, any technology and any profession includes a part which is nowhere written down, one has to live with it in order to see and to learn it, one has to come to the conferences in order to meet and to understand the community, in order to grow into it. In view of the present-day flood of conferences and the increasing number of journeys – which become less and less pleasant so far as transportation and accommodation are concerned – it is highly necessary to critically evaluate traditional events as well as new proposals, but a consideration of the human value of meetings must not be forgotten.

3. The computer

What is, in fact, this machine which we call computer? Well, today it can be assumed that everybody present in this room has read a lot of books on computers, matched to his level of specialization. Most of the details he has learned about computers are irrelevant to this conference, and no particular introduction is required. If I give a kind of definition, then it is only in order to turn our attention to what I consider the relevant facts.

3.1. Symbol replacement

Information processing can be seen as systematic symbol storage and symbol replacement. Chains of numbers and letters go into the input and are stored in the memory. Each elementary step in the computer consists of the transportation of two memory entries into the processing unit where, conforming to precisely defined rules, numbers or letters are replaced by other numbers or letters, and the result is moved back into the memory.

There are many replacement rules, not only in arithmetic and algebra

$$6 \times 7 = 42,$$
$$6 \times 7 = 2, \text{ carry } 4,$$
$$(a + b)^2 = a^2 + 2ab + b^2,$$
$$\mathrm{D}x^n = n \cdot x^{n-1};$$

they are almost everywhere

H_2O = water,
ÖGB = Österreichischer Gewerkschaftsbund,
IFIP = International Federation for Information Processing,
UNIDO = United Nations Industrial Development Organization,
UNESCO = United Nations Educational, Scientific, and Cultural Organization.

While the given examples are only simple rules, there exist very complicated ones in any formal system and even in only partially formal systems. In fact, the human world was full of programmed processes long before the invention of the computer. Scientific calculation, bookkeeping procedures, instruction manuals for all sorts of devices, the recipes in a cookbook, the score of a symphony – programs wherever one looks. Before the computer, they were executed by a combination of controlling human beings and controlled or automatic tools. The computer will take over more and more of this, including tool control, because computers can get real time input information and can send output information in real time to effectors. This can be seen as a replacement process too: the input becomes a replacement of a fact by its description, which includes measurement, and output becomes a replacement of the description of an action by its execution, which may include feedback-control. A computer equipped with such input and output facilities to the real world is called a process control computer and in its most general form it becomes the general automaton for processing information, energy and material.

The model of such a general automaton is, of course, the human body which is operated to a high percentage by programmed processes. The computer is not at all unnatural in its general function, it only increases systematics, precision, speed and power. The computer is inhuman in its super-human strength, but much more so in its restriction to level No. 2, to the logical and physical nature of the process structures. Within this level No. 2, the computer is almost universal – but unlike the human being, the computer does not watch its actions from level No. 1. This is important – this is my subject in this paper.

3.2. The logical structure of the computer

The title of one of the books by Arthur Koestler calls the scientists *Sleepwalkers* (Koestler, 68) and the book demonstrates, from ancient Greece to Galileo, how scientists took the right steps without good reasons or for the wrong reasons. This thought also applies to the computer.

For when the electronic engineers chose binary operation, and electronic circuits conform to switching algebra, they ignored the fact that they were building their instrument on the grounds of the propositional calculus of logic. It is not important that the computer uses the binary number system, but it is important that the computer offers all facilities of propositional calculus up to the theory of algorithms. John von Neumann, the famous American mathematician from Budapest, recognized this and made it explicit – the electronic engineers even invented switching algebra without knowing that they were reinventing propositional calculus. But whatever this story is, the net result was that the computer can compute – within certain practical limits – any computable number and can decide any decidable logical problem.

3.3. Programs

There is one precondition, however. Somebody – a human being – must have written the program for the computation or for the decision process.

Such a program is a sequence of computer instructions, either written directly in machine code or written in a programming language and translated into machine code by a so-called compiler. The program is written for the execution of a certain job. If the program leads to a virtually infinite class of input values and in each case to a solution, then the program is called an algorithm. Information processing is the universe of algorithms.

The essential fact is that the program is an object of class No. 2. Whatever the computer can do, it necessarily is a result, a derivation of logical knowledge. The circuits of the computer contain nothing but elements of logic – negation, disjunction, conjunction, unit-time-delay; even the most sophisticated circuit is nothing more than a combination of these four basic elements. Any program, consequently, necessarily, is built up from yes-no-decisions and combinations of basic logical function. Authors frequently forget this when they go into metaphysical explorations.

Of course, there is also the computer as an object of type No. 1 which I can hold like this desk and on which I can put my manuscript. But information processing within this real object is only on level No. 2. The interpretation of the processing on the outside may be on level No. 1 and often is. We think too little of the gap, and this is easy to explain.

4. The flexibility of hardware and software

Programming and digital electronic circuitry are of a flexibility nowhere else reached in technology. This yields the illusion that the computer is as flexible as the human being – a colleague robot, as a German book title formulated (Radwit, 65) – the illusion that man and machine can be matched to any desired degree and that this matching comes automatically. A look at the real situation tells us differently.

I can still remember the day when I first produced an electric impulse of a duration of only 20 microseconds; this was in 1944 and few people in Central Europe at that time would have known how to do it. I reached one microsecond soon after, and in 1950 we had for the first time at our Technische Hochschule an impulse of 50 nsec. The whole digital technology is brand new and, while the user accepts a nanosecond technology computer in large-scale integration as a normal product, the electronic engineers know quite well that it is a kind of miracle that it works at all.

4.1. Electronician-oriented flexibility

Having this in mind, one understands the computer technology of the pioneer days: the electronic engineer was so happy he could deliver a working model that he was convinced that the solution he had found was the best possible one – unless he himself had some plans to improve it. Unfortunately, the first customer was an extremely flexible thinker: the mathematician. Whatever the electronic engineer would bring forward, the mathematician would welcome it with praise and he would make the best use of it. Because mathematical thinking is perfectly matched to the machine.

4.2. Mathematician-oriented flexibility

But the mathematician has an inherent basic property: he is lazy. Again and again he invents methods to reduce labor. There is no need to multiply – the laborious calculator can reach the result by sequences of additions. Because mathematicians of earlier days were lazy, they invented multiplication. Before the pioneer computer, the mathematician became angry about the need for a lot of basic writing and bookkeeping work in programming; lazy as he is, he wanted to program in familiar algebra instead of in the engineer's machine code. So the mathematician invented algorithmic programming languages. Within a short time, the computer offered every flexibility for numerical calculations when equipped with a compiler for ALGOL or FORTRAN.

4.3. User- or profession-oriented flexibility

The bookkeepers had no formal language ready for programming when the computer was invented. But under the pressure of the US Government a programming language for their needs came into existence, COBOL. Once they became accustomed to it, COBOL became an excessive success, although the mathematicians found this language distasteful.

But with the extension of computer use into many more professions, those professions slowly realized that they wanted to be as lazy as the mathematicians and have their own programming language, oriented towards their profession, giving maximum flexibility for their problems with a minimum of programming effort. But few professions are as creative and well organized as the mathematicians. It turned out that it was quite difficult to satisfy big user groups with problem-oriented programming languages. It was not the mathematical sections which caused the headache – they were soon written in one of the algorithmic languages. The problem was on the organizational side and with input and output in particular. The mathematician, well-trained in abstraction and in complicated structures, was much easier to satisfy than the average employee of an average computer customer. This group of users does not accept the hardware nor the software as offered by the electronic engineers and mathematicians. New aspects have to be taken into account – the flexibility of electronics and programming must be used to fit the user as he is.

The physiological aspects of key-boards and optical displays have to be studied, the psychology of programming and the attractiveness of a notation must be considered for software design. The inadequacy of products which had been satisfying for a decade became an important issue of academic study and provided an opportunity for the manufacturer, in particular the small manufacturer who could concentrate on a subset of users.

4.4. Worker- or personnel-oriented flexibility

With the demand for more and more computer personnel it is no longer possible to select the people around the computer so that they match it – the flexibility of the machinery in hardware and in programming must be oriented towards the worker on the equipment. Noise and heat, complication and abstraction – many aspects of the work on the computer became a matter of consideration and investigation.

And a new key-word appeared: job satisfaction. The early days were so full of excitement that nobody would have understood the term. With many computers in tiresome standard three-shift operation there is little excitement, but a justified request for improvement.

4.5. The price to pay

This conference will deal with the better matching of the computer to the people around it and to the users in general. The discussions should not neglect the price to pay. And I do not mean amounts of money; for an improvement of the operation, management will be ready to find the finances. I mean the price in terms of inherent general consequences.

Profession orientation, for instance, certainly is possible, but it will yield a proliferation of application classes, a loss of visible similarities. Less generally applicable solutions not only are more expensive – all too personalized solutions will pile up a second Tower of Babel, much higher than the first one, a tower of Babylonian programming language confusion.

Worker orientation is also possible, and a lot should and will be done.

From a certain point on, however, too much adaptation will result in overspecialization and this will rebound back onto the worker in the form of career and position difficulties. Flexibility is a human virtue and should be cultivated.

There are many discussion items for this conference. Flexibility of hardware and software can be used to make many improvements, but it has certain limitations which are difficult to understand. They are, however, extremely important for the evaluation of the social impact of the computer and I want to discuss them in more detail, repeating and paraphrasing some of my introductory arguments.

5. Semiotics – The scientific theory of languages

In his famous paper *Computing Machinery and Intelligence* A.M. Turing (50) tried to prove that we will have to admit that computers do think, as soon as we are no longer able to tell whether there is a human being or a computer on the other end of a communication line. Turing's method of proof is very clever: he defines the rules in his experiment in such a way that the proof system is of type No. 2. The positive result, under this condition, is not astonishing. Like a lot of cybernetic literature, it makes the reader underestimate the gap between levels No. 2 and No. 1, and it does not take into account certain insights of the philosophy of the 20th century which I consider very important for understanding the computer and for the subject of this conference.

I cannot take the time for a systematic development of the relevant ideas, I must restrict myself to a short-hand version of a paper I gave four years ago (Zemanek, 72) and discuss very briefly,

(a) semiotics, the scientific theory of languages;

(b) the form and content of computer symbol chains, distinguishing five kinds of information;

(c) certain aspects of the philosophy of Ludwig Wittgenstein.

In any man–machine-system when man talks to a machine, a language is required, and when the computer talks back, a machine language is required, not necessarily the same. Understanding these languages helps to understand the man–machine relation.

Language theory or *semiotics* (Peirce, 31–35; also Morris, 55) distinguishes primarily three levels of investigation, called *syntactics, semantics* and *pragmatics.*

5.1. Syntactics

Syntactics is the level of syntax, and is very close to the notion of grammar: the set of rules governing the relationships between different signs. Scientifically syntactics is defined as *dealing with the combination of signs without regard for their specific signification or their relation to the behavior in which they occur.* The rules of combination – symbols to words, words to sentences, any kind of elements to certain patterns – are, in the ideal case, clear and free from exceptions. Whether a formal text is syntactically correct or not can be checked quite easily and even automatically. Given the rules and certain selection criteria (either controlled from a higher level, like meaning, or just stochastical selection), formal texts can be generated by the set of rules and given formal texts can be parsed (taken apart into the syntactic elements) by automatic mechanisms.

5.2. Semantics

Semantics is the level of meaning; it describes the relationships between the signs and the objects to which they refer. Semantics is defined as *dealing with the signification of signs in all modes of signifying.* The rules of verification – how to check whether the relationships expressed by the symbols or words conform to those in the described world – in general, are a problem (and we shall come back to this problem later); in the ideal case, which can only be a constructed language, there might be a set of rules on how to establish the meaning of a text. All investigation of *semantics* can aim only at an objective meaning, since its definition excludes subjective components.

5.3. Pragmatics

Pragmatics is the general level of investigation, and includes everything else – the use of the language, the user, its history, and all other aspects. Pragmatics is defined as *dealing with the origin, uses and effects of signs within the behavior in which they occur.* In natural languages, this is where any investigation has to start: finding out how the users use the language and then progressing further, discovering its grammar, for instance. With constructed languages it is inviting to start off by playing with sets of syntactic rules, but the best way is starting from pragmatics: which functions are wanted, what goals are to be achieved. In both cases, *pragmatics* is that part of language investigation which is least suitable for systematic treatment.

It is obvious that these three definitions are hierarchical, each following definition includes the preceding one; the borderlines between the three levels are not always well defined and clearly visible, but as a principle and as a thinking tool, semiotics has proved to be very convenient and efficient.

5.4. Natural and constructed languages

Natural language is a wonderful tool. Everything can be expressed and described – formulation may be difficult, of course, but this is another aspect of language. Considering the versatility of natural language, it is indeed astonishing that constructed languages like algebra and programming languages were introduced and became successful. The explanation is another variation of the basic distinction. Living language is a perfect means for dealing with objects of type No. 1, while the logical and constructed universe requires also languages of type No. 2. A disregard of the distinction may have disastrous consequences, at the least it does not help to resolve problems.

It is not the case that natural languages do not have constructional aspects. The philologist comes closest to engineering when he analyses the structure of sentences. Syntax is formal and a set of formal grammatical rules can come very close to the live language. However, exceptions will always remain. The syntax of a constructed language, in contrast, is perfect.

The essential difference is on the semantic level. The linguists, up to now, have not been able to approach semantics formally to a satisfactory degree. My opinion is that the semantics of natural languages cannot be defined. This is, and will remain for ever, a gap between daily life and science. And this gap has crucial consequences for the computer. The problem is not obvious. Let us proceed pragmatically and see how the computer deals with its information.

6. Form and content

It might appear to the non-technical reader that the binary code for numbers, letters, symbols and operations or instructions is a typical example of technical standardization and unification, whereas nature in its beauty would maintain diversified methods of information transmission and storage in the living organism. But this is not so.

Sensory organs are transformers from optical, acoustical, chemical and mechanical signals into a highly standardized and uniform nervous telegraphy where electro-chemical impulses of only one constant shape occur. This telegraphy has an analog character (so that I personally have difficulty in understanding how my brain can make a binary decision), but apart from this not very important difference, the principles of nature and technology are equal: all sorts of contents are coded into the same form and the internal signal as such does not communicate its content. The meaning depends on the position in space and time and on the context.

This leads to the conclusion that since we can feed any kind of information into the computer, all kinds of information can be processed with the reliability and precision for which the computer is famous.

This is true, however, with one important restriction: it can be achieved only with information of type No. 2, with formal information. Informal information processing has not yet been successful.

It is appropriate to ask how the computer can have been so successful while so little attention has been paid to the level distinction. I will answer this question by discussing five kinds of processed information, namely:

6.1. numerical information,
6.2. physical information,
6.3. formatted information,
6.4. texts in natural languages,
6.5. texts in formal languages.

6.1. Numerical information

Processing numerical information is handling numbers, adding them, multiplying them, subtracting and dividing. All these operations are perfectly logically defined and the computer circuits conform to this logic. Also any higher form of mathematics is only a short-hand notation for the basic arithmetic operations to be performed. Any formula can be translated into these basic operations, and this is exactly what the computer does.

Consequently, there will never be semantic problems with numerical calculations, and the syntactical problems are resolved. This perfect situation is not applicable if non-numeric processing is intended. Theorem proving is an example of such information processing, and indeed progress is not very fast there. But in the end, all the algebraic and logical operations offer themselves for projection on the basic numeric and logic operations, and even if the advance is difficult, it does not encounter insurmountable obstacles.

6.2. Physical information

Physics has a clever method for reducing most of its laborious information processing to numerical calculation: the physical dimension. Any physical quantity can be expressed as the product of a numerical value and a unit of measurement. And all the units of measurement are either basic units or else they are interconnected by simple factors of time and length units. The principle of the physical dimension, invented in 1822 by the French mathematician and physicist J.M. Fourier in his book on the Analytical Theory of Heat (Fourier, 1822) resolves the semantic problem in physical calculations. For in any calculation, before the physicist entrusts it to a computer, he is obliged to make sure that the dimensions are in order.

This would, of course, be no longer true, if the physicist tried to use the computer for the development of equations or of physical concepts. But this has hardly been attempted up to now.

6.3. Formatted information

Bookkeeping has another very clever trick to reduce information processing to numerical calculation: the reduction to formatted information. All the books of accounting and financial administration are nothing but sophisticated forms and an entry can go into only one of the columns, the meaning of which is predefined and does not lead to problems of information processing. Operations are between formally defined fields of the forms and so are restricted to numerical calculations.

A most simple example for a formatted value is the ordinary date. It consists of year, month and day: 1974-04-01 or 01-04-1974 or 04/01/1974. This illustrates the danger of insufficiently defined formats or unstandardized formats. And here we have the semantic problem of formatted information.

You will have tried to fill in a census form and felt the uncertainty of what to write in certain fields. If you indicate a wrong profession, you will be counted into the wrong sum and two end-sums will be wrong. Sometimes, in spite of all the efforts of the census officers, the semantics of a field are not clear enough. But the computer which will process the information is not aware of any problem, the computer follows the algorithm.

There are many examples of ambiguities. Think of the decimal classification in documentation. A new field like cybernetics may shake the whole system. And even primitive notions like calf and veal in meat import and export statistics turn out to have difficult problems of definition, although everybody believes that he knows what the terms calf and veal mean.

6.4. Texts in natural languages

Mechanical translation was the first kind of natural language processing, suggested in 1947 by A.D. Booth and first practically demonstrated on 7th January 1954 in Washington. The leading linguist of this project was Prof. L. Dostert and the computer scientist was Dr. C.C. Hurd. A vocabulary of 250 words from different fields of science was punched and permitted a rough translation from Russian into English. This demonstration made big headlines and soon equally big hopes were around. Until, in 1960, Prof. Y. Bar-Hillel from the University of Jerusalem said (Bar-Hillel, 60; Appendix III, pp. 158–163) that there is no likelihood of a high-quality fully automatic natural language translation. He said this after having been for many years a strong supporter of automatic translation.

The computer had suffered a giant defeat, the importance of which many people have not understood until today. Bar-Hillel's change of judgment did not only come from a lack of success after many years of hard work, it came even more out of a philosophical insight. Its nature is precisely our basic distinction, which Prof. Bar-Hillel showed me by means of an example. The score of a symphony, he said, is not identical with the symphony itself. Indeed, the score is an object of type No. 2, a formal description of the composition, while the performance of the symphony by an orchestra is an event of type No. 1 – human beings interpreting the score in a way that an automaton can never do.

Natural language is a symphony, and I believe that this example explains a lot about the limitations of the computer.

6.5. Texts in formal languages

While mechanical translation of natural language experienced its defeat, translation of formal languages became an obvious job for the computer. Each compiler is a program for the translation from a programming language to machine code and a true case of text processing.

Programming languages are built around a central part which is the translation of formulae of logical and numeric algebra into machine code. The main difference from historic algebra is the time element: the computer requires a clear definition of the sequence of steps.

The present period of development can be described as the extension of application fields, and this means the creation of new programming languages and programming systems covering problems and professions beyond numerical mathematics, allowing the formulation of jobs in the language of the new field. In many cases this means the construction of models for this field exclusively on level No. 2. Human processing permits the interconnecting of formal parts by informal interfaces; computer processing requires total formality.

There is, furthermore, a meta-problem. It is not sufficient to have a formal language. This formal language must be formally defined, and so a formal meta-language is required, both for syntax and semantics. Formal definition of syntax was first resolved in 1959 for the programming language ALGOL 58 by the Backus normal form. Formal definition of semantics is a difficult problem; it was resolved much later, between 1965 and 1970. The meta-language developed for this purpose is now generally known as the Vienna Definition Language (Wegner, 72) and was used to write a formal definition of full PL/I (Lucas and Walk, 69).

6.6. Conclusions

Much more could and should be said on the requirements of formality in information processing. The five kinds of computer information which have been described clearly indicate that both intuitively and rationally formal information was selected for computer application – and where informal information was tried, the application was not successful. This finding would permit immediate conclusions. But before doing so, I want to show how our basic distinction, and experience with different kinds of information, is supported by philosophy.

7. Philosophy

Philosophy is an outcome of doubt rather than of confidence. The philosopher tries to understand the world because he finds the world confusing. He searches for a principle or a mechanism which will explain the universe in a logical way.

Ancient Greek philosophy searched for a basic principle, but was less concerned with certainty. If certainty was hoped for, this stemmed more from a religious belief than from a thinking effort.

It was an offspring of the Renaissance that philosophy aimed at certainty and perfection. Leibniz, almost 300 years ago, formulated the rationalist's hope in the following words (Leibniz, 1840):

> Therefore, when a controversy arises, two philosophers will have no more dispute than two computerists. It will suffice for them to get writing tools and an abacus at hand, and to say to each other (in a friendly tone, if they please):
> Let us calculate!

The *Empiricists* like Locke, Berkeley and Hume did not search inside the human mind; they hoped to get the irreducibles from outside, from direct sensations. Their programme was not only close to the one of science, they indeed prepared the thinking of the scientific era.

Starting from celestial mechanics, one field after another was cleared in the empiricist's sense and early in the 20th century, all elements were ready for a common view of logic, mathematics, linguistics, physics, chemistry and psychology – for a logical and atomistic philosophy. A young man recognized this situation and conceived such a philosophy. It could be called a formal definition of the universe of nature and mind, an attempt to remove our basic distinction by showing that level No. 2 is all we can speak about.

7.1. The "Tractatus" – the philosophy of perfection

The young man was the Viennese L. Wittgenstein, born in 1889 and educated as an engineer. He had very broad interests and covered many fields in his studies. Whatever he did, he did with incredible intensity. He became a student of B. Russell in Oxford and of the psychologist K. Buehler in Vienna. What the *Principia Mathematica* did for logic and mathematics, what the idea of the *atom* and *quantum* did for physics and chemistry, what *associationism* intended for psychology, he generalized to an overall philosophical system. In 1921 he first published his *Tractatus Logico-Philosophicus* (Wittgenstein, 22), and for the next 15 years he was convinced that his work had closed the books of philosophy – the objective of his work from the beginning. He had given to his treatise the title and the form of a legal *Abhandlung* – it was a trial of philosophy.

The *Tractatus* is in fact a synthesis of the theory of propositional calculus and the theory of the sentence as a picture of reality. One of Wittgenstein's basic assumptions is that there are elementary sentences, atom-like statements, which he calls *elementary propositions* and which are logically and factually either *true* or *false*. A *proposition* is a logical combination of *elementary propositions*. The syntax of the well-formed picture of reality in a scientific language is, then, the set of all well-formed logical combinations of all *elementary propositions*. And its semantics is the subset of those combinations which are facts. It may be a considerable amount of work to find all *elementary propositions* and to check all logical combinations of them in order to establish if they are factually true or not – but the method is a perfect algorithm for the construction of a perfect picture of the world, which is built up of the facts. Once this algorithm is accepted, everything within the scheme becomes self-evident and tautological, and one cannot speak about anything outside the scheme in a scientific or philosophical language. Mystical *somethings* behind the scheme may appear or may be *shown* (e.g., that the world does exist at all) – but the rule is to pass over such *somethings* in silence.

The most extreme followers of Wittgenstein's thoughts went one step further and denied the existence of anything outside the *Tractatus*-like construction: there is no meta-physics whatsoever. In particular the *Wiener Kreis (Vienna Circle)* endeavoured to work out a complete construction of the world in the sense of the *Tractatus* and rejected Wittgenstein's mysticism. The school in general is called *Logical Empiricism* and its centers, besides Vienna, were Oxford, Chicago, Berlin, Copenhagen, Helsinki and Paris. The theory of languages was studied, including the investigation of meta-languages and the logic of semantics. Wittgenstein's *elementary propositions* were called *protocol sentences* (e.g., "on 15 July 1932 at noon the temperature in Amsterdam was plus 15 degrees centigrade") and a unified language for science was envisaged. This was almost an anticipation of computer programming languages.

Indeed, it is perfectly correct to say that what Wittgenstein tried to construct is the universe found today in the computer, where everything is reduced to a protocol decision between *true* and *false*: to the bit, the atom of the computer world. And everything more complex is a true logical combination of such bits. The computer, as a matter of fact, implements the philosophy of Wittgenstein. What the computer does say is clear and what the computer cannot talk about it through necessity passes over in silence.

One could hope – and some people do – that the era of cybernetics and of information processing will bring the crowning of 400 years of rationalistic effort: the execution of Wittgenstein's algorithm and the production of a perfect description and understanding of reality by science. But the hope is illusionary.

7.2. Imperfection versus perfection

Wittgenstein was not only the philosopher who pushed the philosophy of perfection to the extreme. He is also unique for not only realizing that he had been wrong, but also creating a second and new philosophy, published after his death as *Philosophical Investigations* (Wittgenstein, 63). Here the semantics of a word depends on the *language game* within which it is used. The idea of a formal definition of semantics in natural languages and environments had failed.

The failure is not in the logic of the *Tractatus*, it is in some of its hidden assumptions; if all of them had been correct, then the *Tractatus* would in fact have been the end of philosophy.

The first wrong assumption was the existence of atom-like elements in reality, language and philosophy. Like the atom of physics, the elementary propositions relating to the natural word, the protocol sentences have the property of becoming a complex universe in themselves when investigated more deeply. The clear yes-no-decision without decomposition is a privilege of the artificial, of the constructed world, of logic and formal definition.

But even within a static structure like an axiomatic system, the perfect order, which the *Tractatus* expected, cannot be reached; as a friend of Wittgenstein and member of the *Wiener Kreis*, the mathematician K. Gödel, proved in 1931 (Gödel, 31). Even in a simple system of axioms covering only whole numbers, there are sentences which cannot be decided.

The *Tractatus* requires that semantic truth must be verified. Another Viennese philosopher, related to but not a member of the Vienna Circle, Sir Karl Popper, has shown that general verification is not possible (Popper, 59).

There is no perfect logical picture of the natural world and the philosophy of perfection is not the solution for understanding man and the universe. Philosophy is open as it always has been.

And this supports our basic distinction: maybe one day in the history of philosophy and science we will return to the ancient Greek ideal of unity between humanity and science – for the foreseeable future the gap between objects of type No. 1 and objects of type No. 2 will remain. And since the computer definitely belongs to type No. 2, we shall also have to live with a gap between information processing and daily life. Which is a true consolation. Because this assures us that the computer will never outdate and outgrow the human being, it will remain a tool in our hands, to be applied to our benefit or our damage, and the choice between these two possibilities is a human choice.

8. The social consequences

The computer, like any other tool, is a constructed device in a living environment, nearer to the human brain than any other machine, but clearly distinct in its absolutely formal properties. The computer makes technology more powerful than ever, and at the same time displays the weakness of any technical solution. Such an instrument, mass-produced and mass-applied, must have interesting and important social consequences. This conference will deal with many of them. I have the privilege of discussing a small and arbitrary selection.

8.1. Information as a merchandise

The computer together with modern communications technology has turned information into a merchandise which is produced, stored, transported, collected and distributed, sold and used, and which has many degrees of quality and freshness. It can cost a lost of money and it can be the subject of crime.

We tend to be very proud of the amount of information at our disposal and of its unprecedented precision and security. I personally believe that we receive too much information of unprecedented unreliability.

It is true that we know the speed of light to 9 decimals: 299 792.458 ± 1 m/sec; that is one part in 300 million. And since this is formal information, I am full of confidence that the value is correct. However, I do not yet know when I will make use of this information a second time.

If I hear or read news, it may have travelled to me with the speed of light, but even the greatest optimist will not attach the same kind of precision and reliability to this news. Language is not improving these days and semantics is not only decaying, it is manipulated and destroyed. If you think of the scrolls of the Dead Sea which prove that texts have been conserved over centuries with each word in its original form, then you might at least begin to share my doubts in the information of today.

Moreover, we suffer today from an oversupply of information. I do not only receive the information I want to receive, but from all corners I get unwanted information. From sign boards, from elevator loudspeakers, from technical noise sources, and from many other sources.

The computer should be a shield against this oversupply. It is an information reduction device by its nature. Its output should be matched to my input channel which has a capacity below 50 bits or 10 letters per second. The computer should deliver to me an amount of information I can absorb. The same should be true all over society. But there is still a long way to go. The computer can collect incredible amounts of facts – my problem is to find a way to select and recollect precisely what I want to know. Again: still a long way to go.

The computer can collect a lot of information on me, not all of it true, and I might not even like all the true parts. I should have a right to something like information justice – but there is still a long way to go before I will achieve this. We must recognise that information has now become a merchandise.

8.2. System complication

The systems of our society are growing – some of them in advance of computer influence, some under the influence of the computer.

An example of the first kind is the public transportation systems. Have you recently tried to use a bus or a streetcar in a European city after an absence of a number of years? It may be that you arrive in the dark at a stop and that you find there a little ticket automaton, but you do not know how to handle it, how much money to insert, which of the alternatives to select. The engineers and administrators who planned the system did their best to make the system efficient and inexpensive, but the result is far too complicated; and made worse by the fact that each city has a different system.

Is it pessimistic to predict that a similar situation will develop in future information handling systems, unless we are all very careful about the human aspects of hardware and software?

An example of the second kind is electrical power networks. Analog and digital computers can run a system of a degree of complication which hardly anybody can imagine, not even its designers. It was not only in reference to the famous New York black-out that Prof. A.P. Speiser formulated a principle which may become very important in future development (Speiser, 72):

> In systems of high degree of complexity, there can occur conditions of instability, even under perfectly normal operating circumstance, in which an almost arbitrarily small perturbation can have catastrophic effects.

I believe that we live in a world of overcomplicated systems of technology and administration, but there is no easy way to reduce complication. The computer can be helpful, but more important is a new mode of thinking, to which the computer can contribute. The computer cannot simply replace a group of human employees – the whole stream of information with which the computer is to work must be reconsidered. Similarly, the computer cannot simply be used to administer a complication which was built up by unscientific behavior, by natural power and neglect – we are once more confronted with our basic distinction.

8.3. A contradiction to resolve

Unfortunately, however, this last variation of our basic distinction leads us into a contradiction. What I said about complicated systems is true for our highly technical world: there is no easy way. While human properties and values are in danger of being destroyed by the physical and technical mentality, the protection of the individual and of human society can be achieved only by the methods and tools provided by science and technology.

But contradictions should never be considered as dead ends, contradictions are dead ends only in logic, in the human world they are challenges. What is required on a large scale is what this conference tries to do on a limited scale: to humanize our world of civilization and technology. This cannot be done by logical sets of rules or by systems of a mechanical character of type No. 2. The way into the future is directed by the unsophisticated principles of human behavior, centuries old and of type No. 1. Because science and technology may develop slowly or fast – man remains the same.

References

Bar-Hillel, Y. (1960). The present status of automatic translation of languages, in: F.L. Alt (ed.), *Advances in Computers*, Vol. 1, New York: Academic Press, pp. 92–163.

Berkeley, E.C. (1949). *Giant Brains or Machines that Think,* New York: Wiley.

Fourier, J.M. (1822). *Théorie analytique de la chaleur,* Paris.

Gödel, K. (1931). Über formal unentscheidbare Sätze der Principia Mathematica und verwandter Systeme, *Monatsh. Math.* 38, pp. 173–198.

Gödel, K. (1965). On formally undecidable propositions of the Principia Mathematica and Related Systems, in: M. Davis (ed.), *The Undecidable*, New York: Raven Press, pp. 5–38.

Homer, Ilias XVIII.

Koestler, A. (1968). *The Sleepwalkers*, London: Hutchinson, 624 pp; in German: *Die Nachtwandler – das Bild des Universums im Wandel der Zeit*, Bern: Scherz Verlag, 560 pp.

Leibniz, G.W., De scientia universali seu calculo philosophico, *Erdmann's Opera*, Vol. 1 (1840), pp. 82–85; Gerhardt's Philosophische Schriften, Vol. 7 (1890), pp. 198–203.

Lucas, P. and Walk, K. (1969). On the formal description of PL/I, *Ann. Rev. Automatic Programming* 6, part 3, pp. 105–182.

de la Mettrie, J.O., *L'homme machine*, see: A. Vartanian (1960). *O. de la Mettrie's L'homme machine*, Princeton: Princeton Univ. Press, 264 pp.

Morris, C. (1955). *Signs, Language and Behaviour,* New York: Braziller.

Orwell, G. (1949). *1984,* New York: New American Library; in German: Konstanz: Diana Verlag, 297 pp.

Peirce, C.S. (1931–1935). *Collected Papers*, Vol. 1, 1–6, Cambridge: Harvard Press.

Petzval, J. (1843). *Bericht über die Ergebnisse einiger dioptrischer Untersuchungen*, Budapest: Hartleben, xx+43 pp.

Popper, K. (1959). *The Logic of Scientific Discovery,* London: Hutchinson, revised Ed., 1968; 480 pp.

Radwit, K. (1965). *Kollege Roboter,* München: Ehrenwirth, 270 pp.

Speiser, A.P. (1972). Computers and technology, in: H. Zemanek (ed.), *The Skyline of Information Processing*. Proceedings of the Tenth Anniversary Celebration of IFIP, Amsterdam: North-Holland, pp. 23–36.

Turing, A.M. (1950). Computing machinery and intelligence, *Mind* 59, pp. 433–460; also in: J.R. Newman, *The World of Mathematics*, Vol. 4, New York: Simon and Schuster, pp. 2099–2123.

Wegner, P. (1972). The Vienna Definition Language, *ACM Comput. Surveys* 4, pp. 5–63.

Wittgenstein, L. (1922). *Tractatus Logico-Philosophicus*, London: Routledge & Kegan Paul, Engl. Transl. by D.F. Pearson and B.F. McGuiness.

Wittgenstein, L. (1963). *Philosophical Investigations*, Oxford: Basil Blackwell, 232 pp.

Zemanek, H. (1972). Some philosophical aspects of information processing, in: H. Zemanek (ed.), *The Skyline of Information Processing*. Proceedings of the Tenth Aniversary Celebration of IFIP, Amsterdam: North-Holland, pp. 93–140.

E. Mumford and H. Sackman, eds., Human Choice and Computers
North-Holland Publishing Company (1975)

THE DESIGN OF COMPUTER SYSTEMS:*
Man's Vision of Man as an Integral Part of the System Design Process

Bo HEDBERG

School of Business Administration, University of Wisconsin, Milwaukee, Wis., U.S.A.

and

Enid MUMFORD

Manchester Business School, University of Manchester, Manchester, England.

1. Computer systems and work design: Problems of philosophy and vision

At this moment in time two sets of *values* present in society are in conflict with each other. On the one hand we have a powerful technical value system which tells us to make maximum possible use of technology so that we may become more wealthy and comfortable. On the other hand we have a humanistic value system which tells us to beware of technology for it is a mirage which will lead us to disaster rather than success. Somewhere in between these two value systems is another which says technology is essentially neutral; whether it produces gains or losses depends entirely on the decisions that are taken on how it shall be used. Supporters of this middle position are a group of researchers from seven European countries who are working together in an attempt to influence one form of technology – computers – to

* This paper is published on behalf of an international research team which is carrying out a joint research project on Computer Systems and Work Design. This project is an optional study associated with an international research project on Automation and Industrial Workers administered by the Vienna Centre, Austria. The present study was carried out while Bo Hedberg was a research fellow at the International Institute of Management, Berlin. The Swedish bank study is financed by this institute. Funds for additional Swedish studies are provided by the Swedish Savings Banks' Foundation for Economic Research, and I.B.M. Svenska AB. In Britain finance is provided by the Social Research Council.

move in a direction which produces human as well as technical gains. This paper is a report on one aspect of our research. We argue that computers and *information technology* represent a powerful resource for improvement at all levels of society, but for this improvement to come about, alternative ways of using the technology must be identified and choices made in terms of human psychological needs.

The rapid development of computer technology has led to an overemphasis on possible technical gains, and human needs and values have been neglected. Our international group, which comprises research teams from Austria, Denmark, France, Germany, Great Britain, Poland and Sweden, believes that the time has now come to change direction and to consider how computer systems can be used to provide individuals with more *job satisfaction* and an improved *quality of working life* – in other words, to give a human vision and human goals to a technology that has so far been evaluated solely on its technical successes.

We have given ourselves a broad range of research objectives and in each country are examining the human effects of computer systems by making depth studies in the banking and steel industries. In banking we are investigating branch accountancy systems, in steel, order processing and production control systems. In each research situation we are attempting to establish the following,

(a) *How the computer system came to take its present socio-technical form.** To what extent is the shape and function of the system a product of top management values and beliefs on how work should be organized to achieve efficiency and productivity and how computer systems can assist effective *organization*. To what extent, also, is the system a product of user department opinion on how its work can best be organized and how the computer system can help service its needs. Finally, and most relevant to the discussion in this paper, to what extent is the nature of the system a consequence of the values and beliefs of the systems designers on how computers should be used and how computer based accountancy and production control systems should be structured for effective results. We are particularly anxious to establish if systems designers set themselves any human goals such as an increase in job satisfaction and an improvement in the quality of working life, when designing computer systems.

We are also examining,

* By "socio-technical" we mean the interaction and mutual influence of the man and the machine or the man and the technical aspects of his job.

(b) *How successful has the computer system which we are investigating proved to be in human terms?* Do the employees associated with its operation in the user department show a high level of satisfaction with their tasks and responsibilities? If a high level of satisfaction is found to exist what features in the design system have contributed to this? If employees show a low level of satisfaction, what features in the design of the system have led to this and is an absence of *human design goals* an important element in the system's unsatisfactory human consequences?

If a computer system proves to have human defects in that certain aspects of the employees' task structure and task environment are causing dissatisfaction, then we hope to establish,

(c) *if the computer system could have been designed differently and in such a manner that these human problems would have been avoided.* Would another design approach have led to a better socio-technical solution or are there technical or other constraints which limit the design alternatives available for the human part of the system. By technical constraints we mean technical features which must be incorporated if the system is to work yet which force a particular kind of pattern of tasks on the users of the system, the nature of these tasks determining job functions and responsibilities.

One of our principal research hypotheses is that computer systems associated with the solution of particular business problems allow for different forms of *work organization* and different job structures. In other words, that systems involving computers such as stock control, order processing or production control are not technologically deterministic but permit the designing of these systems in a manner which successfully meets the needs of people. This will include factors related to the performance of work such as fast, accurate, clear information and factors related to needs for job satisfaction such as work interest and challenge.

A second hypothesis, and the one on which this paper focusses, is that we are not at present getting computer systems which are consciously designed to increase job satisfaction, because the reward system and the values which influence systems designers are not of a kind which motivate them to do this. These values may be the systems designer's own individual or professional values or they may be top management or user values to which systems designers have to respond. *In this paper we shall discuss only the values of the systems designers.* We recognise that top management values and reward systems or, in some situations, the values of user management and staff, together with time constraints, technical constraints, financial constraints etc.

imposed by management or by the existing hardware or software support may have considerable impact on the way computer systems are designed, but we believe that the values of the systems designers exercise a strong enough influence over the design process for these to warrant separate examination. It is therefore this aspect of our research which we shall examine here. Using the data collected so far we shall examine the *models of man* which the systems designers in our survey have told us they use.

Systems design means technical and social change. The design group alters important variables in the multivariate system which we call organization. Not only the technology, but also the work roles of individuals, the nature and performance of their task, and the structure which is designed to keep the organizational components together can be subject to change. The complexity of the design task is considerable and the consequences of various design alternatives are often hard to evaluate. It is reasonable to assume that values play an important part in guiding the designers' choice between different design alternatives.

We shall argue that systems are designed in terms of a vision of man and man's needs and abilities which is greatly influenced by the systems designers own values, training and experience. In a situation where the potential users of the system may lack time, EDP knowledge, and perhaps the motivation to become involved in the design process, the systems designer is left to create his own organizational reality and this may not coincide with the reality of people in user departments where new computer systems are introduced. We hypothesize that systems designers, in an attempt to regulate and reduce the variety of the systems design process, build simple conceptual models of the design universe and the people located in it. These models do not typically include human factors such as a desire for job satisfaction.

Such models assist the systems designer to bring order to the design process and when translated into objectives and procedures they determine the manner in which he approaches his work and the criteria which he uses for evaluating the success of his work. But they are likely to be derived from his own value system and, if there are no other active participants to the systems design process, will incorporate concepts of human and organizational needs which are related principally to the organizational reality perceived by the systems designer and not to the view of reality held by workers and managers in the situation where computer systems are introduced.

The thesis of this paper is that if the computer man is left to create his own organizational world and the rules by which it is to operate, then he will not design computer systems which fit the organizational worlds of the workers and managers who use his systems. The result, in the words of Beer

(73), can be a *non-viable* system. A system which cannot survive or which will only survive in a state of instability. Stafford Beer argues that "whatever makes a system survival worthy is necessary to it". We suggest that a necessary component of the successful creation and survival of computer systems which involve human beings is a definition of environmental reality by systems designers which equates reasonably well with the definition held by system users – in other words which incorporates the same models of man. This similarity of perception, if it can be achieved, should produce a better fit between the efficiency needs of the enterprise, which must be met if it is to survive, and the human needs of those workers and managers who use the computer systems. These, too, must be met if they are to achieve psychological health and job satisfaction.

An important objective of our research is to obtain an understanding of the success or failure of the systems design process by examining the following.*

(1) The nature of the models of man (both of the organization as a network of human relationships and of man as an individual) which the computer technologist uses to guide and regulate his systems design procedures.

(2) The origins of these models. Do they come from the system designer's personal value system, from his training, from his professional reference group, or are they to a large extent imposed upon him by the senior management of the firm which employs him?

(3) The nature of the models of man held by people in the user department. To what extent, and in what way, do these differ from the models held by the systems designer? Are changes in work expectations leading to the creation of new models which place more emphasis on work interest, challenge, autonomy and power?

2. Earlier research

The hypotheses in that part of the international project which concentrates on the models of man held by systems designers have been a product of earlier research by other investigators and by the authors of this paper. It may be useful to briefly review here some of the research evidence which has led

* By success and failure we mean the ability of the organizational unit containing the computer system to adapt successfully to its human, technical and administrative environments.

us to believe that a study of system designers values and "models of man" should be part of our current research project. An American researcher Boguslaw (65) has concluded that the "new utopians (the computer systems designers) retain an aloofness from the human and social problems presented by the fact or threat of machine systems and automation. They are concerned with neither souls nor stomachs." He contrasts the approach of the systems designers of the past with that of the systems designers of today.

> The most distinctive characteristic of classical utopian designers is the basic "humanitarian" bent of their value structures. In Sir Thomas More's Utopia, the inhabitants are more concerned with the welfare of their fellow men than with the furthering of their individual fortunes . . . the new utopians are concerned with non-people and with people substitutes. Their planning is done with computer hardware, system procedures, functional analysis, and heuristics . . . . The theoretical and practical solutions they seek call increasingly for decreases in the number and in the scope of responsibility of human beings within the operating structures of their new machine systems.

Another American (Davis, 71) who is one of the major researchers in the field of *job design* criticises the model of man of the technical systems designer as follows.

> No clear objectives concerning roles for men as men are visible, although objectives are clearly defined for men as machines. When man is considered only as a link in a system, design rules do not exist for allocating appropriate tasks to man. Nor are there design rules for designing task configurations to make complete and meaningful jobs . . . . If we turn to how technology is translated into requirements for job designs, we see widespread acceptance of the notion of the technological "imperative", put forth by most engineers and managers. That a substantial part of the technical design of production systems involves social system design is little understood or appreciated.

Hedberg (73) a Swedish member of our international research team and co-author of this paper has completed a great deal of research on the design of computer based *management information systems*. This work has demonstrated to our research group the importance of the values and perceptions of man held by the systems designer. He maintains.

> The decision making process of (MIS) design will include values as well as facts as its decision base. Values and visions of man, desirable structures etc. will to a degree affect the solutions which are perceived and selected . . . . Although the present body of knowledge about man would basically require the information technology in MIS to be designed for human beings, who search for motivation, who have severe problems to cope with large volumes of data and to understand the behaviour modes of complex models of reality, too many MIS are today

designed to control non-motivated people who lack data for decision making but who otherwise are rather well-functioning information processors. It should be very worthwhile to try to pinpoint and describe the values and mental models of man, which today guide the systems design process.

Sackman (71) suggests that this unwillingness or inability to take account of human factors in systems design stems from the manner in which computers were first used and continue to be used. He says,

> The early computers were virtually one of a kind, very expensive to build and operate, and computer time was far more expensive than human time. Under these constraints, it was essential that computer efficiency come first, with people last .... The developing computer ethos assumed an increasing misanthropic visage. Technical matters turned computer professionals on; human matters turned them off. Users were troublesome petitioners somewhere at the end of the line who had to be satisfied with what they got.

We hope through our international research group, to establish if these anti-human attitudes still exist, if they are common to all the countries involved in the survey, and their source. But while recognising the truth of Sackman's remarks it may be that, just as the murder victim can provoke the murder situation, so user behaviour has delayed a building of human variables into the systems design process. Top management has generally not required this of its systems designers while trade unions have been more concerned, in many countries, with negotiating the wage rate for the new system than with intervening in the design process. Similarly, there has been little demand from users themselves for an opportunity to learn and practice systems design or even for the opportunity of stressing their psychological needs to the systems designers.

The Austrian trade unions are, together with the Norwegian trade unions, noteworthy exceptions to the generalization above. Margulies, an Austrian trade union official and a member of our international research team has written in an article on computer education.

> If the hazards of computer use are to be avoided and the chances optimized, employees and their representatives (shop stewards, unions) must be granted an opportunity to exert an influence on decisions and to represent their point of view. Management should be obliged to inform the employees about intended changes and reorganization in time so that, coincidentally with the technical, organizational and financial plans for the introduction or extension of electronic data processing, a social plan of adjustment (personnel plan) could be worked out.

3. A definition of models of man

We are hypothesising that systems designers work from a model of man that is different from the model of man held by employees in departments which use computer systems. We argue that a poor fit between these models of man is likely to make computer systems unacceptable to users. Let us now define our terms and specify more precisely what we mean by models of man.

We must start by differentiating between organizational and individual models. The two terms are often used synonymously but by *organizational model* we mean here an intellectual construct (of a very simplified kind) of how an organization functions. This will include the logic of roles and relationships. The manner in which these are assembled enables the organization to perform its production or service functions, to survive in its external environment and to respond to the demands of the human beings which make up its internal environment. An *individual model* of man is narrower and is an intellectual construct (again simple and usually containing some value judgements) of the needs of the individual human being.

3.1. Organizational models of man

Organizational models can be broadly divided into two types. First, *theoretical models* which are used primarily by academics such as social scientists, cyberneticians and information theorists to assist their understanding of how organizations function. Second, *operational models* used primarily by practising managers as conceptual tools to help them to manage the organization.

3.2. Theoretical models

The range of theoretical organizational models is vast and it is only possible to give one example here, selected from the social sciences. It should be noted that many theoretical models become operational models once they are well established and recognised by practising managers as helpful concepts for understanding the workings of their own organization. Organizational theory goes back into the mists of history but has become formalized in the United States and Europe during the last fifty years. Attention has concentrated on different aspects of organization during this period and a simple theoretical model of an organization provided by Leavitt (64) is a useful aid to understanding these shifts in interest. Leavitt describes an organization in terms of the four basic interacting variables set out in the diagram on the next page.

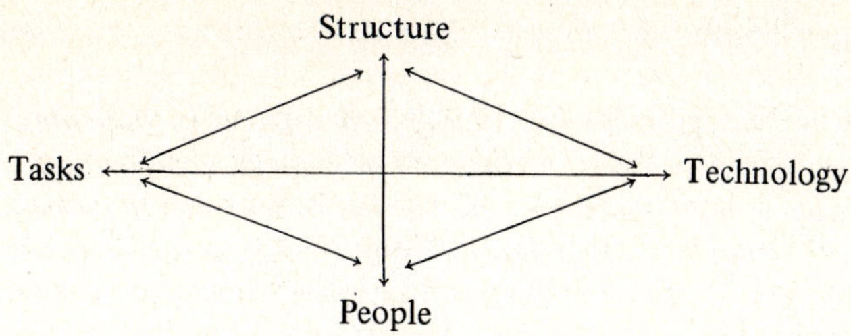

Structure refers to the network of roles and relationships that makes up an organization, in particular the locations of authority and responsibility. Its formal version is usually depicted in the organizational chart to be found hanging on the wall in most Managing Director's offices. Technology is the system of tools and techniques that assists employees to make the organization's product. This will include both machinery and techniques for controlling and processing information. The "people" variable includes the necessary human skills to operate the technology together with psychological factors such as motivation and interpersonal variables such as communication. Tasks are the activities which people perform and which, combined together, they regard as their job responsibilities.

All of these four variables interact together and a change in one will tend to produce a change in the other three. When managers attempt to improve the functioning of their firm or department they do this by manipulating one or more of these variables, using their own operational model of a well functioning organization as a guide. Thus they may alter the structural variable by centralizing or decentralizing, in this way altering the authority and decision structure. Or they may choose to influence the technology variable by introducing new machines and control systems, and they may seek to recruit a more or a less skilled labour force than their existing one to fit their new technical needs. It seems that up to the present the task variable has not been consciously manipulated but has been viewed as dependent upon the technology variable. Thus what have been seen as technological imperatives have determined the patterns of tasks and tasks have only been altered if they were too difficult for the available labour force to undertake. It is only within the last few years that management has become aware of *task structure* as a manipulatable variable that is related to job satisfaction and employee motivation. In our research we are seeking to identify the alternative task structures that can be associated with particular forms of computer technology.

An example of a theory of organization related to the organizational structure is that of Burns and Stalker (61). They produced the concept of "mechanistic" and "organic" forms of structure. Mechanistic indicating a stable, rigidly demarcated form of structure with a system of roles and relationships that alters very little. This form of organization, in their view, was appropriate for a firm operating in a stable product and technological environment. An organic structure, in contrast, is more fluid and without tightly defined jobs and areas of responsibility. This form of organization is very adaptive and is able to cope with a rapidly changing external environment. A firm wishing to operate in an organic mode must avoid introducing the kind of computer system that produces rigid control systems and tight centralization.

A theory of organization relating to technology has been provided by Woodward (65). She argued that the strongest influence on the structure of an organization was the technology it used. Thus batch, mass and process production firms were organized in different ways to fit their technologies. Any major change in technology, such as the introduction of a large scale computer system, would require an alteration in the firm's organizational structure to ensure a good fit between the technology and structure variables.

Organizational theory related to the "people" variable has been greatly influenced by the "human relations" school of thought and is largely concerned with the integration of individual and group needs with organizational needs. This aspect of theory has been developed from the work of American social scientists such as Maslow, McGregor, Herzberg, Likert and Argyris. It considers the nature of the human situation which a firm needs to create if it is to provide an environment which both motivates and satisfies the people who work there. In our international project we are testing the hypothesis that this variable is neglected when computer systems are designed. The "people" variable is also concerned with labour availability, recruitment and training.

Lastly, there is the task variable. This is the pattern of tasks which each individual and group is required to carry out in order to make the organization's product or provide its service. Many social scientists argue that this is the critical variable in job satisfaction for modern man requires a set of tasks which gives him work challenge and interest. This variable meshes tightly with the people variable as the viable organization requires a good fit between the tasks which people are required to perform and their needs and competences. The importance of the task variable has been brought to management's attention through the work of social scientists such as Davis, Lawler and Hackman in the United States, Emery in Australia, the Tavistock Institute and Cooper and Wild in Britain. This variable is of particular interest to our international project for we believe that the creation of a set of interesting and challenging tasks for system users is a key design responsibility for the designers of computer systems. We hypothesise that computer systems are sufficiently technologically flexible to permit tasks of this kind to be associated with their operation.

Considering our Leavitt organizational model as a whole we would argue that the viable organization – the organization that can survive and develop within its environment – needs to establish a reasonable fit between its structural, technological, people and task variables. These must all interact harmoniously with each other, and it must be understood that any alteration in one variable will affect all the others.

3.3. Operational models

Operational models are the visions of the organization and its effective functioning used by managers who base their actions on experience, hunches, rules of thumb etc. and not on theoretical analysis. Such models are often simple, prescriptive and general, based on commonly accepted ideas of how an organization should be run. They are influenced by the history and traditions of the firm and by practices which have worked well in the past. They frequently contain elements of *organizational theory* which have been accepted by managers and taken into practical use. Because of the time required for knowledge to diffuse, this theory is usually old rather than new and it has been said, with some justification, that "the practitioner is the slave of an outdated theory."

Systems designers are changing structure, technology, people and task variables when they design computer systems. They must therefore work with an organizational model of some kind which is related to what they are trying to achieve, even though this may be more operational than theoretical. We believe that the organizational models of the social scientists could be valuable inputs to the systems design process but we accept that their value must be demonstrated. De Greene (73) claims that so far information processing models are the only social science models which the computer systems designer has been prepared to use. We hope that the ideas of social science have achieved a greater penetration into the systems design process than this comment suggests, but recognise that much educational work needs to be done.

We hope that our research will throw some light on the nature of the organizational models which the computer systems designer uses in his work and will show us the extent to which these are based on theoretical analysis or on operational principles culled from tradition, experience, training or hunch.

4. Individual models of man

An *individual model of man* is the way in which we perceive ourselves and other people. In any situation, such as computer systems design, where new organizational structures are being developed and introduced, it is important to understand not only the organizational philosophy behind design goals and procedures but also the perception that the technical design group has of the needs of those affected by the system, but who do not play a part in its design. This perception can then be compared with the employee's own definition of their needs. Of course, when a user department as a whole efficiently participates in the systems design process, then the models of man which define system goals will be those of the system users. This kind of active participation and influence from the users still appears to be rare.

Hedberg (73) points out that some hypotheses about man exist in all technical designs, although these may be more or less explicit and more or less sophisticated. He argues that as new technologies and new systems become well established and mature in their environments, so the models of man which are incorporated into these become richer and truer representations of man and his needs. An examination of developments in technology since the industrial revolution provides many examples of this process. The first phase of the industrial revolution can be described as a period of (1) *technical optimism*. "Here is the technology, let us build the machines." Very little concern was shown for the human part of the *man–machine* mix when new production systems were being designed.

Then came the realization that machines could injure men and a phase of (2) *concern for safety* began. Measures were taken to ameliorate the latent physical conflict between men and machines through the introduction of safety measures and the formulation of safety legislation.

Next it was recognised that although serious physical injury could be averted, long term discomfort through badly designed machines or poor working conditions could also have a detrimental affect on the worker's physical *and* mental health. We then entered (3) *the ergonomic phase* of the maturity cycle and man as a physio-anatomical system began to be incorporated into the design process.

Lastly, it became clear that even if work was carefully designed to fit human physiological characteristics, the worker still had psychological characteristics such as emotions which would affect his attitudes to his work and his behaviour in the work situation. He could for example, feel boredom or resentment. Man as a *motivated system* then started to influence the technical design process and we moved into (4) the *human-oriented* design phase.

"Human beings have emotions; attitudes and aspirations, let us build machines that will help human self-realization."

This last approach owes much to the development, by behavioural scientists, of a *self actualization* model of man. These researchers believe that human beings require opportunities for personal growth and development and for a realization of their intellectual potential if they are to achieve job satisfaction and psychological health.

Hedberg argues that the systems design associated with computer technology is at an early stage of this maturity process. It would appear to be moving slowly out of the technical optimism stage and to be moving into the ergonomic stage with an awareness of problems of man-machine interaction, particularly when display terminals form part of a system. However, it is still far from human-oriented in a wider sense.

Today, many systems designers and managers, appear to work with a model of man which is not human need-oriented but based on *compliance*. This model assumes implicity that an organizational system does not have to specifically cater for human needs such as job satisfaction because rewards and punishments can be built into the operation of the system and these will secure acceptance of the system. Catering for human needs as a system goal is often not seen as relevant to systems design, because it is believed that the human being can be manipulated into accepting virtually any system which does not contravene his personal values too grossly. In consequence training and planning are perceived as more important tools for systems implementation than user participation. The systems designer often describes himself as a salesman who markets a completed product. Training programs and user involvement are thought of as ways to get user acceptance, and not primarily as means to secure user ideas and influence.

Compliance has been a common behaviour pattern and may still exist where employees have a value system which includes deference towards management and an acceptance of overall organizational goals; but the realities of most industrial situations suggest that these are rapidly becoming the values of the past, not the present. One of the problems of the computer systems design process may be that systems designers work from a position of technical optimism combined with a compliance model of man. At the same time the system user is developing a personal self actualizing model and will soon reject technological change that contravenes this.

We would stress again here that the behaviour of systems designers has to be understood within the framework of their own work situation.

Although they may have personal ideas on what constitutes an ideal system design; technical, economic and other constraints define their freedom to act. The influence of organizational factors such as management climate, budgeting procedures, reward systems etc. in determining the actual outcome of the design process has not so far been subject to extensive study. At this point in time we can only assume that the values which are implicit in the ultimate designs reflect not only the professional values of the systems designers but also the values of other groups located in the firm and in the community.

5. Research evidence

Later publications will contain a comprehensive analysis of the findings of the different national research teams on the conceptual models of man held by top management, systems designers and the employees using computing systems, in each of the firms investigated. This evidence is not yet available. However, the British and Swedish research teams have collected data on the values and models of man of their computer technologists and these are set out below. Depth interviews with systems designers in the banking industry suggested to the British researchers that it would be valuable to establish if a larger sample of systems designers saw man as a motivated being striving for opportunities for self development in work or if the opposite view was generally taken and man was seen as a limited individual with a low level of competence and a need to be checked and controlled. In order to establish which of these models of man was used by systems designers, questionnaires were sent out to systems designers in other British industries. These systems designers were sent a postal questionnaire which asked them a number of questions directed at ascertaining how they approached the human side of the system design process. Unfortunately the response rate was low and out of 135 firms contacted, only 41 replies have so far been received.

In Sweden the same questionnaires were used to cover the whole population of systems designers in a commercial bank. 25 computer specialists responded. They had all been involved in the design and implementation of an advanced computerized system during the last three years.

The low rate of response in the British Sample could be interpreted in one of three ways:

(1) British systems designers are too busy to fill in questionnaires,

(2) they are not interested in the human aspects of their work or,

(3) they felt that they were unable to answer the questions that we posed.

Whatever the reason, it is clear that the sample who have replied are highly selective and it is a reasonable hypothesis that they represent those who are particularly interested in the human aspects of their work.

6. The organizational model of man held by the majority of systems designers

In an attempt to elucidate this, systems designers were given two sets of statements, representing the extremes of an opinion scale (graded 1–7) and asked to indicate where they stood on the scale. The results are set out below. Table A shows some relevant descriptive statistics for the distribution of answers. Diagram A sets out the average view of the respondents. The statistical means of each distribution are connected by the graphs.

Table A
Organizational model of man (description of answers)

Item	Mode M		Mean μ		Median $\tilde{x}$		Standard deviation σ		Range $\{x_M - x_T\}$	
	S	UK	S	UK	S	UK	S*	UK**	S	UK
A	6	2	5.10	3.46	5	3	1.31	1.75	6	7
B	6	5	5.20	3.73	5	4	1.36	1.64	6	7
C	6	5	5.70	4.51	6	5	1.00	1.45	4	7
D	6	3	4.95	3.63	6	3	1.40	1.53	6	7
E	5	3	4.55	3.07	5	3	1.36	1.57	5	7
F	7	6	6.35	5.68	6	6	0.73	1.46	3	7
G	6	5	5.10	4.63	5	5	1.31	1.38	5	6
H	6	3	5.50	3.85	6	4	1.07	1.41	4	7

S = Swedish Study (N = 20), UK = British Study (n = 41).
* $\sigma_S = \sqrt{(\Sigma(x-\mu)^2 \cdot f)/N}$, where f is the frequency within each class,
** $\sigma_{UK} = \sqrt{(\Sigma(x-\bar{x})^2 \cdot f)/n-1}$.

The highest consensus in the British sample was on statements C, G and H and the greatest variance on A. In the Swedish sample consensus is high on statements C, F and H. Answers to statements B, D and E are more scattered. In general the Swedish answers show smaller variances than the British ones. While standard deviations range from 1.38 to 1.75 with an average of 1.52 units in the British sample, standard deviations in the Swedish study go from 0.73 to 1.39 units with an average of 1.19. The British respondents make use of almost all steps of the scale. The average range equals 6.9. There is no case where the Swedish respondents use all seven steps of the semantic differential scale. The average range is 4.9. The relatively high overall spread of the answers, and the fact that the British response rate is as low as 30%, should be kept in mind when interpreting the results. The ultimate reports from the

DIAGRAM A: Organizational Model of Man

Use the following scale to indicate what you believe to be the best form of department structure for non-specialist, non-management staff (put an X on the scale for each pair of properties).

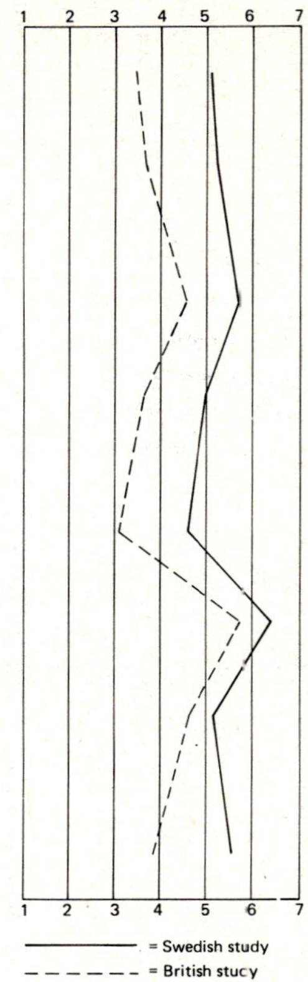

A	Jobs should be clearly defined, structured and stable.	Jobs should be flexible and permit group problem solving.
B	There should be a clear hierarchy of authority with the man at the top carrying ultimate responsibility for all aspects of work.	There should be a delegation of authority and responsibility to those doing the job regardless of formal title and status.
C	The most important motivators should be financial e.g. high earnings and cash bonuses.	The most important motivators should be nonfinancial e.g. work challenge, opportunity for team work.
D	Job methods should be carefully defined by O & M department, management services or supervision and adhered to.	The development of job methods should be left to the group and individual doing the job.
E	Targets should be set by supervision and monitored by supervision.	Targets should be left to the employee groups to set and monitor.
F	Groups and individuals should be given the specific information they need to do the job, but no more.	Everyone should have access to all information which they regard as relevant to their work.
G	Decisions on what is to be done and how it is to be done should be left entirely to management.	Decisions should be arrived at through group discussions involving all employees.
H	There should be close supervision, tight controls and well maintained discipline.	There should be loose supervision, few controls and a reliance on employee self discipline.

Computer Systems and Work Design project will be based only on population data and enable us to use traditional statistical tests and comparisons.

Statements on the left of the scale represent, using the terminology of McGregor (60), a Theory X view of the firm. A tightly structured organization, with precise job definitions and clear lines of hierarchical authority. Statements on the right represent a Theory Y position. A flexible organization, which has a great deal of control located with employees instead of supervision. It can be seen that the British systems designers are not consistent. At the task, or operational level – the work which the employee does, they favour well defined, structured and stable jobs; they want job methods to be carefully defined by O & M, Management Services or supervision; they want targets to be set and monitored by supervision, and they want close supervision, tight controls and well maintained discipline. Yet at the same time they favour the downward delegation of authority and the provision of nonfinancial motivators such as work challenge.

The areas where they want structure and definition are those over which they have a great deal of influence when they design systems, namely job content and work controls. Yet it can be argued that by imposing a tight structure and tight controls they eliminate opportunities for challenging work and for group decision taking. This could suggest a perhaps unrecognised conflict between the way they design systems and their personal, more democratic values.

The Swedish sytems designers are somewhat more consistent in their Theory Y-oriented view of the firm. However, the profiles of the two graphs are rather similar. All observations from the Swedish sample fall on the Y side of the British data and on the Y half of the scales. The majority opinions of the two groups are close to one another on statements F and G where the variance in both studies is relatively low. The opinions are quite far apart for statements A, B, D and E, where the variance in both studies is relatively high.

Although the majority of the Swedish systems designers feel that jobs should be flexible and permit group problem solving (statement A), that authority and responsibility should be delegated (statement B) and that job methods and targets should be decided upon by the group or by the individual himself (statements D and E), the spread of opinions on those items is noticeable. Likewise while the majority of the British respondents favour delegation of authority and responsibility (statement B) several members of their group question that position.

The data seems to indicate that Swedish systems designers are consistently more Y-oriented in their perception of the ideal organization than their

British colleagues. The latter are less willing to let the employees of an organization take responsibility for job definitions, job methods and work targets. At the present point in time the limitations of our data prevent us making too definite conclusions about differences. However, the welfare gap between the two countries seems to have some correspondence in an opinion gap between the two professional groups concerning worker demands and quality of working life. If there is a bias in the British material, it seems reasonable to assume that the group which answered would be more Y-oriented and aware of human needs than the average British computer specialist.

Computer systems and the way they are designed clearly have a considerable impact on the structure of an organization – the way it arranges its functions into departments, the way these departments and the people who work there relate with each other and with the outside world. In the early days of computer usage it was suggested that computers would bring some dramatic changes to organizational structure. For example, that there would be a strong move towards the centralization of operations, that many functions would merge together, and that the shape of the management pyramid would undergo considerable change as computers took over the control functions of middle management.

At the present time the management literature is full of powerful normative theories on how organizations should be structured if they are to operate effectively. Beer (72) has a cybernetic model which he calls the "viable system", other theories are provided by management and behavioural scientists. We were therefore interested in finding out the organizational design principles that were used by our systems designers. We asked two open ended questions.

(1) Describe briefly some of the properties which you consider important to a well functioning organization.

(2) When you design a system in what ways do you think you are contributing to the well being of the organization?

The answers to the first question are interesting because few British systems designers appeared to have any concept of structure as it is defined by organizational theorists – that is as a network of roles and relationships serviced by technology, and arranged in a manner which enables the organization to perform its production or service functions and interact with its external environment. Out of 56 suggestions in the British sample there were only four references to structural properties of this kind. These covered the allocation of decision responsibilities and the need for a well designed management hierarchy. 64% of the British answers referred to personnel or human relations factors such as good management-staff relations, good interpersonal communication, good opportunities for promotion. Referring back to our organizational model it seems that British systems designers are most conscious of the "people" variable as a factor contributing to organizational success and less aware of the structure and task variables.

The Swedish systems designers were somewhat more aware of organizational structure. Out of 34 suggestions from Swedish respondents, 15% were primarily concerned with structural aspects like decentralization, delegation of authority etc. Just as many (15%) were primarily influenced by an engineering or cybernetic systems concept of organization and stressed the importance of operational goals and efficient feedbacks in a well functioning organization. Twenty-three percent of the Swedish respondents were mainly concerned with management-staff relations and good interpersonal communication. All in all decentralization and a simple systems model seem to dominate the Swedish systems designer's perception of the well functioning organization. However, few of the respondents believe that they can assist decentralization through their systems designs. Some of the answers actually state that respondents are afraid that they tend to cause centralization and take away people's control of their work. The designers feel that they can contribute to organizational efficiency through the development of good decision bases, efficient feedbacks and controls, and explicitly formulated goals for various functions within the organization.

In answer to the second question, the comments fell into the following categories.

Systems design contributions to organizational well being

	N	Greater efficiency	Better information for management	More job satisfaction	Financial savings	Staff savings
British	62	31%	27%	18%	15%	10%
Swedish	23	45%	35%	15%	0%	4%

Job satisfaction was seen as increasing as a result of the systems designer's ability to reduce the amount of routine work.

These comments suggest that at the organizational level systems designers perceive themselves as having a rather limited role. Their contribution is to assist the organization to become more efficient through speeding up work procedures and providing information that is useful to management.

It seems as if the British systems designers have no conception of themselves as organizational designers using computer systems to produce new organizational forms. They possess no intellectual constructs which would enable them to assume this kind of role. But here again we find the same interesting contradiction which we noted in Diagram A. They place most emphasis on the human relations climate and personnel policies of the company as assisting its effective operation and they believe they can assist this to some extent through removing boring work and thus increasing job satisfaction. Yet, they see their principal work activities as increasing efficiency through stream-lining procedures and providing better information. They do not appear to appreciate the potential of computer technology for improving the overall quality of working life. They do not design their systems to facilitate good human relationships.

Although the assessment of contributions to the organization is similar in the two groups, the Swedish systems designers mention more often their role as change agents in an organizational context. Several of the respondents use terms like organizational change, change processes and organizational development. A few give as an important contribution that they try to provide their clients with a better understanding of the totality of their organization. The zero value given to "financial savings" in the Swedish data should be interpreted in the light of the designers recent experiences with a large, advanced but expensive real-time system which was designed to improve services rather than to cut costs.

One of the authors of this paper has made an earlier study of the attitudes and values of computer systems designers in eight companies (Mumford, 72). In this investigation she found that their operational design philosophy approached most closely to that of an engineering or cybernetic systems model with homeostasis through order and control perceived as a major goal. She found also that no explicit human models were ever incorporated into descriptions of the systems design process. Typical definitions provided were.

> It is the solving of problems, basically with a computer solution in view. It involves detailing the problem, proposing a solution and specifying how jobs will be done with the computer, both by machine and manually.
>
> To produce the required output from the given input while minimising the sum of computer time costs, related labour costs and machine costs; yet allowing flexibility and practicality and ensuring accuracy.

When asked to define their role in terms of its technical and human relations content, many systems designers (in one firm as many as 53%) perceived it as having only a technical content. Where a human relations content was recognised this was seen more in terms of successfully selling the system to users than in designing it to meet human needs.

7. The individual model of man held by the majority of systems designers

In order to find out how systems designers perceived the individual users for whom they were designing systems, they were asked to complete another opinion scale. The average opinions on this scale are set out below. Table B shows some relevant descriptive statistics. The statistical means of each distribution are connected in the graphs of Diagram B.

Table B
Individual model of man (description of answers)

Item	Mode M		Mean μ		Median $\tilde{x}$		Standard deviation		Range $(x_M - x_T)$	
	S	UK	S	UK	S	UK	S	UK	S	UK
A	3	3	3.72	3.93	3	4	1.429	1.490	7	5
B	5	4	5.12	4.12	5	4	1.225	1.417	6	7
C	4	4	4.40	4.17	4	4	1.233	1.448	5	6
D	5	4	4.92	4.22	5	4	1.197	1.226	6	6
E	4	5	4.48	3.80	4	4	1.026	1.483	6	7
F	3	2	3.04	2.95	3	3	1.182	1.303	6	7
G	3	5	3.28	4.15	3	4	1.312	1.440	6	6
H	5	3	4.88	4.17	5	4	1.242	1.303	6	6
I	5	3	5.12	3.90	5	4	1.300	1.113	6	5

S = Swedish Study, UK = British Study; N(S) = 25 = population; N(UK) = 41 of 135.

The right hand side of the scale (items A–I) represents McGregor's Theory Y man – a responsible, self achieving individual who can take full control of his work environment. The left hand side of the scale is McGregor's Theory X man – a different kind of individual who likes order, wishes to work within tightly specified boundaries and does not want to have a great deal of personal control over his activities.

As in the "Organizational Model of Man" case the British systems designers are closer to a Theory X view of the people for whom they are designing systems than are their Swedish colleagues. The latter are still on the Y half of the scale in all cases but two. However, the variance is sometimes considerable both in the Swedish and British answer distributions (Table B).

DIAGRAM B: Individual Model of Man

Use the following scale to describe the average human being (non-specialist and non-management) for whom you design computerized systems (put an X on the scale for each pair of properties).

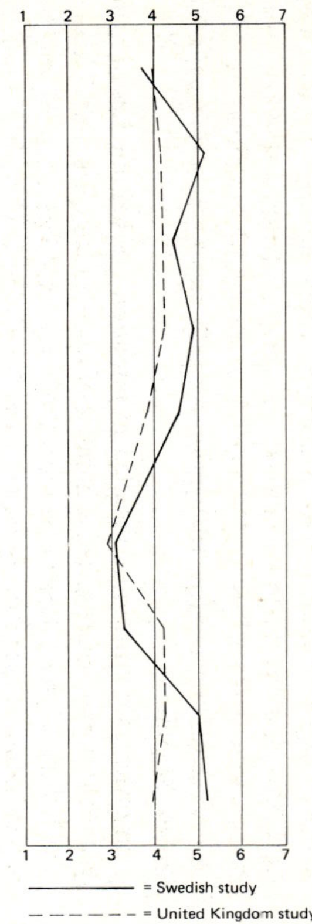

A	Leaves other people to take most of the decisions on things which affect him at work.	Will protest if he is not consulted on all matters which affect him at work.
B	Capable of handling only a limited range of tasks in his job.	Capable of doing a job involving a variety of different tasks.
C	Not concerned about having social contact at work.	Regards opportunities for social contact at work as important.
D	Can tolerate boring work.	Demands interesting work.
E	Works best if the pace of the work is outside his control.	Could be given complete control over the pace of his work.
F	Needs or wants to have a well defined job (area of operation) which he sticks to most of the time.	Works well and enjoys working in a job (area of operation) which is not clearly defined.
G	Needs to be told what to do next and how to do it.	Can organize the sequence of his work and choose the best methods.
H	Unable to undertake responsibility for decisions, and take initiatives.	Able to undertake responsibility for decisions, and take initiatives.
I	Has a low level of skill and/or knowledge (expertise).	Has a high level of skill and/or knowledge (expertise).

Although basically Y-oriented, the Swedish systems designers are not sure that their clients would function well within less structured, or well defined jobs. They also feel that to a certain extent their clients need to be told what to do and how to do it. The resulting model of man, as provided by the Swedish sample, is clearly not entirely consistent with the same group's model of the organization. Although they state that employees in an ideal organization should be free to determine their job methods, set their own performance targets etc., their model of the average employee does not really assume that the capacity for doing so is at hand.

It should be noted that the "Organizational Model of Man" questions (Diagram A) were concerned with future visions of a better organization. The "Individual Model of Man" (Diagram B) is concerned with the present state (the average human beings for whom you design computerized systems). The gap between the British and Swedish average answers is less noticeable in the description of the present characteristics of the users than in the descriptions of future organizational visions. This might imply that the Swedish computer specialists find themselves in a more pronounced conflict situation between societal values which favour Y-oriented organizations, and their own perception of the actual humans they have to work with than is the case with the British respondents.

In order to obtain more detailed information on their models of man, the systems designers were asked a number of open ended questions. These were,

(1) Give a short description of the basic characteristics of the human beings (non-management, non-specialist) for whom you typically design computer systems. What strengths and shortcomings do they have? How do these strengths and shortcomings affect your design approach?

(2) Describe briefly some of the factors which you consider contribute to employee job satisfaction?

(3) When you design a system in what ways do you think you are contributing to an increase in employee job satisfaction?

There was considerable unanimity concerning the basic characteristics of the user populations. 81% of the British comments referred to shortcomings like institutionalization (13%), resistence to change (29%) and limitation of outlook (39%). 41% of the Swedish comments were primarily concerned with the same factors: institutionalization (8%), resistance to change (14%) and limitation of outlook (19%). 22% of the Swedish systems designers mentioned a lack of EDP knowledge or knowledge about new models or methods as the primary weakness of their clients.

The strength of these individuals was seen as their considerable knowledge of their own job. A job which many had done for a number of years. (Mentioned by 32% of the Swedish respondents.) Their principal weakness was described as a dislike of change together with a reluctance to divulge information to the systems designers unless this was specifically asked for. Inability to make existing demands explicit and to think in "systems concepts" were other weaknesses mentioned. These strengths and weaknesses affected the system design by influencing the systems designers to make the systems as simple and error proof as possible with input forms easy to complete and output easy to understand. A number spoke of introducing computer systems gradually in order to get them accepted, others of trying to make their systems flexible and related to user work needs.

Yet the question on which factors contribute to job satisfaction produced answers totally at variance with the narrow, conservative kind of individual the systems designer saw himself as designing systems for. We shall analyse the answers in terms of a model of job satisfaction developed by Mumford (72). This measures job satisfaction on five variables. (1) the knowledge fit – the extent to which an individual's skills and knowledge are used and developed. (2) the psychological fit – opportunities for achievement, recognition, responsibility, advancement and status (Herzberg, 68). (3) the efficiency/rewards fit – the extent to which the individual receives the kind of resources, controls and financial rewards that he thinks is appropriate. (4) the ethical fit – opportunities for involvement and participation. (5) the task fit – is the job designed so as to provide meaningful, interesting and challenging work in the performance of which it is possible to take decisions and use discretion? We received the following pattern of responses from the systems designers.

Task factors were mentioned most frequently in the British study as con-

Factors which you consider contribute to job satisfaction (number of comments)

	N	Knowledge factors	Psychological factors	Efficiency/reward factors	Ethical factors	Task factors	Other
British study	112	2%	21%	13%	7%	32%	24%
Swedish study	46	4%	17%	26%	15%	24%	13%

tributing to job satisfaction, particularly the need to have a meaningful, challenging job and work interest. Psychological factors came next with emphasis on recognition, achievement and opportunities for advancement. In the "other" category working conditions and "good" management were mentioned frequently. Task factors played an important role also in the Swedish study. Efficiency/reward factors such as proper resources for action were, however, considered to be even more important. Ethical factors like opportunities for self determination and participation were mentioned more frequently by the Swedish than by the British respondents.

In answer to the question "when you design a system in what way do you think you are contributing to an increase in employee satisfaction", the British majority response was "by making the job less routine". The computer was seen as taking over the very simple work, leaving the user with more interesting activities, such as dealing with exceptions. However, a number of the systems designers in both the British and Swedish samples said that they did not think that they were contributing to job satisfaction. 25% of the respondents in the Swedish group felt that they could contribute to employee job satisfaction by removing repetitive and simple jobs, by matching the needs and demands of the clients (35%), by allowing the potential users of the system to participate in the design process (10%), by designing a technically perfect and well-functioning ("simple" and "reliable") system (20%), and by decentralization and delegation of authority through the system (10%).

These answers are extremely interesting for they suggest that at both the organizational and the individual level the systems designers in our sample operate with two models of man – one operational, one theoretical. One which they use when actually designing systems for users, the other which they produce when asked to consider the subject of human needs such as job satisfaction at an intellectual level. The first, operational model of man is close to McGregor's Theory X concept. In terms of organizational design it implies tightly structured jobs which are defined by the systems designers or their O & M colleagues. It also implies targets and controls set and imposed by supervision, and not by the employees themselves. At a theoretical level we get a totally different organizational model, one which has rather few structural concepts embedded in it but which sees the successful organization in terms of good human relations.

There is a similar dichotomy when we look at the individual model of man. Here the *operational model* used when designing systems takes a Theory X form with users perceived as limited, conservative human beings who operate within a narrow skill range and have great resistance to change. The *theoretical model*, which perhaps coincides with the systems designers' own needs, is totally different from this. We now see McGregor's self actualising Theory Y man, interested in self development and with a strong desire for challenging work.

8. The user's point of view

We now need to ascertain which model of man the user holds. Does he too see himself as limited and conservative, requiring a secure, Theory X, type of work situation, or does he have a different vision of himself and his own abilities? This data is in the process of being collected by the International Research Project, but is not yet available. In the meantime some evidence exists already.

Investigations carried out by the Computer Research Unit at Manchester Business School suggest that while different groups of workers hold different models of man, increasingly expectations are moving in the Theory Y direction and there is a strongly expressed desire for more interesting and challenging work. *When asked what factors would be most important to them in their ideal job*, clerks in six British firms gave the following replies.

Task factors (Work interest, variety, scope for initiative)	Rewards/controls (Good supervision, pay, job security)	Psychological (Freedom from pressure, promotion opportunities, social relationships)	Don't know
59%	20%	15%	6%

9. Conclusions

The evidence that has been collected so far supports our original hypothesis that systems designers use a restricted Theory X type model of man when designing computer systems. We need to explain this fact although there is not space in this paper to go into detail. It can be argued that systems designers are subject to many influences which affect the way they define their occupational role and the values they use when acting in this role. They derive their values and philosophy from their training, their professional colleagues, the technical literature which they read, the expectations of top management and the kinds of demands which user departments make of them. The most interesting fact which emerges from the research evidence collected so far is that at an intellectual and theoretical level, which perhaps expresses their own interests rather than those of the users of their systems, they have a completely different model of man. They now see a much more mature, sophisticated individual with a desire for challenge and achievement and a need to have control over his own work situation. *Yet this model is not extensively reflected in their work.* The gap between the operational and theoretical models of man and organizations might also indicate the conflicting loyalties of the systems designers. On the one hand they are responsible to the society in which they live and influenced by the ongoing debate and a relatively fast moving set of values concerning the *quality of working life*. On the other hand they are responsible to their superordinates and have to act within the punishment-reward system and value system of the firm. The time lag between these two sources of norms might place the systems designers in a relatively difficult loyality conflict. Some of the respondents indicate their frustration on this matter.

Our problem would seem to be how to change the model of man which the systems designer uses at the operational level to that which he uses at the theoretical level. Does the answer lie in a new approach to the training of systems designers, to more trade union and user intervention in the systems design process or to a new value system on the part of top management? Probably all of these are required. From the user's point of view an answer may lie in the increase in his competence and power. The systems designers in our sample saw their users as narrow and conservative perhaps because these users were too passive and non-initiating. Yet involvement in the systems design process requires a knowledge of how to analyse problems, use computers and design systems which few user departments as yet possess. It requires also a willingness to insist on being involved in the changes that are taking place, something which a user department that sees itself as having little power in comparison with the computer department may be reluctant to do. The present models of project management are seemingly not sufficient. The expert-client relation too seldom contains real communication. In the *hostage model* a number of potential users are included in the design group, without any real possibility of their influencing the outcome. They do not have the expert power to impose their opinion, if the EDP experts want to use technical constraints as an argument for doing things their way. Neither do these project hostages have any real chance of recognising and understanding the set of action alternatives which are available for tackling the various problems calling for decisions during the design process. In the *indoctrination model* the users are introduced to EDP, the systems concept etc. Quite often they gradually convert into systems designers and lose their links with the group they were supposed to represent.

The most important thing seems to be to establish real communication between experts and clients in design groups and to change the content of the joint discussion. Rather than discussing the tools, the users should help establish the goals. The *value system* rather than the actual computerized system should be the focus of interest. Perhaps the strongest influence that will change the practical model of man held by the systems designer will be when the users get up and shout "we are not as you think we are". They may need both trade union and top management support to enable them to do this.

References

Argyris, C. (1957). *Personality and Organization,* New York: Harper and Row.

Beer, S. (1972). *Brain of the Firm,* London: Allen Lane, The Penguin Press.

Beer, S. (1973). Fanfare for Effective Freedom, Third Richard Goodman Memorial Lecture, Brighton Polytechnic.

Boguslaw, R. (1965). *The New Utopians,* Englewood Cliffs: Prentice Hall.

Burns, T. and Stalker, G.M. (1961). *The Management of Innovation,* London: Tavistock.

Cooper, R. (1973). How jobs motivate, *Personnel Review* 2, pp. 4–12.

Davis, L.E. (1971). Job satisfaction research: The post industrial view, *Industrial Relations,* May, pp. 176–193.

De Greene, K.B. (1973). Models of man in systems in retrospect and prospect, Paper presented to 5th Congress of the International Ergonomics Association, Amsterdam.

Emery, F.E. (1969). *Systems Thinking,* London: Penguin.

Hackman, J.R. and Lawler, F.E. (1971). Employee relations to job characteristics, *Journal of Applied Psychology* 55 (3), pp. 259–286.

Hedberg, B. (1973). MIS-design as a change process. A sociotechnical approach, International Institute of Management, Berlin, Preprint Series No. 1/73–16.

Hedberg, B. (1973). Computer systems and the quality of working life, Paper submitted to the North American–European Ecumenical Conference on The Technological Future of the Industrialized Nations and the Quality of Life, Pont-à-Mousson, France, to be published in *Anticipation,* Geneva 1974.

Herzberg, F. (1968). *Work and the Nature of Man,* London: Staples Press.

Leavitt, H.J. (1964). *Managerial Psychology,* Chicago: University of Chicago Press.

Likert, R. (1967). *The Human Organization,* New York: McGraw-Hill.

McGregor, D. (1960). *The Human Side of Enterprise,* New York: McGraw-Hill.

Margulies, F. *Computer Education: Its impact on Man and Society* (to appear).

Maslow, A. (1964). *Motivation and Personality,* New York: Harper.

Mumford, E. (1972). *Job Satisfaction: A study of computer specialists,* Longmans.

Sackman, H. (1971). *Mass Information Utilities and Social Excellence,* New York: Auerbach.

Wild, R. and Birchall, D. (1973). Means and ends in job restructuring, *Personnel Review* 2 (4), pp. 18–24.

Woodward, J. (1965). *Industrial Organization: Theory and Practice*, London: Oxford University Press.

E. Mumford and H. Sackman, eds., Human Choice and Computers
North-Holland Publishing Company (1975)

TRADE UNIONS AND COMPUTERS

Alfred DALLINGER

Gewerkschaft der Privatangestellten, Vienna, Austria

In October it will be 25 years since Norbert Wiener's book *The Human Use of Human Beings* was published. Recalling this fact on the occasion of this conference not only constitutes a tribute to the "Father of Cybernetics", it also serves as an indication that the questions raised in 1949 are still unresolved and need to be tackled more urgently still. Wiener states the thesis of his book to be that society can only be understood through the study of the messages and the communication facilities which belong to it. Upon explaining the principle of feed-back, he writes:

> In this respect our views on society differ from those propounded by many fascists, successful businessmen, and politicians. (This terminology has to be viewed in the spirit of 1949.) People of this type prefer an organisation in which all information emanates from the top and where there is no feed-back. The subordinates are degraded to become effectors for an allegedly higher organism. I should like to dedicate this book to the protest against this inhuman use of human beings. It is easier to set in motion a galley or a factory in which human beings are used to a minor part of their full capacity only, rather than create a world in which these human beings may fully develop. Those striving for power believe that a mechanized concept of human beings constitutes a simple way of realizing their aspiration to power. It maintains that this easy road to power not only destroys all ethical values in humans but also our very slight aspirations for continued existence of mankind.

How true! is what we should like to exclaim when regarding today's situation in factories, in public life and in business. The development of the means of communication has not been attended by corresponding measures with respect to mutual paths of communication. The computer in particular has become – even more than anticipated 25 years ago – a tool for monopolizing information rather than for democratizing it.

Even so, many profound changes have taken place since the times of

Norbert Wiener. To the extent that the technological forecasts have been confirmed, Wiener's socio-political warnings have become the object of closer attention. Computers have ceased to be utopia, they have become reality and an integral part of our daily life. We have become more aware of hazards and opportunities implied in man's use of the computer. If Norbert Wiener had been a lonely caller in the wilderness, today an army of natural scientists, sociologists and economists is engaged in thorough and exacting research to determine the impact of computers on man and society.

We as trade unionists may justly claim to have pointed out these problems at an early stage. Originally, this was done by our colleagues in the labour unions in the U.S. who were the first to be confronted with automation and its effects. As early as 1953, the congress of the UAW (United Automobile Workers) adopted such a substantive resolution; at that time several labour unions in the U.S. launched profound studies on the socio-economic aspects of automation. In 1955, the U.S. Congress conducted a "hearing" on these problems; again, the union representatives, while fully approving of automation, cautioned against the negative impact of uncontrolled technological development and demanded stringent measures to avoid serious setbacks. "We would like to harness automation through social responsibility", was the way in which the former head of the automation department of the AFL-CIO formulated these goals.

In Great Britain too, the automobile workers were the first to point out the hazards of automation and the first to make the public aware of them. In 1954 the TUC, with the aid of the "Scientific Advisory Committee", initiated studies on the basis of which the TUC Congress in 1955 adopted such a resolution.

In the Federal Republic of Germany, the trade unions in 1956 began to pay closer attention to these problems, in particular IG Metall imparted major impulses to this work by establishing a department for "Automation and Nuclear Power" – headed by Dr. Günter Friedrichs. Additional incentives came from international seminars organized by the latter.

At its fourth national congress in 1959, the Austrian Trade Union Movement dealt in detail with the problems of automation. In the resolution adopted, the members pronounced themselves in favour of technological progress ("workers are not enemies of technological progress. . .") while at the same time advancing participation on the part of the workers in all relevant decisions. We believe that this is the only way to avoid pitfalls and to make full use of the advantages of automation – for the benefit of the workers and in the light of material, social and human aspects.

Thus the trade unions in different countries have developed a similar approach to the problems of automation. The time lag in stating their respective positions may be explained by their different economic levels and their uneven rate of technological progress. Differences in conduct and action are primarily due to differences in conduct and action on the employers' side.

I therefore believe that a distinction between "good" and "bad" trade unions, between those favouring technological progress and those interested in higher wages only is somewhat unjust. No trade union genuinely concerned with its proper task, i.e. the representation of workers' interests, can unconditionally agree to all technological changes. In each and every instance we must ask what these changes might entail and in each and every instance the answer will decisively influence action taken by the trade unions. Of course the response carries a lot of weight in its actual implication rather than in its verbal manifestation. The idiom frequently used in our country that "no answer is also an answer" still holds valid, and this is precisely what we get in the majority of cases.

Let us recall that in the early stages of EDP installations, labour saving was the declared and principal objective of manufacturers, sellers and users of computers. Naturally, the concern about maintaining jobs dominated all considerations and measures put forth by workers and their representatives. Until 1950, indifference based on disbelief in a comprehensive and rapid introduction of the computer prevailed. This changed suddenly with the spectacular qualitative and quantitative development: automation now became synonymous with anxiety and fear.

News from various countries seemed to confirm this attitude: Millions of unemployed in the United States, mass lay-offs in the British automotive industry, a gigantic increase in productivity, examples of computer application with dozens of employees becoming redundant; all this disproved the prognoses of many "nice nellies" who claimed that automation would involve a few branches of industry only, that it would proceed slowly and affect but a few jobs. Due to the continuous boom and the policy of full employment advanced by trade unions, the wave of automation in most countries did not lead to major unemployment. Still, the number of workers in industry in the Federal Republic of Germany remained stationary at about 8.34 millions between 1962 and 1972 whereas production during the same period (at constant prices) rose by 64%. Had production remained at the same level, there would have been 3–4 million unemployed in the Federal Republic as a result of automation. These figures plus the so-called symptoms of crisis at the turn of 1973–1974 (artificially caused by speculation and manipulation but nevertheless dangerous) prove the instability of our economic system and the potential danger of technological unemployment that still prevails.

Even if global full employment can be maintained, there is still individual anxiety about individual jobs. Against the background of a total of 8.34 million industrial workers in the Federal Republic of Germany we have to consider a shift from the 24 branches of industry with a diminishing level of employment (drop between 1962 and 1972 approximately 600 000) to the 11 expanding branches of industry which in 1972 employed approximately 600 000 more workers than in 1962. Not only these 600 000 persons had to change their occupation; even within individual enterprises and departments there has been a continuous process of change. Constant developments in technology also require constant readaptation of the individual. Those unable to go along, fall by the wayside. This holds true for bookkeepers and payroll accountants whose work is to be taken over by the computer; it also holds true for programmers whose knowledge becomes obsolete to the extent to which software systems, operational systems and languages are changed or renewed. This equally applies to the simple punchcard operator who is being replaced by new methods of data collection. Even under optimal employment conditions older workers are left behind during this migration. In the past we used to say that life begins at fourty; today we practically have to admit that life ends at forty – at least for those who have to look for new jobs at that age. The age structure of an Austrian computer sales company provides a good example to support this argument (Fig. 1).

Almost 80% of the staff are below 35. Adding the group between 35 and 45 covers 94.1% of the total number of employees. The other age groups in this company do not amount to more than 5.9% even though 25% of the overall Austrian population are found within this range. Shouldn't we consider the future of these people? Thus the net result of a constant employment level is but a very superficial aspect that must not by any means pacify trade unions. The millions (or in Austria the tens of thousands) of displacements with their profound social, material and psychological implications for those affected do confront us with a genuine problem. Long-term personnel planning with workers' participation along with all other types of planning measures are required when a computer system is introduced or changed; for us this constitutes a priority demand. It is the only way to avoid risks to the employees and to surmount the difficulties in these transitions. It is the only way to assure that the workers' interests are safeguarded and the only way to avoid a completely negative approach to technological innovation.

When the trade unions in our country began dealing with the problem of automation, there were only a handful of EDP installations in Austria. On the other hand, there were many experts trying to prove that automation would not make any headway in Austria. Quite a few people believed these experts.

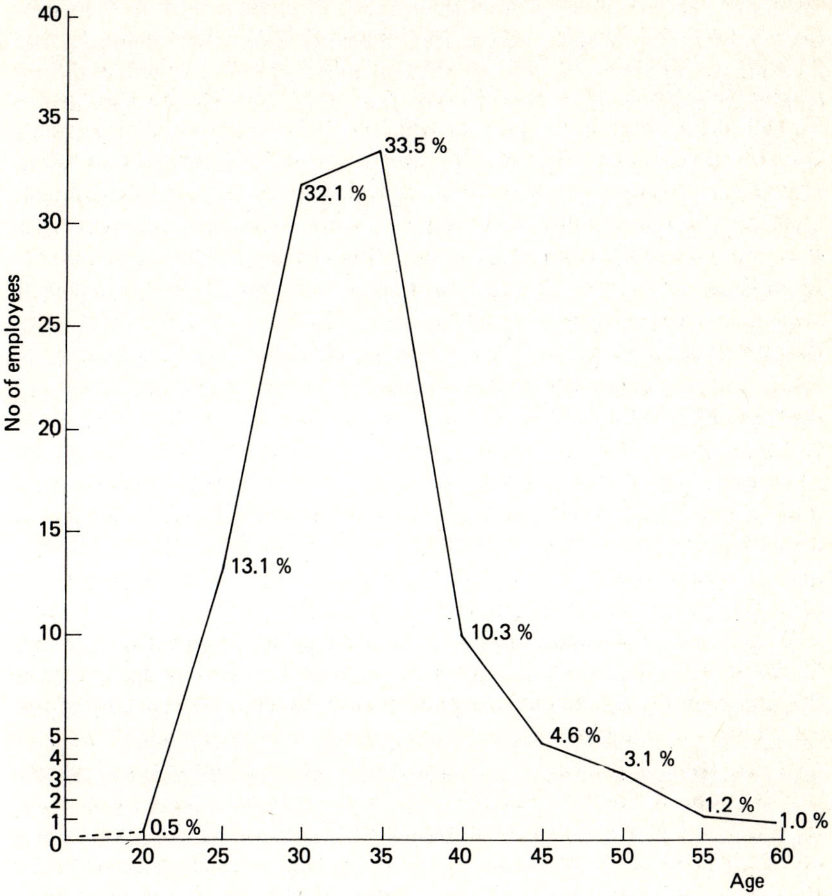

Fig. 1. Age distribution of employees in an Austrian Computer Sales Company.

The computer boom that set in shortly thereafter, with an annual growth rate of 20 to 30% or even more, brought about a basic change in the attitude of employees and employers alike. The labour saving aspect as a motivation for introducing computers reverted to the background compared to the expansion of capacity and performance, compared to the ability to cope with rising requirements, with the ability to improve the information system. The computer became an instrument for data processing.

At about the same time the public's attitude changed. Even though anxiety and fear had never been totally eliminated just as labour-saving aspects had never quite disappeared from the employers' catalogues of requirements, there did arise a profound wish to find out more about technology. At that time many institutions – not all of them well-founded – appeared and offered EDP training; they took a great deal of money from the uninformed public without fulfilling their customers' high professional and financial hopes. It was quite a while before public institutions (ministries, common interest groups and trade unions) offered courses independent of these companies on a non-profit basis; it was not until some time later that the public was sufficiently forewarned against the risks involved in such private training institutions. On top of that, the trade unions offered (and still offer) to their officers and shop stewards courses in information processing in which these people learned about the basic concepts and functions of hard- and software. These courses also met with a lively response just as did regular lectures about new developments in data processing organized jointly with the University of Technology or our "Automation Club".

At the same time we continued to be concerned with the working conditions and the work design for EDP personnel. In too many cases when building or remodelling premises for EDP installations it was overlooked that not only computers had to be accommodated but that people had to work there; human beings who needed sufficient space, proper illumination, a low noise level, ergonomically correct seats, a comfortable climate and adequate rest periods. Unfortunately, it is still the rule, for example, to design the air-conditioning equipment according to the requirements of the computer whereas the staff has to accept draughts, dryness and similar discomforts. A broad study carried out two years ago on the working conditions of punch-card operators revealed some frightening factors. At this time – in cooperation with various universities and institutes – we were trying to check on the eye stress caused by working on visual display units. The use of these devices is still in the incipient stage in our country and we hope to be able to provide guidelines and limits on the basis of this study for that type of work to be taken into consideration as soon as visual display units are generally introduced. From all this we may infer that in line with our approach to technological change we are trying to keep in step with these developments or even to stay a little ahead of them. The fact that our opposite numbers on the employer side make this rather difficult by withholding information from us as long as possible and by keeping us out of the decision-making process whenever they can is, of course, an entirely different matter.

Computer development has certainly not been concluded but rather continues at a very rapid pace; who would be better aware of this than the participants in this conference? This implies that the interrelationship between man and computer is a major interest not only to the trade unions and social scientists but also, I believe, to computer scientists.

The computer which was initially regarded as an improved calculating machine, first took over work in various fields without changing the structure of the organization or the character of the work performed in different divisions. In many instances the EDP-department remained a foreign body within the enterprise, something of an elite with a mysterious air about it but with no tangible influence on day-to-day business. This has now changed fundamentally. Integrated information systems, data banks, on-line terminals, multi-programming and many other developments have turned the computer into an instrument with multiple application. In many enterprises there is no longer any important department that does not provide information to the computer, that does not receive processed information from the computer, in other words, that does not make use of the computer in one way or another. Thus, the number of persons dealing directly or indirectly with computers or the number of those whose work has been changed by the data processing systems or the administrative measures involved, has expanded considerably. In turn, the computer is now much more dependent on personnel who have developed a very realistic or even pragmatic relationship to this machine – even though these people are neither thoroughly trained in EDP nor necessarily aware of the consequences of errors or inaccuracies.

This growing interdependence on the one hand implies the danger of major difficulties which in extreme cases may even lead to failure of the system. On the other hand interdependence is the great chance to take an important step toward the goal of "humanizing" work.

Our present industrial system which started with the industrial revolution of the 18th and 19th centuries when the material basis of capitalism was created, has been characterized by a tremendous development of the means of production (tools, machines, production methods, and sources of energy) while man's development continuously lagged behind. In the pre-industrial age heavy physical labour was the principal factor in production. But even then every single production process required some mental effort in addition to physical labour. As a rule, however, it was the producer himself who planned his own work, implemented and completed it. Mental and physical labour constituted an integral whole which made possible some development of personality and required and made feasible some creative activity.

In contrast, mass factory production of the industrial era led to an increased division of labour, to a separation of mental and physical effort. Creative activity remained the preserve of a relatively small group of higher employees while most of the white- and blue-collar workers in production became appendages of the machine. Their work – in extreme cases – was confined to the brainless and soul-destroying repetition of unchanging tasks.

Thus the worker lost his personality and his personal relationship to work. In the work processes there are no decisions for him to make. Every step is prescribed and the machine to which he is subordinated is not his property. Others dispose of the product which he helps to create. Very often he does not even know what the product looks like when it leaves the factory or what it is being used for.

In his *Das Kapital*, Karl Marx writes: "Even facilitating work becomes a means of torment since the machine does not liberate the worker from this task but rather strips work of its content."

Increasingly, people resist this dehumanization. The elementary need for realization and full development of one's own personality for purposive, gratifying and creative activity is coming more and more to the foreground once material want has been overcome and the physical necessities of life are assured. The revolt against work on the assembly line in the United States, Sweden and France, the protests against the monotony of performing always the same manual tasks illustrates this trend. So do the riots at the universities and the strike of the metal workers in Nordbaden for improved working conditions under the slogan: "Man must be more important than productivity and profit."

The scientific and technological revolution of our age invites this great chance of reversing the trends of the industrial system. The new technology no longer requires the division of labour nor does man need to continue being an appendage of the machine. Wherever within the industrial system man became an automaton, automats are now in a better position to perform this work quicker and with less friction. Man turns from a servant of the machine into a supervisor, maintenance man and partner. Man finds a task adequate to his nature in the dialogue between man and machine, in the interrelationship of the man–machine system.

Thus the construction and design of this man-machine system, the role assigned to man, has become a priority problem the resolution of which is not only a matter of concern to trade unionists and sociologists but also to a growing extent to computer scientists. This happens to be so because the idea is gradually gaining ground that computer systems – in order to function properly – require man's attention. With the rising complexity of systems this fact becomes ever more relevant. But of course, systems call for man's attention in a different way from before. They do not call for button pushers devoid of thinking but for the type of person who is endowed with reason, able to make his own decisions and aware of his power to act deliberately. In our updated terminology we would call this model the "motivated man".

You know that there are many tests and studies being carried out on man's motivation in order to find out what makes him happy and content. I must admit that I am increasingly sceptical about these studies. It is not hard to find out what makes a man discontented and unhappy. Contentment and happiness, however, are made up of so many components that in most instances it is impossible even for the person himself (and even less so for an outsider) to draw up a complete and integrated pattern. To me it seems the epitome of misconception to try and tell someone else how he is to become happy.

I have been told that in an American plant a group of sociologists for the umptieth time wanted to conduct an investigation; they were received by the firm's employees with a poster stating "Do not feed the animals". If we have reached the stage when our search for man's true happiness imparts the feeling that man is to be an object of curiosity in a zoo – then we are obviously on the wrong track. We will only be able to reach our goal if we give people the chance to do their own thinking, to make their own decisions and to implement them. All those who have engaged in creative activity of some kind know from their own experience that the opportunity for decision-making is the most attractive aspect of one's work.

Why shouldn't it be possible to initiate preparations for a new data processing system by informing those involved in its use about the qualities, possibilities and limitations of the system and then asking them to consider in small working groups what part of their work they would like to assign to a computer and what other tasks they would like to take on instead. I do not know how good the proposals of such groups will be and I am not sure that all staff members will accept such an assignment with the same amount of enthusiasm. We must recognize the fact that desire and ability to do creative work are by no means general phenomena. For us this means having to bear in mind that everybody ought to be afforded the *chance* to work creatively. Considering all the badly operated and incorrectly used data processing installations, the above mentioned method must at least lead to some sort of improvement.

However, we have to accept as the basic hypothesis the premise advanced by Mrs. Mumford in her lecture, i.e. that "computer systems associated with the solution of particular business problems allow for different forms of work organisation and different job structures. In other words, the systems involving computers . . . are not technologically deterministic but permit the designing of these systems in a manner which successfully meets the needs of groups which will operate them . . ." It seems to me that the great challenge for modern engineers and scientists is to work out such alternatives and to bathe them in the limelight of discussion. The major question that remains to be considered in this context is the measure of freedom of choice and decision left to these experts.

When speaking about the humanization of work, we ought to avoid two misconceptions: One would be to regard computers only as a tool for increasing productivity and thus eventually for increasing profits. As traditional methods of incentive are losing their effectiveness, "motivated by their intrinsic need for positive performance and identification, workers will on their own direct their efforts toward achieving the objectives of management" (Frankfurter Zeitung: "The So-called Humanization").

The other misconception would be to presume that humanization of the job will not only eliminate physiological and psychological drawbacks, but banish all difficulties and job problems. Such a situation would basically contradict man's need for creative activity. It would also disprove our basic practical experience that leisure time predominantly constitutes a continuation of working hours. Those who are forced to lock out their mind while at work, in other words those who leave their creative ability at home when they go to work, will rarely be creative during their leisure time! Not man's liberation from work, but man's liberation from inhuman conditions is our goal. Much in the same way as the state can eliminate hardships and offer chances but should never try to remove all obstacles, company organisation is not in a position to do so either. If work is to be interesting, it must include challenges, tensions and problems. This is one of the reasons why I believe it to be wrong to redesign work from the outside. If I were to adapt an old slogan of the workers' movement to modern times, I would say that the humanization of work can only be carried out by the workers themselves.

From the philosophical approach Prof. Zemanek has proved that computers can never replace man and that only man is able to cope with the distinctions between a model and reality.

On the other hand, Dr. Sackman will show what a powerful tool the computer may be for man – opening up the path towards "Human Choice".

Mrs. Mumford has described how far away we still are from realizing socio-technical systems, a task left to be accomplished by computer experts and system designers. If their systems are to function, then these systems have to be adapted to thinking, creative human beings and to offering these thinking, creative individuals a chance for self-fulfillment and development.

I have attempted to show that this task cannot be solved for the working man but only with him and that his needs as a human being must take precedence over technological and economic considerations.

For this reason modern trade unions concentrate on demanding participation for workers in all technological and administrative decisions. To put it differently, we want the employers to provide full information in good time – that is in the planning stage of a computer system or better yet, when it is first considered, prior to specific planning. We also want the employees to be represented in all in-company committees dealing with the planning and development of computer systems. Let us deal right here with the objection that shop stewards do not have enough expert knowledge to participate and that therefore it would suffice to inform them once the social consequences have become apparent, consequences which become manifest much later. First we would like to say that in management decision-making power does not always go hand in glove with comprehensive knowledge. On the other hand, shop stewards who are able to acquaint themselves in courses offered by the trade unions, with the basic concepts of electronic data processing, also have experts at their disposal within the trade unions who may support them and give them information. However, the principal argument we put forward is that the shop stewards' committee is not designed for nor does it intend to interfere in technological and administrative details. Its primary task is to see that from the first moment of planning the human problems are placed on the agenda. The committee also has to pass on information to those concerned and to stimulate them to consider and formulate their own demands; in other words, to see that the process of humanization of work is initiated by the workers themselves.

We feel that we can cope with these tasks provided computer experts and scientists help us and in their own interest participate in optimizing the man–machine relationship. In designing the ever more complicated systems of information processing or automatic manufacturing, man and machine must be regarded as integral parts of a whole system. The ideal is no longer the perfect machine that should be interfered with as little as prossible by man but rather the optimal fit of technological and human capabilities. If a process deviates from the programmed routine, man with his capacity for abstract thinking, creative analysis and carefully considered decisions enters his proper sphere. And it is this sphere that will tax man's mental capacity, will make it possible to develop his personality and make him content on the job – the first step toward overcoming alienation.

If computer and social scientists would cooperate with employees and their representatives in order to get firsthand acquaintance with their wishes, proposals and considerations, and in order to base their activity on these criteria, it would mean that a decisive step toward humanizing work had been taken. On their own behalf and in the interest of the technological progress to which they are dedicated, experts in all fields ought to become the most fervent and determined advocates of workers' participation.

E. Mumford and H. Sackman, eds., Human Choice and Computers
North-Holland Publishing Company (1975)

COMPUTERS AND SOCIAL OPTIONS

Harold SACKMAN

The Rand Corporation, Santa Monica, Calif. 90406, U.S.A.

1. Introduction

World War II not only spawned the atomic age for mankind, it also gave birth to the modern electronic digital computer. The explosion of physical power was accompanied by the less dramatic but more profound explosion of information power. And as major advances were made in the scientific and technological growth of atomic power, so were equally spectacular advances made in information power.

Only a relative handful of scientific and technical people used computers at the end of World War II. Now we are on the verge of mass information utilities – the universal extension of computer services to the general public. What are the options, real and potential, for social choice with computers?

The initial approaches to this question were speculative and predisciplinary. Computers and society made good material for science fiction Sunday supplements with roller-coaster chills, thrills and spills for the avid reader. Only in the 1960's did fantasy give way to more serious efforts to assess the impact of computers on society. Professional conferences were held and working committees were established on social implications within the computer field, in allied areas, and in government. The first books on computers and society appeared in the late 1960's and seem to be exponentially increasing in the early 1970's.

Fads, fancies, and fears were generated for the public eye, stemming more from the immediate payoff of sensationalism than from informed analyses. There were periods when computers were thought to make possible completely automatic, pushbutton wars (e.g., at the 1960 time period when the SAGE air defense system became operational in the United States); beliefs that computers could "soon" easily translate any language into any other language; insistence that automation would make the work force obsolete and annihilate the Protestant ethic; computers were anthropomorphized by the optimistic as helpful symbiotic partners and by the pessimistic as Machiavellian mechanical overlords that will ultimately enslave or destroy the human race; management information systems were inevitably going to drive out middle management. More recently, with the proposed centralization of federal statistical services in the United States in the mid-1960's, the spectre of computerized invasion of privacy arose; and with the universalization of computerized billing, banking and record-keeping at local and national levels, a hue and cry has been raised over the depersonalization and dehumanization of numbered men. The computer world has aided and abetted many of these trends with too many irresponsible promises of glittering things to come from the hawkers of computer services. Nevertheless, the gross cost of computer-related goods and services has continued to grow exponentially, from a virtually nonexistent industry at the end of World War II to over 20 billion dollars per annum worldwide today.

Amidst this hurly-burly scene of rapid growth, confusion, broken promises, rampant fears, and animistic superstitions, the field of computers and society has found it extremely difficult to achieve respectable status with professionals and the public. Only recently have several distinct areas of systematic inquiry emerged, some even giving promise of amenability to scientific method. It is the task of this theme chapter to review four areas of significant advance that are beginning to emerge. The four approaches that have been singled out are:

(1) Computers and Social Problems,
(2) Computers and Education,
(3) Computers and the Individual,
(4) Regulatory Issues – Computers and the Law.

This fourfold set is not put forth as a comprehensive and mutually exclusive classification scheme for computers and society. It simply represents key areas of the general field where significant work is in progress with reasonable promise of substantive developments to come.

The first category refers to the application of computers to major social problems. The emphasis is mission-oriented. It is not on the negative note of what computers are doing *to* society, but on the more constructive note of what computers can do *for* society to ameliorate our most pressing problems. Since this is the most comprehensive area, it receives the most attention.

The second category is computers and education where much has been done and where we are at a critical crossroad in social alternatives for extending the benefits of computers to all of society. The third area, computers and the individual, like the first, is extremely broad and uneven, but has achieved sufficient stature and importance to be treated as an entity in its own right. The fourth category is already fairly well-defined with a rapidly growing literature – regulatory issues – including computers and the law broadly considered.

It should be apparent that there is unavoidable overlap among the four categories, and that common themes are likely to run through them. This introduction to these areas will prepare the reader for more detailed treatment of subsequent chapters in this book, and help develop a sense of the thrust of computers and society, its leading issues, and the prospects for enlightened social choice.

2. Computers and social problems

The essence of this area is defined by two questions. First, what are the leading social problems of our day and age? Second, how can computers be used to help people understand and solve such problems? The first question presupposes a classification of social problems, and the second requires an analysis of current and projected computer usage.

The above task was tackled as a project under the aegis of the American Federation of Information Processing Societies; the final product was a book entitled *Computers and the Problems of Society* (Sackman and Borko, 72). The project also involved an invitational conference consisting of contributing authors exchanging their ideas. The results of this conference and book are very briefly sketched.

A classification scheme of social problems was developed as an organizational guideline. This scheme is shown in Table 1. No special claims are made

Table 1
Classification of social problems

(1) *International Problems*	(3) *Environmental Problems*
(a) International cooperation	(a) Urban problems
(b) Hot and cold wars	(b) Ecological balance
(c) World population growth	(c) Biomedical
(2) *Economic Problems*	(4) *Humanistic Problems*
(a) Commerce and industry	(a) Education
(b) Individual consumers	(b) Politics
(c) Management and planning	(c) Individualism
(d) Mass communications	

for this loose taxonomy – it served its purposes effectively in delineating broad areas of human problems, the development of computer services in these areas, and the prospects of projected computer assistance in ameliorating leading problems. Other classifications have been proposed such as the social problem matrix put forth by Platt (69), where problems are categorized by "intensity" and estimated "time to crisis".

The scope of this theme chapter does not permit any comprehensive discussion of results. Only general trends can be sketched following the four broad areas shown in Table 1. In the international arena, the most advanced computerized information systems, particularly in real-time command and control, have been developed for military purposes. Unfortunately, equal and opposite computer power has not been allocated to wage peace, foster international cooperation, nor stem the erosion of the quality of life with the advancing tide of global population.

In the economic arena we also find a humanistic mismatch. Some of the most advanced computer systems are found in commerce and industry, as in on-line banking, industrial process control of petrochemicals, and the proliferation of management information systems (Head, 72). The problems of labor, the white-collar worker, the individual consumer, and the plight of the underprivileged have hardly been touched by the great potential of computers to protect workers, consumers, and upgrade the standard of living of the poor.

The environmental area is a relatively newer application for computers. Ecological, urban and biomedical problems have been subjected to intensive computer-aided simulation, forecasting, and planning efforts with increasing public support. Perhaps the most advanced computer systems have appeared in medical applications, building upon NASA manned-spaceflight experience, as in real-time monitoring of critically ill patients in emergency hospital wards. A humanistic lag also exists in computer services for environmental problems which receives only spotty support from meager government, institutional, and municipal budgets.

The last category in Table 1, humanistic problems, is the most uneven, and predictably, the most neglected area of all. The most advanced computer applications are probably found in education. Despite all glowing claims and promises of cheap and powerful computerized education driving out traditional "manual" education, we have not yet arrived at cost-effective computerized configurations. Politics is beginning to respond to the vast potential of information as the new seat of power, and to the unprecedented opportunities for participatory democracy with online voting via mass computer utilities. (See *The Information Utility and Social Choice* (Sackman and Nie, 70).)

Last but not least is the promise of the transformation of individual perception, cognition and effective human intelligence for Homo sapiens over the long run. Will computers be used to elevate the collective wisdom of the human species?

It is apparent that this effort to match computers against the challenge of social problems ends in raising more questions than it answers. However, a number of integrative themes emerged from the disparate problem areas. These common themes may be grouped under three heads – social values, methodological approach and technology.

For all the many computer shibboleths that were shattered, a fundamental belief persisted among the experts that computer technology will continue to make significant advances in man-computer decision making, problem solving, learning, and ultimately in uplifting effective human intelligence. Although there was much disagreement over particular techniques and the rate of progress, the basic article of faith was the expectation that the computer would amplify the power and range of human intelligence. There was no agreement whether such intellectual advance would necessarily be good or evil.

As cautionary measures toward more beneficent human evolution, it was urged that computers be employed as early warning devices for diverse social indicators to alert all of society to emerging problems in time to solve them. An ancillary social value expressed in many different problem contexts was participatory social decision making aided by public computer networks. The implicit assumption was that over the long run the democratic ethic would lead to the greatest good for the greatest number, more or less in line with Winston Churchill's dictum that democracy is probably the least worst of all known forms of government. These social values, however, were tempered by the qualification that the technological-professional contributors may have world-views quite different from social majorities (e.g., Churchman, 72), and that none of us could predict public attitudes in the era of universal computer services.

In the methodological area, several agreements were obvious across diverse problem domains. A non-surprising outcome was that computer applications to social problems are inherently interdisciplinary in nature – real-world problems have a perverse disrespect for compartmentalized disciplines. Diverse problems have many similar methodological elements in problem detection, formulation and solution, and the structure of effective social planning is often similar across different problem domains. For example, social experimentation with institutional or community prototypes, and the extensive use of simulation and gaming were frequently cited as early warning methods of choice to try out new computer-aided solutions on a limited scale before accepting them for widespread application. None of these methods were put forth as panaceas, and abuses of each were easy to find.

In the technological areas there was much criticism of the failures and shortcomings of existing computer technology. Exaggerated claims for computer oversell were heavily scored. It was admitted that large and complex computer systems have persistently encountered crushing software problems resulting in failure and abandonment of many systems with marginal cost-effectiveness for many others. (One of the working groups of this conference devoted most of their effort to this issue.) Management was charged with abdication of responsibility to middlemen in many computer systems, such as systems analysts and programmers, who were not prepared or competent to deal with the user community and the organizational mission. This delegation of authority to technicians was viewed as bankruptcy of leadership.

Even with all these reservations over the management and development of computer technology, there was a clear acceptance of the imminence of mass information utilities as the next major breakthrough – the extension of on-line computer services to the general public in the natural environment of the user, at home, at school, and in the office. It was agreed that the technological building blocks were available (e.g., broadband CATV communication links to all homes, cheap and easy to use terminals, TV display services, and the necessary computer power and data storage). The major challenges ahead are the development of computer readiness in the general population, and field-tested, cost-effective configurations for community implementation.

A final outcome of this effort was the realization that mission-oriented computer users in a particular problem area are in the best position to systematically add to our knowledge and capability in the application of computers in their problem domain. This seeming tautology has major implications for the thrust of future work – effective leadership in the formulation and solution of social problems is the proper responsibility of those closest to the problem, not the computer expert.

3. Computers and education

There are two sides to computers and education that are actively growing and developing. One is the application of computers to the educational process, and the other is the teaching of computer and information science in schools and on the job. We are confronted with social choice in what computers are doing to education, as opposed to what education is doing to computers. The distinction is not frivolous.

About a decade ago there was a kind of general euphoria in the United States that the application of computers to education would solve most of education's ills. CAI (computer-aided instruction) would patiently move at the pace of the individual student, it would keep records of progress, diagnose errors, branch off into corrective exercises, and bring each student up to his maximum capability. CAI proved exorbitantly expensive, on-line consoles cost dollars rather than cents per connected hour, learning improvements over traditional manual methods were ambiguous and problematic, critics such as Oettinger (69) pointed out the fallacies of the philosophy of the "technological fix" to cure the ills of education, and a whole generation of educational researchers and technicians became chastened and disillusioned as research monies from the federal government dried up in lean years. There is a shift in research from CAI to making sources of knowledge more accessible to students, and to other educational computer applications such as simulation and gaming, and to new forms with mixed media, especially with television. Much effort is being directed to economies of scale in anticipation of mass educational information utilities.

Perhaps the most promising of the emerging prototypes for large-scale computer-aided education is the TICCET system developed by Mitre Corporation at Reston, Virginia (Stetten and Volk, 73). Mitre plans to extend TICCET to Stockton, California, utilizing existing two-way cable television lines for interactive color video displays using the home TV set for a variety of competitive CAI services. If their proposal is funded, they hope to service 1000 families, with a rated system capacity of 100 simultaneous users. They hope to work toward interactive educational services that would be commercially feasible at one to two dollars per connected hour at the home console. The prototype would be conducted as a social experiment, with results in the public domain.

Looking at the other side of the coin, we can ask "what is education doing to computers?" There has been steady progress in the appearance of computer centres in the universities for teaching computer science; the size and power of a computing centre has become a status symbol. Departments of computer science are proliferating with rapid establishment of Ph.D. level programs. In many colleges most undergraduates are required to take at least one introductory course in computer science. About 15% of secondary schools in the United States offer introductory computer courses. The question arises, "Are students receiving proper indoctrination and instruction in the use of computers?"

This question is more than academic. For better or worse, introductory computer courses not only provide basic computer concepts and techniques, they also generate polarized attitudes toward computers. The attitudinal fallout may be more important for society over the long run than the initial skills that are developed. For example, the major social problem for mass information utilities is not the technological problem – we know we have all the technological building blocks – it is the problem of public acceptance. No one can force a citizen to have computer services in his home if he doesn't want it. So the question arises, "What is education doing to foster favorable attitudes toward beneficial applications of computers?"

Here there is cause for concern on two basic counts. First, introductory computer courses as now organized and implemented, are likely to turn off students in large numbers with negative attitudes. Reason: such courses are conceived and administered as an introduction to computer programming, as opposed to computer science and social uses of computers in the broadest sense. Computer programming is neither the essence nor the whole of computer science. Most citizens, whether departments of computer and information science like it or not, will be users of computer services, not programmers. They want fast, reliable, easy, effective, mission-oriented computer aids; they are too often turned off by laborious coding and unforgiving debugging in producing their own programs as class assignments.

Table 2
Positive and negative student attitudes toward computers and computer programming

Positive Attitudes	*Negative Attitudes*
Understanding program concepts.	Inadequate access to computer facilities.
Understanding the speed and power of computers.	Unreliability of hardware.
Insight into the structure of syntax.	Programming is too complicated.
Learning how to debug and test programs.	Poor support services.
Appreciation and respect for computers and computer science.	Computers are wasteful for many types of easy problems
Programming is logical.	Too much work, too time-consuming.
Learning how a computer works.	Batch and/or timesharing are poor ways to use computers.
Appreciation of computer language.	Painstaking care and attention.
Batch and/or timesharing is easy.	Computer is an antagonist.
Successful communication with computers.	Batch and/or timesharing are unreliable .
Sence of triumph over computers.	Disappointment in not solving a well-understood problem after great effort.
Understanding flow charts.	Antagonism toward computer language.

The author, for example, found 26% of a sample of 415 cadets in an Air Force Academy study expressing negative attitudes toward computers and programming as nothing less than "the most important insight" they achieved in their introductory class experience (70). See Table 2 for a listing of positive and negative attitudes reported by these students. The upshot is plain for all to see – we need to design courses aimed at winning friends and influencing people toward socially desirable uses of computers in introductory courses. A shift toward a broader introductory course offering, one that emphasizes computers from the user's point of view, stressing all and not just the programming part of computer science, a course that features social implications, would go a long way toward getting off on the right foot.

The emphasis on computer programming as the fit diet for the neophyte stifles much wider extension of introductory computer courses for all schools because of the very expensive and hence limiting requirement of a school computer facility to suppcrt student programming. If the aim of introductory computer courses is computer readiness through computer appreciation, then such courses can be effectively taught without hands-on programming experience. Computers are prohibitively expensive for schools with declining budgets in austere times. If computer support isn't necessary, then virtually any school can afford to develop an introductory computer course, even at the elementary school level where it is urgently needed. Today's elementary school children will be in their prime in the year 2000. Such courses, for students of all ages, would go a long way in developing constructive computer readiness in the general population for the era of mass information utilities.

4. Computers and the individual

There are many approaches to the vast and amorphous area represented by computers and the individual, and as indicated earlier in the discussion of humanistic problems, perhaps the least amount of work has been done in computer applications for the ordinary citizen. The extension of computer services to all individuals in the form of mass information utilities provides a useful focus to this area leading to possibilities for constructive social planning. The major impact of the computer on the individual will be determined by the manner in which computer services are introduced to him and the ways he learns to use them as such services become more diversified and more universal.

At the end of World War II, practically no one used computers. One generation later in the 1970's, only about one percent of the population of advanced industrialized nations has significant working interaction with computers (this figure could be expanded or decreased depending upon how "significant interaction" is defined). With the advent of mass information utilities, this figure will move through some two orders of magnitude with consequences we can only dimly discern at this point.

Even at this relatively early point before the advent of mass computer services, the computer has demonstrated a wide-ranging impact on the individual. But the impact has been problematic. Many have predicted shorter work weeks and an increase in personal leisure with advancing automation. The record is unbelievably complicated, ruling out the early simplistic expectations. Although production of goods requires less and less manpower per unit, the rise of services in post-industrial society, as described by Bell (73), seems to absorb available manpower leading to new economic configurations.

The decline of the individual, the obsolescence of privacy, dehumanization, and depersonalization have also been predicted for the citizen increasingly alienated from his society, partly as a result of computerization. What we find instead is a more or less increasing standard of living, with rising expectations in the Third World, and greater rights accorded to minorities, women, children, students, homosexuals, and even to the mentally defective, the mentally ill, criminals, and other "forgotten" groups. We find a growing assertion of individuality among the young. The role of the computer in these changes is, at this point, probably secondary and derivative, and in any case, almost impossibly difficult to determine. The name of the game is not what computers are doing to society, but what society is doing with computers. The issue is social choice.

Whatever the impact of computers on society now, it will be much more profound when everyone or nearly everyone will be using them in the era of mass computer services. There are two basic social alternatives for the grand design of individual computer services. One, already well underway, is economic exploitation of the individual market for information services via two-way CATV. The heart and soul of this approach is simply private profit. The other, almost nowhere in sight, is deliberate social planning of individual services for maximum benefits to every citizen over the long run. The heart and soul of this approach is the supreme worth of every individual. The design of mass information utilities is no less than our design of the new individualism.

This potential for reconstructing a new individualism raises the issue of a bill of human rights for individual use of computer services in the public domain. The notion of a "computer bill of human rights" was raised numerous times during the conference and in several of the conference working group reports. Unfortunately, the conference was only able to explore this area only in a very rudimentary way. The consensus of opinion seemed to be that the time is ripe to help formulate such a bill of rights in key areas such as education, work, and social services, and that the presence of such a formulation would facilitate the development of social policy with computer services. For example, some labour union representatives at the conference believed that such a bill of rights would have helped them in developing long-range quality of life standards for working conditions in highly computerized occupations. International statements of human rights, such as those promulgated by the United Nations (67) need to be updated to anticipate the future human condition.

5. Regulatory issues – computers and the law

As computers spread into the warp and woof of society, they become increasingly affected with the public interest and a growing need for public safeguards. Regulatory issues arise in law and within computing as a profession. Considerable time and attention has been devoted to this area which is quite active at this time. These issues may be classified under three broad heads which are discussed in turn – professional certification, user safeguards, and public utility regulation. (See Leininger and Gilchrist, 74, for an authoritative, recent look at computers and the law based on a conference at the Stanford University Law School.)

Professional certification refers primarily to internal standards and codes of ethics within the computer world. The various national computer societies have developed codes of ethics for their professional following. This is undoubtedly a useful initial step, and an act of responsible leadership. However, professional societies are primarily oriented toward the production and dissemination of technical knowledge and can hardly be expected to be effective watchdogs and policemen over their membership.

Another approach to professional certification is the development of standards of professional competence. The traditional form is educational certification. The colleges and universities are beginning to produce large numbers of graduates at junior college, baccalaureate, master's and doctoral levels in computer and information sciences, including emphasis on overlapping areas such as engineering, mathematics and business.

Industry has been loathe to enforce rigorous educational standards because of the economic advantage of obtaining cheap labour and providing quick training on the job for specialized in-house applications. Many fly-by-night programming schools have mushroomed into existence to exploit easy access to a career in computing. The number of machine operators and programmers without formal training constitute a large part of the total computer personnel labour force with a strong vested interest in resisting exclusive educational standards.

The software industry is notorious for poor quality control and exacerbated management problems. The situation becomes increasingly critical as software costs continue to exceed hardware costs, proportionately and absolutely. The certification issue for computer professionals is bound to come to a head as the colleges and universities increasingly take over the total educational job for the computer world, and as better trained professionals drive out those with marginal credentials on the job and in the professional societies.

Another approach to certification is to validate delivered computer systems and information services. The American Federation of Information Processing Societies has been very concerned with this problem and is supporting an effort to develop guidelines for computer system test and evaluation. That is, users of computer systems will have a set of established guidelines to help them determine whether they are getting effective or shoddy information services. Unfortunately, software reliability and validity, and computer system cost-effectiveness is still much more of an art than a science, and establishment of acceptable standards for system quality control has a long way to go. However, the recognition of the crucial value of objective system test and evaluation in the computer user community is a major advance in its own right, and a concerted effort in this area is bound to develop powerful approaches that will protect users from abortive computer investments.

The quest for system quality control spills over into the area of user safeguards, the second certification category. The user needs better assurance that services will perform as promised as mentioned above. He also needs protection against charlatans and fraud. Professional certification, when it becomes a potent force, should go a long way toward eliminating computer quacks.

Much time and attention has been recently devoted to use safeguards for the security and privacy of personal and proprietary data files. Security of data is an old game as any professional who has worked with classified information can tell you. No system is foolproof, and you get what you pay for. Some system designers use a rule of thumb that security costs should not exceed 10 percent of total system costs. The field is marked by security measures, counter-measures, and counter-counter-measures reminiscent of wartime command and control (see, for example, Peterson and Turn, 67).

Linked with security issues is the so-called invasion of privacy. This issue is treated in three papers in these proceedings, only a few key points are made here. Privacy has unfortunately been an emotionally charged issue marked more by heat than by light. It has not received an objective operational definition amenable to measurement and evaluation including the work of Westin (67) and Miller (70). There are no quantitative empirical baselines to measure social indicators in this area. It has been placed in the pantheon of untouchables with the good, the true and the beautiful. The individual's right to withhold information about himself is counterbalanced by society's right to know, particularly in democracies. There is no doctrinaire triumph of good over evil by pitting one side against the other – the solution of choice is selective compromise for specific issues in specific contexts based on working experience. It is unfortunate that the public has only been exposed to the threatening side of privacy (e.g., derogatory dossiers); the opportunities are at least as great for unprecedented protection for each individual in computerized files if systems are deliberately designed for such protection. Here again, the issue is not what computers are doing to people, but what people want to do with computers. The issue of privacy is social choice.

The third area of regulation falls into the domain of public utility law. In the United States, communications has been regulated as a public utility since 1933. With the marriage of computers and communications, particularly with data transmission, data telecommunications has become increasingly subject to regulatory decrees.

A major economic conflict is brewing over the fate of CATV regulation as a public utility. The CATV operators would like to enjoy freedom to carry their own programs and to transmit standard TV fare without royalty penalties. The telephone system sees CATV as a major treat, particularly in the computer/communications area. Broadband CATV channels capable of carrying color video have about 100 000 times the information-carrying capacity of voice-grade telephone lines. The TV broadcasting industry and the computer industry are sitting it out on the sidelines to see which way regulatory law is oriented before making major alliances and investments. The economic fate of mass information utilities, the richest plum of the marriage of computers and communications, hangs in the balance.

The issues and choices are extremely complex in this area. It is not possible here even to summarize current status (for further details, see Sackman and Boehm, 72).

Computer-accessible information is a new type of public utility. It is not a homogeneous commodity like gas, water or electricity. We need new thinking leading toward a reconstruction of public utility law to meet the challenge of mass information utilities.

6. Conclusion

This theme chapter has reviewed four areas where significant work is in progress in shaping the field and determining the direction of computers in society. These included the umbrella category of social problems, and the subsidiary areas of education, the individual, and regulatory issues. These areas are so vast and complex that only an impressionistic survey was possible.

Several common themes arose. The major theme is that the public can no longer afford to be passive in the growth and proliferation of computer services. It must play a more active role in shaping and designing the great computer systems and networks of the future in the image of man's highest aspirations. The stakes are too great – we can no longer simply muddle through.

A second theme is the imminent emergence of mass information utilities for Everyman. Computer services in the natural environment of the user will eventually radically transform our homes, jobs, education, and leisure – our life style as we know it, leading to the emergence of a new individualism. It is up to society to decide how to shape this new computer-aided individualism rather than let it be the unwitting creation of the blind forces of the economic marketplace. Labour unions and the rank and file worker have a pivotal role in asserting their stake in mass information utilities.

A third theme is growing dissatisfaction with the failure of the computer world to keep its own house in order. There has been virtually no exemplary pursuit of excellence, neither in professional standards nor in services for computer users. System failures large and small are legendary, professionals are not effectively certified to insure competent workmanship, managers have abdicated leadership to technical specialists, software development and its certification has been neglected, and the computer world is only beginning to develop a social conscience commensurate with its social promise. It would be unfortunate if government has to take the initiative with wide-ranging measures to compel the industry to meet its growing obligations to society.

A fourth theme is that the initial speculative treatment of computers in society is beginning to move out of the predisciplinary stage into more systematic applied scientific disciplines. Computer users, particularly in the various sciences, are incorporating computerized techniques transforming inquiry in their own domains, and allowing them to explore the social implications of their technologies more effectively. This is evident in international, economic, political, legal, environmental and educational arenas. Social experimentation in prototype communities is beginning to emerge, assisted in no small way by computers for the collection, reduction and analysis of data. Social planning, particularly for urban problems, is making major strides with computer-assisted techniques.

The issue is deliberate social choice, leading to responsible social planning, and continuing social accountability. The day is short, the task is long, and the mirror of man hangs in the balance. When you peer into the face of the computer, do not be surprised to discover the reflection of yourself.

References

Bell, D. (1973). *The Coming of the Post-Industrial Society,* New York: Basic Books.

Churchman, C.W. (1972). Management and Planning Problems, in: H. Sackman and H. Borko (eds.), *Computers and the Problems of Society*, Montvale: AFIPS Press.

Head, R.V. (1972). *Managers Guide to Management Information Systems*, Englewood Cliffs: Prentice-Hall.

Leininger, J.E. and Gilchrist, B. (eds.) (1973). *Computers, Society and Law: The Role of Legal Education,* Montvale: AFIPS Press.

Miller, A.R. (1971). *The Assault on Privacy,* Ann Arbor: University of Michigan Press.

Oettinger, A.G. (1969). *Run, Computer, Run: The Mythology of Educational Innovation*, Cambridge: Harvard University Press.

Petersen, H.E. and Turn, R. (1967). System implications of information privacy, *AFIPS Conference Proceedings* 35, FJCC, pp. 111–117.

Platt, J. (1969). What we must do, *Science* 166, November 28, pp. 1115–1121.

Sackman, H. (1967). *Computers, System Science, and Evolving Society*, New York: Wiley.

Sackman, H. (1971). *Mass Information Utilities and Social Excellence*, New York: Mason and Lipscomb.

Sackman, H. and Boehm, B. (eds.) (1972). *Planning Community Information Utilities*, Montvale: AFIPS Press.

Sackman, H. and Borko, H. (eds.) (1972). *Computers and the Problems of Society*, Montvale: AFIPS Press.

Sackman, H. and Citrenbaum, R.L. (eds.) (1972). *Online Planning*, Englewood Cliffs: Prentice-Hall.

Sackman, H. and Nie, N. (eds.) (1970). *The Information Utility and Social Choice*, Montvale: AFIPS Press.

Setten, K.J. and Volk, J.L. (1973). *A Study of the Technical and Economic Considerations Attendant on the Home Delivery of Instruction and Other Socially Related Services Via Interactive Cable TV: Volume 1: Introduction and Interim Summary*, M72-200, McLean: The Mitre Corporation.

United Nations (1967). *Human Rights,* New York.

Westin, A.F. (1967). *Privacy and Freedom,* New York: Atheneum.

MANAGEMENT CHOICE AND COMPUTERS

E. Mumford and H. Sackman, eds., Human Choice and Computers
North-Holland Publishing Company (1975)

INTERFACE PROBLEMS IN MAN–COMPUTER INTERACTION*

K.D. EASON, L. DAMODARAN and T.F.M. STEWART

Department of Ergonomics and Cybernetics, University of Technology, Loughborough, England

1. Research on the interface

Human factor specialists began to take a serious interest in the interface between man and computer when it became possible for interaction to take place via on-line computer terminals. The presence of a piece of hardware meant that man–computer interaction could be viewed as a branch of man–machine interaction. Thus it became apparent that previous research on the displays the machine provides for the user, and the controls by which the user operates the machine, was relevant to this new field of study. This interest has led to much work on the appropriate output devices for man–computer interaction (printer, alphanumeric visual displays, graphics, etc.) and appropriate input devices such as special purpose keyboards, light pens, and joy sticks.

Once the question of how to achieve effective interaction between man and computer had been raised, it quickly became apparent that it involved issues not found in man–machine interaction. Nickerson (69), for example, has drawn attention to the many human factor issues associated with computer language, and Miller (68) to the importance of such system variables as computer response time.

The literature on the human issues associated with the interface between man and computer is growing rapidly but it is largely fragmented. One author is concerned with errors in data input, another with keyboard layout, and still another with character display. The result is more of a catalogue than an integrated body of knowledge and still less is it a theory of man–computer interaction.

* This research was supported by a grant from the Social Science Research Council.

One of the reasons for this state of affairs is that man–computer interaction can take many forms and the interface issues may not be the same for all forms. The computer is a general purpose information processor which can be used for anything from storing a single piece of information to solving the most complex mathematical problem. The users interacting with the computer over this range of tasks are, in many ways, interacting with different machines. Interaction with a computer can show as much variability as riding a bicycle compared with piloting a jet airliner. The issues that concern the user in one situation are unlikely to be the issues of concern in another situation.

It is our belief that, before present knowledge about interface issues can be made coherent, it is necessary to generate classifications of the different forms man–computer interaction can take, and of the interface issues associated with each form. This paper presents some classifications we have developed in the course of studying the forms of interaction employed by the users of 26 computer systems in Great Britain.

We did not feel we could embrace every form of interaction in one study so we restricted the survey to the forms used by one major category of users. These people are *the naive users of the computer*, whom we define as individuals working within an organisation, who are not experts in computer technology but who use the computer as a tool to assist them in their work. Thus programmers interacting with computers are not considered in this paper. The objectives of this survey were to ascertain the purposes for which naive users interact with the computer, the form of interaction employed, and the issues associated with each form of interaction.

2. Classifying forms of interaction

There are a number of conditions that must be fulfilled if man and computer are to interact. First it must be possible for man to communicate with the computer using the input mechanisms (vision, hearing etc.) and output mechanisms (hands, voice etc.) at his disposal. Secondly, in order that the meaning of the communication can be comprehended at both ends of the channel, man and computer must share a symbolic coding system. Finally, if we assume that we can design a computer system to fulfil these conditions, it is necessary to ensure the man can develop the appropriate skills and learn the procedures to operate the system.

This way of describing man–computer interaction, which emphasizes the user's viewpoint rather than that of the system designer, leads us to identify the three components of interaction which are outlined below, and which were used to classify the forms of interaction encountered in the survey.

2.1. The medium of interaction

The physical characteristics of the communication between man and computer we have called the "medium" of interaction. In the survey we made a basic distinction between users who had access to an on-line computer terminal and those who employed less direct means of communication. Terminals were then subdivided according to the type of output provided (hardcopy or display) and the type of input devices used (type of keyboard, light pen, etc.). Non-terminal interaction typically involved coding sheets or data preparation forms as input and printout as output. However, some users had no contact with one or both of these media because they used another person to act as an "interface" with the computer, preparing data for input and/or interpreting outputs from the system.

2.2. The mode of interaction

The symbolic nature of the communication between man and computer we have called the 'mode' of interaction. The striking feature of the modes of interaction employed by naive users is that they provide only restricted access to the power of the computer. Most users employed a set of specially developed procedures which enabled them to conduct interaction related to their work but did not give access to the other facilities computer technology could provide. Some of these modes were more restrictive than others and we developed the classification shown in Fig. 1 to reflect the differences in scope and flexibility of these different modes.

In Fig. 1 the modes of interaction are in three groups, those emphasizing data input, those emphasizing the receipt of output, and those concerned with instructing the computer in the methods by which information is to be processed. In each group two modes have been identified. In the *input group* there was one mode which limited the user to the entry of data (DIO) and another where the user entered data but also obtained outputs from the computer (DIPO). The *output group* had one mode in which the user automatically received outputs (POO) and another in which the user could request the kind of output he required (POR). It is only in the *instructional group* that the user could actually manipulate and change the data. One of the modes in this group (IDP) gave the user a subset of processes he could perform on data. The limited range of facilities of this mode was broadened

Fig. 1. MODES OF INTERACTION

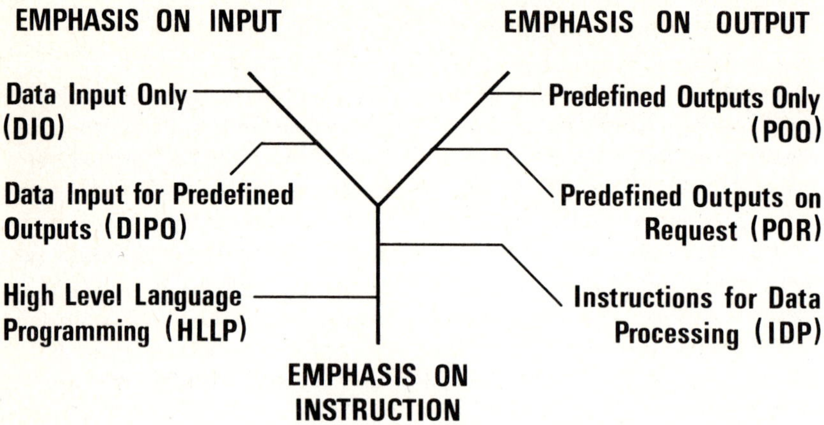

considerably in the next mode when users employed high level languages such as FORTRAN or ALGOL. It is possible to identify modes of interaction of still greater power, e.g. machine languages, but anyone capable of interaction of this type should not be regarded as a naive user.

2.3. User support

The final component of interaction is the method by which the user develops the necessary knowledge and skills to understand and use the computer system successfully. We have called this "user support".

We analysed the kinds of support a user needs in two ways. First we made an analysis of the function for which the user needed support. The user had, in some cases, to develop the necessary skills to operate a terminal, and he also had to master the procedures for operating the system. Similarly he had to ascertain which system facilities were appropriate to his task. He also had to know what to do in the event of system malfunction, and how to escape from the system if he got into difficulties. He had to know who to turn to if he needed help and finally, if he found the system could not perform the functions he required, he needed to be able to convey his requirements to those responsible for system operation and development.

The second kind of analysis was of the way these forms of support were provided. In some cases the system itself provided some of the necessary support. This was accomplished in two ways; by the provision of supporting documentation or by including the support in the interaction that took place between the user and the system. The functions which were most often served by these means were those which specified the procedures for using the system and the facilities available. User manuals containing this information were common-place and some systems were attempting to include this information within the system. However none of the systems that we surveyed were able to answer all user needs for support by these means and all had some kind of support provided by members of staff.

In examining "human" support systems we made a basic distinction between formal and informal mechanisms of support. A few of the systems surveyed had formalised user support services or user liaison groups who undertook many of these functions. In most systems however only one or two functions were formalised, usually training (often only when the system was first implemented) and hardware maintenance and repair. Other functions, if they were provided at all, were provided through the development of an informal network of contact between systems personnel, experienced users, and new or inexperienced users. In many systems we found "local experts"; users who, by virtue of long experience or a special interest in the system, were regarded by their colleagues as the source of all knowledge about the system.

3. User types

A total of 254 computer users were interviewed in the survey and, in addition to classifying the forms of interaction they employed, we also classified the user according to the kind of job held. We placed users in three broad categories.

(1) Clerical Users ($n = 103$). This included a wide variety of jobs, for example, invoice clerks, accounts clerks, stock clerks, and bank cashiers. All of these jobs were characterised by their routine, repetitive, nature and their relatively well defined use of the computer.

(2) Management Users ($n = 82$). Management users of the computer ranged from managing directors, through a middle management level, to first line management and supervision. The sample was predominantly first line and middle management partly because of the inaccessibility of senior management, but also because many of them claimed to be relatively unaffected by the computer. Brady (67) found that senior management in the U.S.A. were similarly not directly affected by computer systems.

Fig. 2. MODES OF INTERACTION

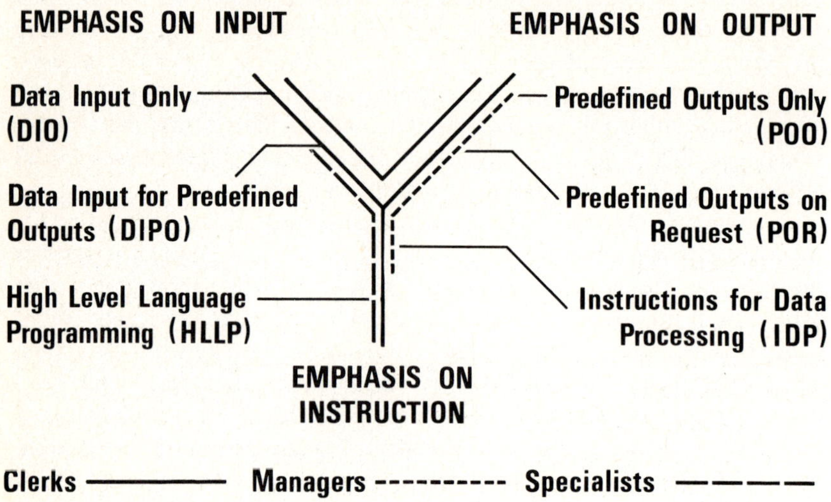

(3) Specialist Users ($n = 69$). This category of users included the various kinds of problem solver to be found in industry and commerce; people who had a specialist discipline to call upon such as engineering, design, operations research, economics, statistics etc. These people were not computer specialists but, because of their own disciplines, they did have specific requirements of computer aid.

A strong correlation was found between modes of interaction and the different user types as is shown in Fig. 2. Most of the clerical users employed the modes of interaction where the emphasis was upon input, although a substantial minority used output modes. Managers, by contrast, were primarily concerned with output modes although there were 24 who made use of evaluative models and were thus operating in a limited instructional mode. Specialists dominated the instructional modes although a few were limited to the more interactive versions of data input modes.

4. User problems with forms of interaction

User interviews in the survey consisted of two parts; an analysis of the form of interaction employed by the user, and an examination of a range of issues which might affect his response to the computer. These issues were of the following four kinds:

(1) Task Fit Issues. An examination of how well the computer system was able to provide for the task needs of the user. This section of the interview included questions about the relevance, accuracy, completeness and timeliness of information provided by the system.

(2) Ease of Use Issues. This section examined how easy outputs from the computer were to read and to analyse, and how easy it was to operate the system. When a terminal was in use there were additional questions concerned with terminal operation, work place design etc.

(3) User Support Issues. This section consisted of two kinds of question, those concerned with the support given to the user when the system was in operation, e.g. for advice or when a breakdown occurred, and those concerned with the role of the user in the design and development of the system.

(4) Indirect Consequences of the System. A wide variety of questions which explored the possible ramifications of computer use for the user, his job and the organisation. Examples included issues of job satisfaction, promotion opportunities, new skills developed etc.

The survey revealed that some issues were of critical importance to some users but were relatively unimportant to other users. The results are presented in detail elsewhere (Eason et al., 74) but a brief presentation of the results pertinent to the man–computer interface are given below.

4.1. The medium of interaction

120 users interacted with the computer via some kind of on-line terminal. Of these, 56 were clerical users, 50 specialists and only 14 managers. This is indicative of the fact that, although the potential of management use of terminals has been stressed by a number of influential authors, e.g. Licklider (65), Morton (68), they have yet to be generally accepted in the management environment. Where the managers in the survey had experienced use of terminals there was a strong tendency to relinquish direct interaction and utilise a "human" interface to operate the terminal on the manager's behalf.

Although human factors studies of man–computer interaction have concentrated upon the medium of interaction, few users found terminal operation a major problem. The most frequently cited problem was the full alphanumeric keyboard which, with its usual mysterious array of special function keys, was a formidable tool for the non-typist to handle. A factor of annoyance to virtually every terminal user was the almost universal lack of consideration given to the furniture associated with a terminal. We found very few examples of attempts to design a complete work station for the user, with adequate seating, desk space, and storage for manuals and working documents.

4.2. The mode of interaction

Some of the most interesting differences between users were related to the different modes of interaction used. The input modes were the ones that led to the most adverse comments about indirect consequences. These were the modes used largely by clerks and they usually involved short cycle, repetitive operations. Users complained of excessive routine, limited job satisfaction and of being controlled by the computer. These problems were most severe for users whose interaction was confined to data input. Although they were still present, these problems were less marked for the user who was not only required to input data but received a service from the computer which enabled him to complete other duties, e.g. the bank clerk checking an account balance on behalf of a customer. There were two important differences between this kind of job and the job that consisted of data input only. First the job was more complex and provided more diversity of work and secondly the clerk could regard the computer as his servant rather than his master.

The issues of concern to users of output and instructional modes were not the indirect consequences of the system but its ability to meet task needs and the ease with which it could be used. In order to examine the overall relation between task fit and mode of interaction we constructed a composite score from the results of all questions that reflected a task oriented issue. These scores are given in Fig. 3. They are expressed as percentages of questions that did not reveal significant problems out of the total number of questions posed and hence a high score represents a good task fit.

Our hypothesis was that task fit would improve as the mode of interaction became more flexible and powerful i.e. that the more power the user could command the better able he would be to obtain the service he desires. To confirm this hypothesis, Fig. 3 would have to display an increase in task fit from left to right which is not the result obtained. An analysis of the results for each user type may explain the situation.

The task fit for clerical users decreases as the modes shift from an emphasis upon input to an emphasis on output. This is not surprising because the only task the data input clerk had to perform was the one the computer system had been designed to facilitate. In the DIPO and POO modes the clerk was engaged upon tasks which used computer output and task fit dropped

Fig. 3.
THE EFFECT OF MODE OF INTERACTION UPON TASK FIT

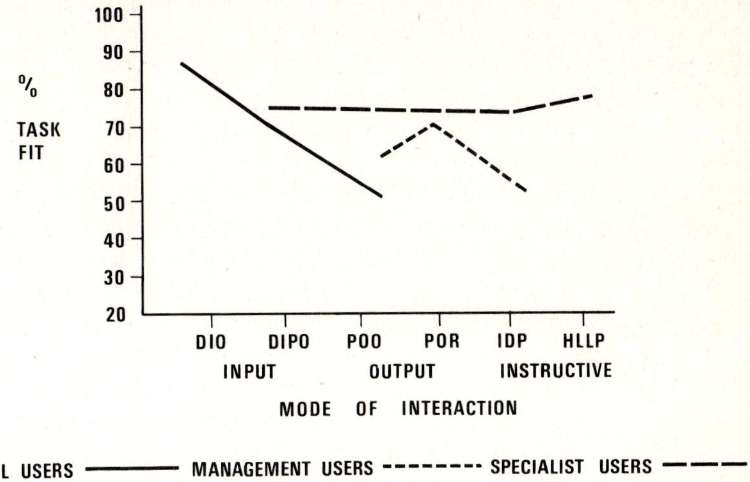

quickly when external tasks were being served. The situation was therefore, that the clerks provided with the more satisfying jobs by virtue of the outputs they used, were likely to be the more dissatisfied with the service provided.

Specialists displayed very little variation in task fit whichever mode they used. This is surprising because, for many specialists, the reason for learning to program was to achieve a better service. Although the HLLP mode showed a slightly higher score than the other modes, there remained a substantial gap between the achievement specialists wanted and that which they actually achieved.

A rather more dramatic picture emerged from the results for managers. Both management and clerical users of the POO mode achieved low task fits. It has been known for sometime, for example see (Ackoff, 68), that management information systems which typically operate by this mode, frequently provide irrelevant and out-of-date information. The user has little direct control over the information he receives or when he receives it. In the POR mode the user gains some control over these factors. The survey results showed that as expected, the POR mode gave users a better task fit than the POO mode. However, the next mode (IDP), which offered further power and flexibility, rather than continuing this trend, led to a decrease in task fit.

Despite the manifest differences between the three user types, they shared one characteristic in their responses to modes of interaction. The modes that were typically provided for their use did not satisfy their needs; personal needs in the case of clerks, task needs in the case of specialists and managers. Unfortunately, when modes were provided that had the potential to meet these needs, the predicted advantages proved difficult to obtain.

There are many reasons for this situation but two are of prime importance. First, as the system becomes more complex, it becomes more difficult to understand and yet, if a manager or specialist is to use it effectively he must understand and accept the assumptions upon which the system operates. Too often, as Edstrom (71) stresses, systems are designed on a normative basis, to provide what the designer thinks is necessary rather than what the user wants. Even with choice available to him, therefore, the user will not obtain what he seeks. The second issue concerns the ease with which flexible systems may be operated. The survey contained a number of questions relating to ease of use issues and a detailed analysis of one of these questions may serve to illustrate a general trend. As Testa (73) has indicated, users often experience difficulty in using the operating instructions of computer systems. Fig. 4 gives the percentage of users surveyed who claimed they had difficulty understanding and operating software procedures.

The software procedures users operated had a variety of functions; for entering data, searching data bases, specifying information to be retrieved, and specifying operations to be performed upon data etc. An analysis by mode showed that clerical users experienced relatively little difficulty, probably because they used the system regularly and they learned the procedures thoroughly. This was not so true for clerical users of the POO mode who were mostly high grade staff who made less frequent use of the computer system. In this respect they resembled management and specialist users who, because they were only occasional users, tended not to master the procedures they had to use. Specialists showed a steady increase in the percentage finding procedures difficult as the modes became more flexible but for management users the increase was much more dramatic.

This was but one indication of a general finding from the survey. Users who sought a better service or a better job by employing a mode which had the potential to meet their needs, were trading one set of problems for another; the problems of using a complex and unfamiliar piece of technology. An interesting and important subsidiary finding was that, for each user type, this problem became critical in a different mode. The specialist users, for example, found the IDP mode a satisfactory mode in which to work whereas management users experienced many problems with it. We conclude that a

Fig. 4.

USERS RESPONSE TO THE OPERATING PROCEDURES OF DIFFERENT MODES OF INTERACTION

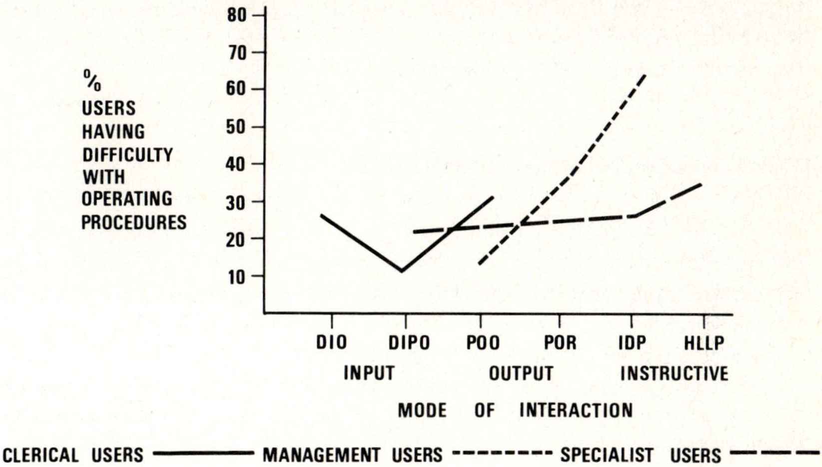

different kind of mental effort/benefit ratio must operate for the different types of user, i.e., specialists are much more willing to expend the necessary effort to use a computer system than are their management colleagues. The mental effort/benefit ratio in general appears to be best explained by Zipf's (65) principle that people adopt a path that involves the least average rate of probable work.

4.3. User support

The user support system operating for most computer systems was a mixture of the formal and informal and proved difficult to define. Clerical systems tended to have formal support teams at the time of implementation but these were often disbanded subsequently. However, clerks more than any other group of users expressed a need for support. Much of their work was centred on the computer and they wished to understand how it worked, the contribution they made, and how it related to the functioning of the whole system. Very rarely were there formal mechanisms for answering these needs.

The support required by specialists and management was more task oriented; it was needed to identify the facilities available and how to use them. Some of the specialist systems were beginning to recognise this need and provide User "Liaison" or "Support" Teams but it was rare to find this in management systems. Where there was no formal provision for these needs users tended to rely on "local experts" for the guidance they require. The importance of the local user support network increased when the users found they could not or did not wish to cope directly with the complexities of the system and preferred to use an intermediary.

5. The consequences of poor interface design

It could be argued that, although this paper has indicated a wide variety of interface problems, these problems are of academic interest only because users were using the systems. There were, however, some aspects of user responses to these systems that suggested interface problems could have serious consequences and these are summarised in Fig. 5.

The consequences were different for clerical users than they were for irregular system users like specialists and managers. Most of the clerical users had little choice but to accept any inadequacies a system possessed and to

Fig. 5.
THE CONSEQUENCES OF INTERFACE PROBLEMS FOR DIFFERENT TYPES OF USER

	USER TYPE	
Consequences	Clerks	Managers & Specialists
For system operation	User adaptation	1. Non-use 2. Limited use of Facilities 3. Human Intermediary
For user	Frustration and loss of morale	Failure to realise system potential

compensate for them as best they could. User adaptation is a phenomena encountered in all kinds of technological systems where flexible man has to work with rigid technology and computer systems are no exception. The cost of continual compensation appeared to be a build up of frustration in the user possibly leading to a loss of morale and interest in the work.

The occasional users of the computer, the manager and the specialist, were much less tolerant of poor sytems. They expected a tool which fitted their needs and they did not expect to modify their own behaviour to fit its needs. A poor interface had many more consequences for these users, the responses being of three kinds:

(1) Non-use of the system. One possibility was that the user, after initial "testing" of the system, would decide not to use the system. Unlike clerical users, management and specialist users often had this option and no doubt many have used it. If there were "users" of this kind in the systems we surveyed, we did not detect them because we sought only active users.

(2) Limited use of the system. One of the features of the flexible, interactive systems was that they offered choice. Many of the users of these systems agreed that they tended to use only a few of the facilities available to them and to disregard the others. It could be argued that the remainder of the facilities were irrelevant to the user but this response was so widespread that it suggests valuable facilities were not being used.

(3) The use of a human intermediary. A response particularly characteristic of the management user, was to employ someone to act as a human interface between the user and the system. In several of the systems surveyed there were moves towards employing this mode of interaction and this method is increasingly common elsewhere. Martin (73) for example, describes an IBM system in which "data secretaries" operate from an "information centre" to supply information requested by high ranking managers. For the manager this approach clearly has much to commend it, relieving him as it does, of most of the ease-of-use problems. It is difficult to know, however, whether such a system, no matter how well organised, will have the same result as an effective man–computer symbiotic partnership.

6. Towards more effective man–computer interaction

This paper has been directed more towards identifying the problems experienced by the naive computer user than towards solving these problems. As is often the case, the survey directs attention to issues upon which further research is necessary, particularly into the dynamics of the user's effort/benefit ratio that appears to play a crucial role in determining the user's response to a system. Nonetheless the survey results do suggest three kinds of issues the system designer must tackle if he is to make more effective man–computer interaction possible by reducing the amount of effort the user has to expend to achieve his objectives:

(1) The Interface. The need for more care in the design of the hardware interface between man and computer is reinforced by the survey results but they also indicate the importance of software interface issues. It is interesting to note, for example that, while there is some degree of standardisation in keyboards, there is no similar standardisation in the software procedures by which such basic operations as data entry, logging on, error messages etc. are handled. As a result, as the user moves from system to system, he has to learn a new "language".

(2) User Support. The more flexible and advanced systems now being provided for users inevitably make heavy demands of the user. Even if system operation can be made easy, the user still has to know the options available to him, understand what each can do, appreciate their validity for his purpose and know how to use them. It will rarely be possible to train users to fully appreciate the potential of the system and learning must often take place while using the system. This process demands that the user is adequately supported through the provision of documentary aids and human advisors. At present these needs are met more by chance than by design.

(3) User Involvement in System Design. The amount of effort a user has to expend to use a system is partly dependent upon his previous experience of the system and partly upon the extent to which it provides a direct answer to his need in terminology with which he is familiar. The best way of ensuring that all of these forms of effort are minimized when the system is in use is to involve the user in the development of the system. User involvement can ensure that the user receives a service he wants, that he understands the service he can obtain, that he can operate the system, and that he is committed to the system before it is implemented and does not view it with suspicion and doubt.

7. Conclusions

The survey results indicate that at present system designers are creating user interfaces which provide only limited access to the power of the computer. By making these limitations the interface can be made sufficiently easy for the naive user to operate. However in many cases, the simpler forms of interaction are unsatisfactory. They either help create repetitive jobs, as in the case of clerical users, or they do not adequately meet the task demands of the user because they are insufficiently flexible and powerful.

Each group of users is therefore in need of more complex forms of interaction. Unfortunately the more complex forms often prove difficult to use and the user cannot or will not provide the effort necessary to master the software procedures of the system. The result is either a self-imposed restriction in the range of facilities used or a reliance upon human beings who act as intermediaries. As forms of interaction become more complex, there is a greater possibility of the computer providing significant aid to all types of user. However the increase in complexity leads to critical interface problems which must be resolved before the full potential of computer aid can be realised. This conference has been about human choice and this paper has shown that we are now developing systems which offer the naive user the opportunity to exercise choice. Unfortunately our present inability to design interfaces for effective man–computer interaction in complex systems means we are often offering choice with one hand and removing it with the other.

References

Ackoff, R.L. (1968). Management misinformation systems, *Management Decision* 2 (1), pp. 4–8.

Brady, R.H. (1967). Computers in top-level decision-making, *Harvard Business Review* 45 (4), pp. 67–76.

Eason, K.D., Damodaran, L. and Stewart, T.F.M. (1974). A Survey of Man-Computer Interaction in Commercial Applications, Forthcoming Social Science Research Council Report, London.

Edstrom, A. (1971). Determining management information requirements, Paper presented at the International Seminar on Organisations and Computers, Dubrovnik, Yugoslavia, 16–18 August.

Licklider, J.C.R. (1965). Man–computer partnership, *International Science and Technology* 41, pp. 13–26.

Martin, J. (1973). *Design of Man–Computer Dialogues*, Englewood Cliffs: Prentice-Hall.

Miller, R.B. (1968). Response time in man–computer conversational transactions, *Proceedings of the Fall Joint Computer Conference*, pp. 267–277.

Morton, M.S. (1968). Visual display systems and management problem solving, *European Business*, April, pp. 37–46.

Nickerson, R.S. (1969). Man–computer interaction: A challenge for human factors research, *Ergonomics* 12 (4), pp. 501–517.

Testa, C.J. (1973). The evolution of man–computer symbiosis, *Computers and Automation* 22 (5), pp. 11–12.

Zipf, G.K. (1965). *Human Behaviour and the Principle of Least Effort*, New York: Hafner, second ed.

E. Mumford and H. Sackman, eds., Human Choice and Computers
North-Holland Publishing Company (1975)

INFORMATION SCIENCE FOR SYSTEMS ANALYSIS

Ronald STAMPER

London School of Economics, London, England

1. Introduction

Managers and administrators are growing doubtful about the claim that computers are easy to justify on economic grounds. They have seen too many information systems that are technically excellent failing to make any effective contribution to the organisation using them. Customers and citizens are growing suspicious about the social consequences of computers. They feel docketed and more open to manipulation, their personal lives exposed both to deliberate prying and to unintentional misinterpretation. These are symptoms of applying a machine-centred "computer science".

Most computer systems are designed on the assumption that they communicate with "mechanistic man", an extension to the machine, conveniently able to take over where the state of the technological art tails off into questionmarks. Though able to imitate machine-like behaviour, man is not a machine. "Humanistic man" uses and responds to information in quite a different way. Most systems design is weak on the problems of the man-computer interface and almost ignores the problems of the interface between the mechanistic and humanistic systems. No wonder we are creating ineffective systems and ones which are possibly socially damaging!

To change this situation we must break out of a mesh of constraints which exist for reasons of history. The development of the computer stimulated developments in a number of branches of knowledge; especially electrical engineering, numerical analysis, the logic of computability and formal linguistics. By the early 1960's these special topics, together with a knowledge of existing hardware and software, had become solidified into what is now called "computer science". Unfortunately, no sooner had the boundaries of this subject been fixed, than the problems of using the computer were to shift from the technical headaches of the early years to the organisational and social worries of today. The practising systems analyst and designer who is forced to go where the practical problems take him is finding himself increasingly out of sympathy with the work of computer science departments in universities and computer-centred professional societies; whilst these institutions cannot lift their intellectual horizons beyond the machine on which they have elected to gaze. What the systems analyst needs today is information science rather than computer science, as Harold Sackman said during this conference.

2. "Information" derived from a more primitive concept of "a sign"

"Information" is a vague notion used with shameful laxity in the field of systems analysis. It is often defined by analogy with a chemical plant: "raw data" is "processed" to yield its valuable content of "information" for the decision-maker. Looking more carefully at what happens when a report is prepared for a decision-maker, we see that words and numbers are selectively rearranged and transformed to yield others which are better able to influence the decision-maker's judgement, which display a different logical structure and which have different statistical characteristics. Both the data and the report consist of signs, tangible marks on paper, probably, which signify things in the world of interest to the decision-maker. Among the properties of such signs are ones which correspond to our vague notion of "information". The concept of a "sign" is a precise one in any context. A sign is whatever is used to transmit information. It is always some recognisable and quite tangible form of matter or energy. Signs are never in any way abstract or mysterious although marvellously varied: a punched card carries information from man to computer, electronic impulses link computers, printed documents pass from computer to man, whilst flowers and side-long looks signify between a man and a woman. The actual physical vehicle, though indispensible, is not important in its own right so much as in its ability to represent something else, that is, to act as a *sign*. In any situation involving information, it is always possible to find a simple, objective, operational way of identifying the signs employed. We can, by equally clear operational procedures, observe and measure the properties of these signs. For example, many different measures of information can be associated with both data and report, by procedures based on their effects on the decision-maker's judgement, or based on their logical structures or based on their statistical characteristics. To ask how much information a set of signs conveys is like asking how large a piece of wood is: there is no single answer to this question, only a number of answers to more precise questions about mass or volume or length. The theory of signs elucidates the more precise questions we should ask about information and develops procedures for finding the answers.

3. The theory of signs or "semiotics"

It is possible to develop a theory of signs capable of yielding an understanding of information that is scientifically rigorous and broad enough to encompass the problems of both human and machine systems. *Semiotics* has a long and respectable history from the Ancient Greeks through John Locke, Charles Peirce, Charles Morris to the present day. In his opening address to this conference, Heinz Zemanek used semiotic analysis to display the gulf between the mechanistic and humanistic systems; elsewhere (Zemanek, 72) he has argued that it is an essential component of the discipline of "informatics". I have myself presented its main ideas in the context of a study of information in business and administration (Stamper, 73a).

Semiotics has always been regarded as a branch of philosophy and, during the formative years of computer science, it enjoyed a vogue in philosophical teaching, especially in the United States. Sadly there was little transfer of ideas. Most information system specialists I know are quite unfamiliar with the subject. It seems essential, therefore, to present a brief but adequate explanation of semiotics in the course of suggesting how it should be applied. The shape of the rest of this paper is strongly influenced by this necessity.

Semiotics as a whole can be divided into four main areas (here I differ from Zemanek in this volume). These are:

Pragmatics: signs in relation to human behaviour;
Semantics: how signs are related to the "real" signs they signify;
Syntactics: the formal relations among signs;
Empirics: the statistical relations among sets of signs.

To analyse an existing information system or design a new one implies a thorough understanding of how the system functions in all these respects; yet how often does the typical computer-centred specialist ask only questions of syntactics or empirics? To ignore, as is commonplace, the problems of pragmatics and semantics is to risk, if not guarantee, designing a formal system ineffectively related either to the surrounding human system or to the reality it is supposedly monitoring and controlling. Poor design is usually the result of omissions and oversights. We should design better systems if we were to force the analyst and designer to consider the problems of pragmatics and semantics, by introducing them into our design check-lists and documentation standards.

To demonstrate this thesis we shall examine carefully one important aspect of systems design (design of files) and more briefly touch upon another (design of printed output).

3.1. The syntactic problems of file design

Suppose we were designing the Real Property File for a Local Authority computer system. The syntactic problems would be those of deciding which data elements should be contained in each record, how they should be arranged and what values they can adopt. Some data elements could be left in natural English but preferably we should employ a strict record format and coded data within it in order to enable the computer to manipulate the data – for example, to correlate records of property with records of their owners or tenants, to group properties by statistical characteristics, even to delegate certain decisions to the machine. This enables a more efficient service to be provided by fewer staff. For example, we are told (Black and Shaw, 67) that Detroit "rated most of its residential areas, structure-by-structure, on a seven point scale ranging from 'sound' to 'extremely dilapidated' in order to get an idea of the extent of residential blight in the city." This simple technique would no doubt save much of the work of deciding upon where to route an urban motor way, for example.

This design for a Property Record would be based upon an analysis of what information was actually used by the many local government officials engaged in such tasks as assessing tax liabilities, deciding upon improvement grants, registering premises for special purposes, compiling electoral registers, planning urban development and conducting health inspections. By defining the formal contents of the file, we are fixing what may be stored within the information system and how it can be expressed. This will rigidly determine the scope of a formal language for talking about a Property within the mechanistic system.

3.2. The empiric problems of file design

Having fixed the content and form of a Property Record, our attention would turn to the volumes of data to be recorded, and their patterns of use. We should find that many departments record the same information about Property and probably we would recommend, on grounds of efficiency, that this re-duplication could be eliminated by storing all Property data in a central file. We might argue that such a unified "data base" would increase accuracy of data because records would be checked more often. We should expect the most recent observation by one department to bring the others up-to-date. Inconsistencies would be eliminated so that better control could be exercised: we could support our argument by citing the case of a house, converted into two flats, which the owner might report prematurely to one department to obtain additional services but tardily to another to avoid tax.

In design work, this analysis of volumes and usage would be applied to computing the storage volumes required, block-sizes, use of buffers and channels, file structure, access and processing mode and so on. If our outlook is that of the computer scientist, these will all be technical problems of the kind in which we shall feel at home. There the problem will rest.

3.3. Only half the problem

Guided in our analysis and design by standards based upon the framework of semiotics, however, we should have been made aware of tackling only half the problem. No questions of semantics or pragmatics had been asked. Today the typical data processing specialist would not be made aware of them.

Eleven years ago that was, perhaps, excusable. I keep on my shelves, as a kind of horror story, a report, produced by the Rand Corporation, called *A Data Processing System for State and Local Governments* (Hearle and Mason, 63). As a result of two years' work, the authors proposed a "unified information system" to enable the various levels of government to pool their data on persons and property for use by departments of public works, welfare, education, culture, police, taxation and others. To support their proposals they adduced all the usual empiric arguments to show that it would be cheaper than the present fragmented system. Furthermore, in pages of earnestly listed "benefits" they make sinister statements such as the following: "Analyses and correlations presently not possible because of lack of accessible data would become relatively simple" (*ibid*. p. 96) and "The system also would provide a comprehensive file for recording the location of objects and events of government interest" (*ibid*. p. 97). After the lapse of eleven years it may be thought that this narrow approach to systems design would be outdated. Unfortunately, studying the problem only from the points of view of empirics and syntactics, the arguments in favour of unified data banks are overwhelming.

Fortunately a number of writers have begun to express their horror at such naivety. Warner and Stone, for example, have cautioned that "if local government is to have its data banks, and it seems that it must, we can only guard such freedom as remains to us by insisting that separate files are *not* integrated, and *not* cross-referenced, so that the *data collected for one purpose is never used for any other*" (Warner and Stone, 70). In the short-term, their advice should probably be accepted, although it runs counter to the advice of the orthodox systems designer. In the longer-term we need a more refined understanding of what factors should govern the sharing of information so that we may enjoy the genuine economic advantages without harm to the organisation or society. This is one end towards which we should direct research into the neglected half of the problem.

3.4. The semantic problems of file design

The incomplete but orthodox approach to systems analysis described above seems to be based upon two false assumptions. About files there appears to be a belief that they are composed of many simple statements that are, individually, easy to understand and either true or false; this view is encouraged by the staple diet of propositional and predicate logic on any computer science course. The remedy would be to teach the systems analyst other forms of logic which are partially developed but still in need of research. About man's use of information the assumption appears to be that, if he is not being stupid, he should respond to signs in a mechanistic way; the computer is a misleading model of behaviour, suggesting that it is wrong to do anything but transform well-defined patterns of signs into others by formal rules or respond to them in any but certain specified ways. The remedy would be to teach how to analyse the complex and diverse interpretations which humanistic man can justifiably give to the same information, as explained below.

Humanistic man is not interested in form so much as in meaning because he uses signs to extend his limited physical and intellectual abilities. Through the use of signs, each of us can know much more of the world than is possible through our unaided and individual senses – one person can see, describe, communicate and many others will "see" as he does. Signs also extend our grasp upon the world – one person instructs and a coordinated team achieves things impossible for any individual. Hence there is a useful dichotomy between those signs which are used with a *descriptive* intention and those used with a *prescriptive* intention. Signs are also used in a human context in two quite different modes. They can *denote* things in the world in a manner that is independent of the human organism; they can also be used to signify *affect*, the states of emotion that lie within the human organism.

These distinctions can be illustrated by a slightly flippant example of property descriptions.

An advertisement for the house in which we now live was written in the usual mendacious style of estate agents:

> Located in the centre of the fashionable Spa, an elegant mid-Victorian family residence, beautifully modernised by present owner comprising . . . . It is set in a walled garden with lawns and terraces.

The unorthodox agent, Roy Brooks, whose frank descriptions of property made his advertisements one of the most popular humorous columns in a national paper, might have written:

> Ten minutes walk from town centre, Victorian house touched but not corrupted by gothic revival, made habitable by competent, do-it-yourself owner. Accommodation . . . . Crumbling walls surround minute garden, used during restoration as rubble tip, now disguised by thin layer of weeds.

The expression "lawns and terraces" was the actual euphemism for the mess accurately described in the second version.

Although they may not exhibit such gross variations as these, there would still be scope for bias in the property descriptions contained in local government records. Consider, for example, the rating given to property in the Detroit databank mentioned above: the route for an urban motorway could be "derived" from "objective assessments" of "urban blight" using "scientific methods of analysis" based on a "computerised model of urban renewal needs". A consensus of honest public servants without any corrupt prompting could result in the road being driven through some area preconceived as ripe for re-development. Many beautiful English towns have been ravaged by a consensus of officials.

To analyse this kind of problem we must recognise, for example, that data can be classified according to their significations:

		INTENTION	
		Descriptive	*Prescriptive*
MODE	*Denotative*	FACTS (I live in Leamington Spa)	INSTRUCTIONS (Take a taxi from the station)
	Affective	VALUE JUDGEMENTS (It is a delightful town)	INDUCEMENTS (You will find it too tiring to walk)

Having made these distinctions theoretically, it is tempting to imagine that these different significations could be made explicit within a computer system by using a code to label each item of information appropriately. Unfortunately, messages used within a human system tend to exhibit all four of these types of signification simultaneously. For example, the house advertisement gives some *facts* larded with *value judgements* so that, superficially, it appears to have a descriptive intention but, in fact, it is primarily prescriptive because the estate agent supplies his message as an implied *instruction* to buy the property, giving, as an *inducement*, the prospect of living among "lawns and terraces".

To design a system which is free from this type of problem one might attempt to restrict it to the handling of objective information, i.e., a data bank composed of facts without value judgements. This is nearly always impossible.

One reason is that the system separates what one can talk about within the formal system from what is entirely excluded; and decisions on what should be excluded themselves constitute value judgements. For example, in describing a person's behaviour it is relatively easy to find brief indicators of human failure, such as arrests, convictions, periods in care, in hospital or unemployed, whereas in simple, coded data-elements, it is difficult to represent positive achievements or those extenuating circumstances that reveal apparent failure as actual success. For reasons of technical efficiency therefore, a computer record will tend to be biased to give a derogatory picture of a person.

Another reason why data banks cannot be freed from value judgements is that many seeming facts serve to reflect value judgements from some other system. For example, an employee maybe attended a grammar school (academic) or a secondary modern school (non-academic) but this "fact" about his ability is a reflection of judgements about the proportion of a school population which should fall into these categories, and in Britain this may vary between 10% and 60%.

To investigate the significations of the data to be held in the files should be a part of the analyst's task. The system should then be designed to ensure that the data are not capable of mistaken or distorted use. As a first practical step to improve the analysis, it would be sufficient to note to what extent each data-element might be capable of being given each of the four kinds of signification: in fact, value, instruction and inducement. To reduce the risk of data being misused, a variety of warning and checking devices would have to be incorporated into the design. These problems are far more complex than the few examples cited above could suggest. Research is needed.

3.5. The pragmatic problems of file design

A file can be viewed as a junction box through which many suppliers of information communicate with many users. Whilst there is plenty of scope for misunderstanding in face-to-face communication, and more scope in written communication, why do we imagine that it should be easier to communicate through a patchwork of information fragments, by means of the files in a formal system? Almost certainly it is not but these *pragmatic* problems have scarcely been investigated.

On the input side, the messages used to update the file will be stripped of much valuable information that would reach the user in face-to-face reporting. By tone of voice and facial expression, the reporter will be able to convey his estimates of the precision, or credibility of what he reports. For example, the loss of this kind of information evoked an indignant response when a computer-based planning system regurgitated all estimates for the completions dates of jobs, some reliable and some tentative, as though they were all firm commitments. Attitudes towards the events, states of affairs and persons who are the subject of the reports are also conveyed non-verbally in face-to-face encounter. This affective information is probably at least as important to a manager or administrator as are the facts he is told.

On the output side, the messages derived from the file will be in danger of being misconstrued for several reasons. Among them will be the loss, on input, of information about reliability. In addition, the user will not be able, as in face-to-face communication, to make allowances for possible bias in the information by taking account of his knowledge of the informant. Also, there will be an absence of contextual information: the computer, unlike a human reporter, will probably not be able to adjust the depth, detail and style of its reports to take account of the predispositions of the user and, thereby, help him to avoid being misled. Face-to-face, of course, the giver is likely to ask the purpose for which his information is to be used; this knowledge, plus indications of misunderstanding, will cause him to adjust what he says and how he says it.

In general, we should expect some organisational disfunction to result from the computer system's inability to cope, as people can, with the varied uses and interpretations which can be given to the same verbal or numeric message. The analysis and design of systems should take account of this problem.

During analysis we normally investigate the relationships between data elements and the outputs in which they will appear. As a practical step towards acknowledging the pragmatic problems, we should extend this analysis to relate each output to its various classes of users and the contexts and purposes involved.

The designer should use this information to reduce the risks of misinterpretation when a file is to be shared by such diverse groups as accountants, policemen, planners, and social workers. He may do this by restricting or extending the content of the file, by limiting access to parts of the file to certain groups, and by careful design of the codes which represent the data. To make systems specialists aware of these problems will be valuable, but we also need research to extend our understanding of them.

3.6. Application of semiotics to design method

Earlier, it was asserted that we should probably design better systems if, into the design check-lists and the documentation standards we employ, we were to incorporate sections which forced the analyst and designer to consider the problems of pragmatics and semantics. An attempt was made to support this assertion whilst introducing the major areas of semiotics during a discussion of file design. The same might have been done with any other aspect of the design problem. For example:

Design of printed output

Syntactic questions: What messages are to appear? Which parts will be standard and which variable? If a message overflows a line how is it to be accommodated? Similarly for page overflow? How are documents and pages to be numbered? What will be pre-printed? What character set is required? . . .

Empiric questions: What is the statistical pattern of use of variable messages or message components? What are the likelihoods of line and page overflows? How many documents produced in the same run will go to the same address? . . .

Semantic questions: What check is there that the document reaches its users? How will the various users act upon the document's contents? What means has the user of checking the document by external or internal redundancies before he acts? Can the document be used in the feedback of information to check that it has been used correctly? . . .

Pragmatic questions: Is the document laid out in a manner to which the users are accustomed? Are the symbols/words/phrases it employs open to different interpretations by the different classes of users? How will the context affect the use made of the contents? Is there an air of spurious reliability about the data which may mislead the user? What training is required for using the document?

In most formalised schemes for systems analysis only the syntactic and empiric questions are included (NCC, 70).

The semantic and pragmatic aspects, whilst not ignored by a competent analyst, are usually dealt with informally. There is a consequent high risk of overlooking issues vital to the system's effectiveness and, when not overlooked, they are the subject of "hints and wrinkles" prescribed by oral tradition instead of being the subject of a rigorous scientific analysis.

4. Semiotics and the education of information specialists

The way we educate our systems specialists today is heavily biased towards the problems of the machine. This surely explains the common failure to design formal information systems so that they can be coupled effectively with the humanistic system.

Historically, it was not until information technology made available new ways of running our organisations that we needed a body of highly skilled information specialists. At first the organisational aspects of the work were simple compared to the technical. The early systems specialists could regard themselves quite justifiably as computer specialists. The technical difficulties are being overcome and, increasingly, the organisational use of information will pose problems more important than those of how to manipulate the data within the machine. The person who is applying the computer to business and administration must become less a computer specialist and more an information specialist; but the growth of an information science with a balanced perspective, including both machine and human problems of systems design, is inhibited by the existing institutions based on computer science.

New institutional foci of growth are needed to assemble the knowledge necessary for the development of systems analysis. Much of the relevant knowledge is available in such disciplines as anthropology, social psychology, linguistics, philosophy, experimental psychology, etc., but the information specialist only requires fragments of the knowledge from all these fields. He needs to learn from anthropology how cultural differences can affect the uses people make of the same sign or symbol. Social psychology can present him with an explanation of the mechanism by which signs retain a stable meaning even in a changing community, a mechanism which also accounts for the differences observed by the anthropologist. To understand how the structures of formal languages might best be related to the structures of natural languages, he needs some ideas from linguistics. The principal source of scientific knowledge about the human problems of using keyboards, reading displays, maintaining attention upon a task, etc., is experimental psychology. Philosophy is perhaps the most important source of intellectual meat for the information specialist: one branch, ontology, goes to the root of some problems of data base definition; another, epistemology, is highly relevant to the problems of testing a design and justifying the use of certain data; others deal with topics such as time, the formulation of command and the nature of information itself. Computer science should be regarded as just another discipline of partial relevance to the information specialist. By assembling fragments from them all he must create an intellectual province of his own.

5. Semiotics and research

These fragments seem to fall within the already established boundary of semiotics, where they help to define tracts of unexplored territory which should be the subject of research. If semiotics were developed with the purpose of understanding how organisations, individuals and society in general employ information, focussing upon mechanisms rather than on particular uses, then we should have a science capable of underpinning the practical work of information systems design. Within each discipline certain problems are perceived to be legitimate ones to study and similar traditions constrain the choice of research methods. The problems of systems analysis are not the proper concern of any of these other disciplines; semiotics can provide the correct framework and inspire appropriate research.

In earlier sections of this paper an attempt was made to hint at the kind of research problems that might be tackled. Space permits me to draw attention to only a few of these and to amplify them slightly. We need to understand better the boundary between the formal and informal systems. First, it must be characterised more exactly; types and degrees of formality could be clarified. We should enquire to what extent the users are aware of the limitations imposed by a system's formality upon the information it supplies, and to what extent they make allowances. We could certainly identify the design decisions which affect the shape of the boundary and probably discover ways of handling systematically the information to which it is impervious.

We need to study semantic distortion. There are in existence many databases shared by users and suppliers of information with disparate interests. The varied assumptions which influence the data supplied and the way they are used should be studied. We may discover that the requirements of some groups of users are incompatible within the same system. We could explore the reduction of semantic distortion obtainable by different kinds of feedback loops between supplier and user of information.

Urgently, we need to improve our techniques of analysis and design. I conjecture that many examples of systems failure, on close investigation, would yield case-studies to demonstrate the consequences of neglecting the pragmatic and semantic aspects of design. A relatively simple study would attempt to develop check-lists and documentation standards which might have some immediate practical impact in these areas. A far more thorough programme of research is needed to discover techniques for specifying the relevant pragmatic and semantic features of a system.

Problems related to these have arisen in the author's current project (Stamper, 73b). The aim of this project is to develop techniques for the accurate description of systems for administering complex rules (e.g. tax and social security systems). This is being done by creating a language, LEGOL, in which to express statute law. A computer system can then simulate the functioning of the related administrative system. The LEGOL language is not a programming language, although capable of being interpreted by a computer in so far as it defines formal operations. The designing of the language brings one face-to-face with the problems of the boundary between formal and informal systems and with the semantic assumptions which we can exploit to achieve brevity and clarity of expression. The LEGOL Interpreter is based upon the use of semantic structures which are added to a normal data-base system, and it permits the storing of information about the real system's empiric, pragmatic and semantic characteristics. The major divisions of semiotics are reflected in major structures of both LEGOL and its Interpreter. Without these and other more detailed distinctions supplied by semiotics, it would have been impossible, in my opinion, to make progress with this extremely elaborate problem.

6. Conclusion

For historical reasons, the education of the systems specialist has a heavy mechanistic bias. Increasingly, however, technical problems are becoming easier to solve and the effectiveness of a system as a whole is becoming more dependent upon the integration of the mechanistic and humanistic components. Unfortunately, the mechanistic bias has been institutionalised as "computer science" and the "computer profession", when the emphasis should be upon "information science" and an "information profession". One obstacle preventing the shift of emphasis is the lack of a clearly perceived, intellectual basis for the skills of the information specialists. It has been suggested here that the time-honoured discipline called "semiotics" can fill this role and provide the information systems designer with the well-balanced viewpoint he now lacks.

8. References

Black, H. and Shaw, E. (1967). Detroit's data banks, *Datamation* 13, March 1967, pp. 25–27; reprinted in Westin, *Information Technology in a Democracy*, Cambridge: Harvard University Press.

Hearle, E.F.R. and Mason, R.J. (1963). *A Data Processing System for State and Local Government*, Englewood Cliffs: Prentice Hall.

NCC (1970). *System Documentation Standards*, Manchester: National Computing Centre.

Stamper, R.K. (1973a). *Information*, London: Batsford; and New York: Wiley.

Stamper, R.K. (1973b). The LEGOL project and language, in: *Proceedings of the Datafair Conference 1973*, London: British Computer Society, pp. 264–276.

Warner, M. and Stone, M. (1970). *The Data Bank Society*, London: Allen & Unwin.

Zemanek, H. (1972). What is informatics? *Management Informatics 1*, Nos 2 and 5.

E. Mumford and H. Sackman, eds., Human Choice and Computers
North-Holland Publishing Company (1975)

INFORMATION SYSTEMS DEVELOPMENT IN A LOCAL AUTHORITY

G.R. WADDELL

Edinburgh Corporation, Warristons Close, Edinburgh, Scotland

1. Background to data processing

The development of data processing within Edinburgh Corporation has been continuous since 1958, when a Central Mechanised Service was set up to process the payroll, accounting and statistical work of the various departments.

By 1964 a full work load was being processed on punched card equipment and the use of computer bureau facilities was extending. Consequently, an investigation was initiated to determine the future data processing policy of the Local Authority.

2. Information systems objectives

The development of Information Systems by Edinburgh Corporation has been influenced by the view that a local authority is a complex organisation concerned with people and the provision of services to meet their needs. The day-to-day administration necessitates the maintenance of very large information files which are very often interrelated but all too frequently left unrelated. With the computer there is a means of providing better information by ensuring that the financial, statistical and other data collected by the individual services of a local authority can be made available for the use of other services. The management of the whole organisation can be improved if better information can be provided on which to base decisions of policy and of day-to-day management.

3. Computer policy

The general computer policy in Edinburgh Corporation is to provide a central service to fully meet the needs of individual departments and in so doing, lay the basis for integrated computer systems to meet the needs of the whole organisation.

The objectives were set in two phases. The short term objectives were:

to establish an extensive data processing service providing access to all major sources of data;

to introduce from the outset of computer development, standard references which are the keys to interrelation and integration.

The long term objectives were:

to develop integrated computer systems from the individual applications;

to set up and maintain central files relating to property, people and any other information identified as the common elements of the applications;

to develop techniques to manipulate data within computer files and permit efficient access to satisfy any information requirements;

to create an environment within which modern management techniques could be employed.

4. Approach to computer development

One of two alternative approaches can be taken in the development of information systems.

The first approach is to carry out a survey of the information requirements of all sectors of the organisation. Arising from this survey a clear definition could be made of the contents of the computer files, identifying the common elements, and the demands which will be made on the information.

This approach has three distinct disadvantages, the first being that:

very few sectors of the organisation could clearly specify or predict their information requirements with any degree of accuracy;

the second is that:

if the requirements could be specified they would probably be considerably out of date by the time the full system was developed and implemented;

and the third is that:

having determined the information requirements it does not necessarily follow that it would be practical or economic to capture the data and maintain it to an acceptable level of accuracy.

In other words there is little value in assessing the OUTPUT from the system till channels have been created for regular INPUT of source information.

The second approach, which has been adopted by Edinburgh Corporation, is to develop a series of data bases as a by-product of selected applications, creating central files of common information, each item being regularly updated as part of a normal process. The aggregated information from all sources is then available for access and analysis to satisfy a variety of additional purposes.

Data Bases must not be created in isolation. They must evolve, from the individual applications within a planned and flexible framework.

No attempt has been made to predict the detailed computer information requirements of Local Government in the next decade, or even in the next few years. Instead techniques have been developed, to tap the main sources of data, to manage the data within the computer, and to retrieve the information for a number of regular processes or enquiries.

This approach, not only ensures the practical and economic maintenance of the data, but also provides flexibility, to cater for all information requirements which may arise at a future date. It also permits the pace and pattern of development to be geared to suit each individual installation.

5. Project development

Development to date has been predominantly directed in projects satisfying the requirements of individual departments.

A wide range of applications has been implemented, providing a data collection, data processing and results service to each sector of the organisation independently.

The common elements of the application files have been identified and classified within a number of data bases. The centralisation of data can eliminate duplication since all applications can draw on the common pool. Savings can also be made by collecting computer data from one source or alternatively, more up-to-date information can be maintained by tapping a number of sources.

A simple example is a property address which can be a lengthy combination of characters to store on every record within all appropriate application files. Substantial savings can be achieved by establishing a street data base as a directory for general use.

If data is to be shared by a number of projects it is essential that rigid standards are adopted from the outset of computer development. Most important is the need for standard references which provide the interrelationship between separately held items of data and permit the integration of independently developed processes. In the example of a street data base a common form of street code must be adopted and held in a standard format within all relevant applications.

The most significant advantage of data bases is the secondary use which can be made of data. It can be used to service new applications which may not warrant the collection of original data. A particular and important case of this is the provision of information for management.

6. Data base chart (see fold-out)

7. Data base development

There are four major factors essential to the provision of an Information Service from data bases

Classification	of data,
Collection	of data,
Management and organisation	of data within the computer files,
Retrieval	of information.

7.1. Classification

The common elements of data have been identified and classified as:

Property
Population
Land
Highways

} Urban Data Base

representing the physical characteristics of the city towards which the services of the Local Authority are directed.

Personnel. The prime resource of the organisation and the major cost element.

Accounting. Fundamental to all organisations is the need for Financial Control.

EDINBURGH CORPORATION DATA BASE DEVELOPMENT

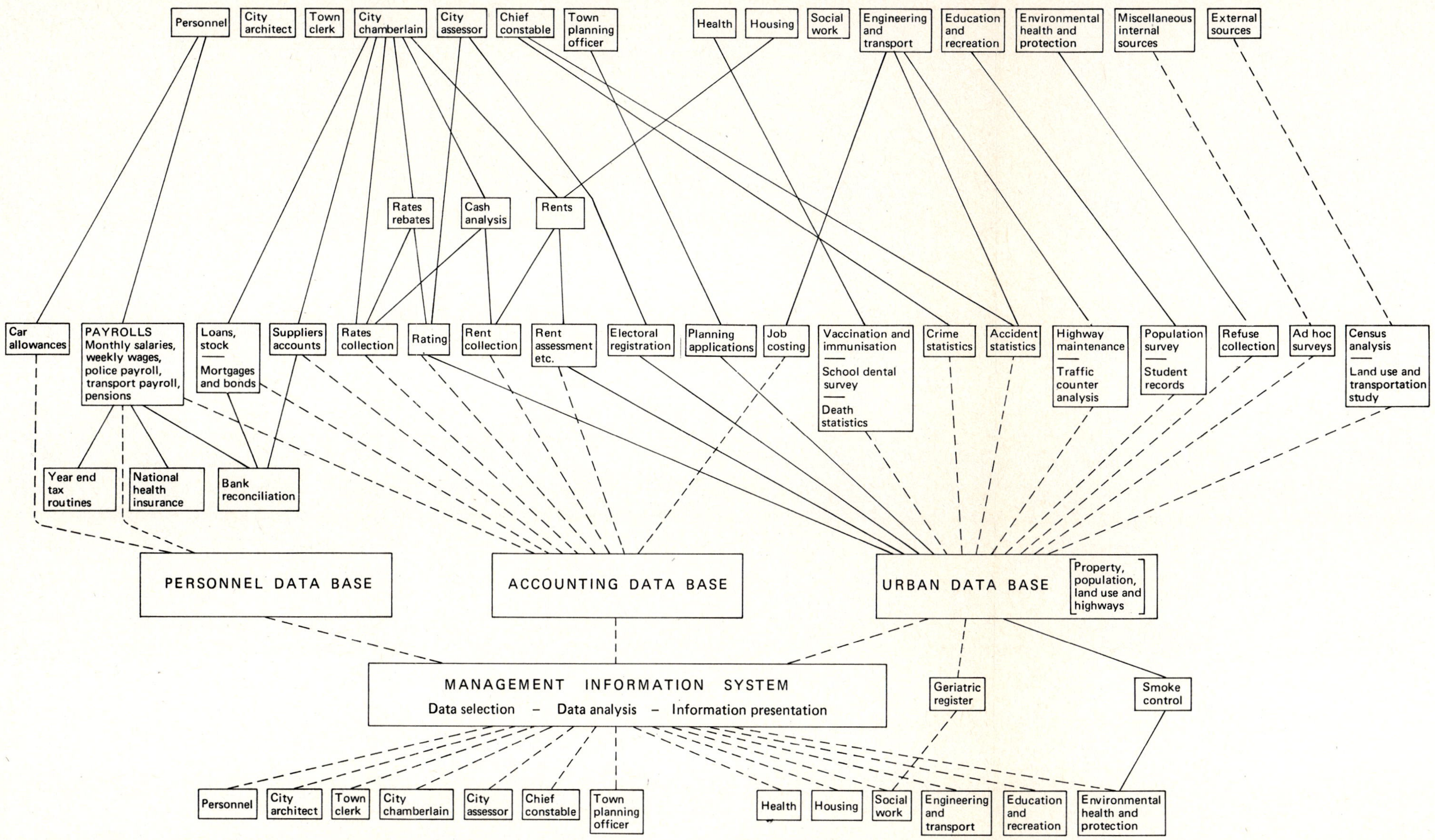

A basic objective of Local Government is to provide the best service to the community at the lowest cost.

The interrelationship of information relating to property, population, personnel and accounting will permit management to measure and increase efficiency of services – and control and minimise costs using Budgetary Control and Management Accounting techniques.

7.2. Collection

Data is collected in common files as a by-product of selected applications.

This is essential to sustain an acceptable level of accuracy.

Initially and for a transitional period the data bases can be created and maintained from the project master files.

When the Information System is operational temporary master files can be extracted from the data bases to permit regular processing without loss in efficiency and alternative use can be made of the data for analyses or individual enquiries direct from the data bases.

In this way a data base can be compared with a warehouse, providing standing orders to retail outlets for regular processing and facilities to aggregate any combinations of data for alternative purposes.

7.3. Management and organisation

The Management and Organisation of the data within the computer files is a vital factor in the development of Information Systems.

In almost all computer data processing to date, data has been held on files appropriate to one process. E.g., Payroll–in Department/Employee Number order.

Data Bases, however, can contain information relevant to a number of processes.

Techniques have therefore been developed to manage and organise the sequence, structure and contents of the files in such a way that conflicting demands can be satisfied within acceptable levels of efficiency.

Practical and economic processing of data bases has been made possible by the availability of very large random access devices at relatively low cost and the development of data base management software by computer manufacturers and software companies.

7.4. Information retrieval

Information Retrieval is the fourth major factor in the development of the system.

The classification, collection and organisation of the data bases are designed to make efficient information retrieval possible. To exploit this potential techniques for selection, analysis and presentation are being developed.

The use of remote terminals, and especially Visual Display Units is a significant advantage for display permitting a conversational like situation between a user and the computer files.

It is, however, only an advantage in appropriate circumstances and is not mandatory for data base access since most enquiries will continue to be submitted in a batch processing mode.

8. Information management

A data base is organised as a series of files, but the structure of these files is not necessarily determined by the requirements of any one application. Instead, the file formats are independent, reflecting the needs of all applications processing the data.

A dictionary is used to define the contents and structure of a data base. Applications do not access the physical files of a data base. Data is accessed using the dictionary and presented for processing to an application in the form of an entity (a record) or entity stream (a file).

This interface ensures that changes to the physical files need not affect the application since the alterations are reflected in the dictionary and the entities are constructed as before. This shielding of the application from changes to a data base is now commonly called Transparency.

Transparency is essential in a data base system providing flexibility in the sequence, structure and contents of the files to cater for current and future conflicting demands and eliminating the repercussive effect of these changes on the applications.

9. Information systems implications – The computer department

It is not a new capability of the computer to provide a general information service. It has always been possible to run up and down files, correlate data from a number of sources, extract, analyse and present the information required. The problem has been that the level of efficiency with which these activities can be executed could result in the excessive use of computer time. The user may not want the results right away but unless the processing time is brief the exercise could be prohibitively uneconomic. The techniques which have been developed for information management and retrieval provide for the efficient, economic and practical operation of data bases. The computer organisation must be able to develop and implement the systems employing these techniques and to operate and maintain the systems with efficiency and economy. It must therefore react and change if necessary to fulfil these functions.

The new and important role of a Data Base Administrator is emerging in computer organisations implementing data base systems. All activities associated with the management of the data bases, including the allocation of unique data identifiers, monitoring and improving data base performance and a variety of housekeeping duties must be co-ordinated to operate the system at a sustained level of efficiency. This role straddles the existing development and operational functions and requires the knowledge of a software specialist, combined with the ability to provide a high standard of documentation and administration.

10. Organisational environment

Having identified the technical solutions to the problems of creating and maintaining information systems, such systems can only be fully exploited within the right organisational environment.

In Scotland the local government organisation is made up of a series of departments which function independently. Computer development in this environment is limited to the provision of a service to these departments or at most an inter-departmental service.

The full potential of computers can only be realised in a corporate structure.

The pattern of computer development in any installation should reflect user demands and should be determined by the objectives and priorities of the various sectors of the organisation and of the organisation as a whole.

Local government users, like any others, are understandably reluctant to share information and must be convinced that the benefits compensate for the problems of control, communication and organisation which will undoubtedly arise.

From the computer point of view the owner of each item of information is clearly identified as the department which submitted it for processing. The decision to integrate files and share information should not be taken in isolation by the computer department, although there is much they can do to anticipate such a need.

The role of computer staff should be to influence and educate users in the new possibilities offered by computer systems in general and data bases and information systems in particular.

In Edinburgh Corporation data processing services have been closely matched to the needs of individual departments but computer staff, acting in the corporate interest, have played an innovating role by laying the basis for integrated systems to provide an information service which crosses departmental boundaries. The computer department, as the most convenient independent sector, has also assumed responsibility for co-ordinating the operational use of data files common to a number of users.

A recent survey of eight major local authorities in the United Kingdom indicates that the role adopted by computer staff in Edinburgh Corporation is by no means unique*. It was established that three authorities were developing information systems as a matter of official Council policy and developments in the five remaining authorities (including Edinburgh Corporation) were taking place in anticipation of a need.

It is expected that the long-term solution to the organisational problems of systems integration will be the reorganisation of local government currently underway in the United Kingdom. The need for Corporate Planning is now widely recognised, and it is anticipated that the previously widespread structure of almost self-contained departments will be replaced by a series of service units co-ordinated under a Chief Executive.

11. Confidentiality

Restricted access to the information on data base files must be imposed for reasons, not only of secrecy or privacy, e.g. personal records, but also ownership and cost, since the collection and collation of source data may have involved significant expense and the information may be a valuable asset.

Confidential computer information must be guarded no less securely than the equivalent manual files and distribution must be authorised by the originator who does not lose ownership or responsibility because he has lost possession.

Computer confidentiality checks should therefore be limited to the reconciliation of a request with an authorisation, which poses three questions.

* See Developments in Management Information Systems – A Survey, Institute of Municipal Treasurers and Accountants (I.M.T.A.) and the Local Authority Management Services and Computer Committee (L.A.M.S.A.C.), July 1973.

(i) Who wants to know?
(ii) What do you want to know?
(iii) How is the information to be presented?

The first point "Who wants to know?" is significant but relatively simple to control. Conventional data processing in batch mode requires the submission of some form of 'run request' or authorisation and the manual distribution procedures provide an in-built security. Remote terminals present additional problems but the use of passwords, badge readers and orthodox locks and keys can provide a variety of adequate safeguards.

The second point "What do you want to know?" if taken in isolation, would normally require each data item to be given a confidentiality classification. This commonly adopted solution creates an operational overhead when checking each request and is restrictive in that it does not permit sufficient flexibility to deal with the third point "How is the information to be presented?", e.g., Information about Corporation tenants could be strictly confidential when presented as individual details but may be much less restricted when presented as anonymous statistics.

A solution to this problem is to control the confidentiality of processes and programs, which embody both the data to be accessed and the form of presentation. This check can be carried out at the initialising stage of a process, with a minimal overhead and complete flexibility, by referring to a simple index of programs and authorised users.

12. Social implications

Discussions on the social implications of computer information systems tend to concentrate on the negative rather than the positive aspects. Concern has been expressed about the growing use of the computer for information storage and handling. A report on privacy submitted to the United Kingdom government made the following points*.

> ... the idea of easy access to personal information is regarded as objectionable by the vast majority of people. ... the computer problem as it affects privacy in Great Britain is one of apprehensions and fears and not so far one of facts and figures. Of these fears about the computer the three which seem to be uppermost in the public mind are its facility to compile "personal profiles" ... seen by some to facilitate the exercise of power over them ... its capacity to correlate informa-

* Report of the Committee on Privacy, London: Her Majesty's Stationery Office, July 1972.

> tion . . . seen by some as infringing the principle that information collected for one purpose should not be available for any other purpose . . . and its provision of new opportunities for unauthorised access to personal information. . . . the fact that computerised information can be tapped via terminals separated by many miles, is seen by some to increase the risk of its falling into the hands of people who should not have it. We think it important, however, to keep the possible dangers to privacy in proper perspective, recognising the immense gains to human welfare which computers can bring . . . adequate safeguards can almost certainly be devised and applied.

Progress towards the wider implementation of personal information systems can no longer be solely dependent on the solution of practical, technical problems.

The level of understanding of computer users and the public must, by education, keep pace with technical development. There must be a general awareness of the human and social implications and the computer staff must act responsibly to generate the kind of public trust currently accorded to other professions.

In the data bases which are evolving in Edinburgh Corporation there is a significant difference in the approach to a relatively uncontroversial area, such as property and the approach to a sensitive area, such as population. A prime example is the referencing systems which have been applied. A standard form of property reference has been devised, which is adopted by all computer applications, to facilitate integration and correlation.

No similar standard identifier has been applied to people, although coding techniques (using name, sex and date of birth) are being used to link population related data.

Mutual exchange of information between various sectors of the organisation can be beneficial but technical feasibility is not the sole criterion. Computer information systems in Edinburgh Corporation continue to be subject to the kind of controls which operate in a manual environment, ownership of each item in the data base is clearly defined and all requests to access any item are routed via the owner, who thus retains total control over its use.

13. Conclusion

In local government the inbuilt safeguard which will ensure that computer facilities are exploited beneficially and are not misused is that the computer users are departments which exist to serve the interests of the community.

The development of individual applications contributing to an improvement in the administration of the local authority is already indirectly benefiting the public.

The development of integrated information systems has additional benefits, permitting exchange of data between departments in a way not previously practical or economic. An example in Edinburgh is the integration of Birth Registration, Education and Health systems to their mutual advantage.

The computer is progressively having a more direct effect with the increasing application of mathematical models to urban and regional planning. In Edinburgh these techniques are used in the evaluation of alternative Land Use/Transportation strategies. Such development is having a significant impact on the decision making process in both local and national government.

The role of the computer is changing. This change will be to the benefit of society. There is a natural progression

from the use of computers as an administrative tool with advantages of efficiency and economy,

through the development of integrated systems providing better information on which to base decisions of policy and of day to day management,

to the computer's role as an aid to strategic planning and projection of alternative solutions – incorporating social factors.

As the computer is increasingly applied in this way, so its impact on the scope of human choice will increase, and only then will its potential be more fully realised.

E. Mumford and H. Sackman, eds., Human Choice and Computers
North-Holland Publishing Company (1975)

BALANCE BETWEEN PROVISION AND RESTRICTION OF INFORMATION WITHIN A PERSONAL RECORD INFORMATION SYSTEM

Cecil P. MARKS

Civil Service Department, Whitehall, London, England

1. PRISM – General description

PRISM – Personnel Record Information System for Management – will hold the personal records of the 500 000 people employed in the United Kingdom Civil Service in a non-industrial capacity. That is to say it includes everyone in central government from permanent heads of Ministries down to typists and clerks, but excludes people working, for example, as machine tool operators or foundrymen in such places as dockyards and ordnance factories. It does not include people employed in local government, the nationalised industries, Post Office, the health service, police, transport or education.

The use of a computer for keeping personnel records is, of course, no new thing, and indeed one of its forerunners, the "Powers" punched-card "accounting machine", was used to analyse the annual Civil Service census records as far back as 1929. Subsequently a continuously up-dated individual personnel record, kept centrally for all Civil Servants on "Hollerith" punched-cards, was instituted in 1947 and this was transferred to a computer in 1968. It is known as the Civil Service Central Staff Record (CSCSR).

Following the report (Fulton, 68) of the review of the Civil Service by Lord Fulton's Committee, a new personnel record was set up to help improve personnel management particularly of the most senior level staff who now comprise an "open-structure". This has three levels, Permanent Secretary, Deputy Secretary and Under Secretary, and all senior staff, irrespective of their old type grading or specialism, are eligible for these posts on merit and ability. To provide essential personnel information, particularly for specialists for whom no central record had previously been held, a new Central Management Staff Record (CMSR) was set up in 1970. This now covers some 11 000 people and besides top level staff includes whole categories of other staff, e.g. statisticians and economists, who are largely managed centrally rather than by the individual Ministries. The most important features of the CMSR record relate to job experience and educational/professional qualifications, a multi-axis system being used for both. Descriptions of the CMSR system have been given by Bridle and Gregersen (71a,b).

Whilst CMSR met some of the needs for personnel information stemming from the Fulton report, a much broader information base was needed to meet more fully the requirements of the rapidly developing personnel management and manpower planning services. In other words it had to be a replacement system for the obsolete CSCSR; but it had not just to meet the information needs of the centre, i.e. the Civil Service Department and the Treasury, but also the personnel management requirements of the individual Ministries. The new system, which came to be known as PRISM, has these key features:

(1) It is an integrated pay and personnel record system.

(2) It operates as a two-level data-base system, serving both levels of management, central and departmental.

(3) The central record is maintained as a collection of 500 000 individual personal records and no attempt is made to hold any form of summary records.

(4) It is maintained on true data-base principles, i.e. single notification of occurrences, data-base recording (not functional file recording) and multiple outputs.

A schematic diagram of the two-level data-base (or data-bank) system is given in Appendix B, which shows the central data-base being fed with information automatically from the ring of peripheral computers. There will be 9 or 10 such peripheral machines maintaining an integrated pay and personnel record system for the various Ministries (Departments); some will serve a single Ministry, others will operate on an agency basis, with one serving up to 50 different Departments. There is a central computer which will have as its main task the maintenance of a central data-base of personnel information on all non-industrial staff, kept up to date with information from the peripheral Departmental computers: this data-base will be the source of personnel information to meet central users' needs. The central computer can be considered as the nerve centre of the information system and is located near London at the Civil Service Department (CSD) Computer Centre at Chessington, Surrey. There is in fact a "twin" installation at this location, the other computer providing an agency service for about 100 000–125 000 people as indicated above. Both computers are models ICL 1904S manufactured by International Computers Limited.

Implementation of PRISM is planned in phases: by the end of the first phase, the target date for which is the end of 1974, the aim is to have all 500 000 non-industrial staff on computer payrolls, with an integrated, "non-pay", personnel record for each person. A sub-set of this combined record called the Central Personal Record (CPR) will be siphoned from the peripheral computers to the central data-base. The contents of the CPR are listed in Appendix C.

The basic PRISM philosophy is to be able to answer any question automatically and quickly within the logical derivations of the data recorded. The intention is that a user will sit at a remote terminal – a Visual Display Unit (VDU) – and, by having an interactive dialogue with the computer, progressively obtain from the huge mass of stored data the relatively small piece of useful information he requires. This process will be directly analogous to the way a man at present uses a terminal linked to a computer to work his way through an intricate mathematical or numerical problem: with PRISM he will work his way through an information selection problem, sometimes with the addition of a mathematical manipulation on the selected data.

If the aim is to answer *any* question which may arise, and recognizing that the variety of possible questions is almost infinite, it follows that data cannot be stored advantageously in any particular order, or in summary or digest form. It follows further that questions would normally necessitate running through the whole data-base (500 000 X 75 data elements) and, since many questions may be coming simultaneously through the various terminals, the problems of queuing and delays might appear daunting in the extreme. The PRISM solution to these problems is to completely "invert" the main file (held in conventional serial fashion), so as to create a "header" for every value of each record element, behind which are held the identities of the people who satisfy that value. The inverted file, called "Countflow", has been described in detail by Bellerby (73).

As mentioned, the main access to the central PRISM data-base will be by terminals, using VDUs in an interactive mode, but there will, of course, also be facilities both for fast bulk printing and for copying the page display from a VDU. Since up to 40 VDUs are planned for the first Phase of PRISM development, and questions will range from the extremely simple (Give the record of a named person) to the quite complex (Produce a matrix nesting in several layers giving an age and seniority distribution of a particular grade), several problems have to be solved.

(1) There must be an immediate response to the user for all "housekeeping" dialogue.

(2) Long and intricate questions must not delay the answers being given to short and simple ones.

(3) Answers to questions must be within acceptable response times at terminals.

(4) The expected traffic must not swamp the system.

(5) There must be a hand-holding dialogue for the lay-user(e.g., a new personnel manager) with some sophisticated and direct methods available for the expert (e.g. a statistician familiar with the data).

(6) Adequate privacy and security safeguards must be built into the system.

Our approach to problems (1)–(4) is to regard questions as if they were transactions, and to deal with them basically as "multi-transaction processing". International Computers Limited (ICL) have developed a system called "DRIVER" for their 1900 Series machines which enables transactions to be regarded as threads carrying beads, each of which is processed individually with the threads being subsequently re-created after all beads are available. This has been modified to meet specific PRISM requirements into a piece of software called PDS (Prism Driver System) which is the main key to fast interaction and to questions "overtaking" each other.

In order for the user, and particularly the inexperienced user, to be able to exploit the full power of the system, it was found necessary to create a special retrieval language. This, called PIRL (Prism Information Retrieval Language), enables the user both to describe the nature of what he wants done in a general sense e.g. create a table, and to specify the required information in his own terms, without a detailed knowledge of the data or how it is stored.

PRISM has been chosen by OECD (Organisation for Economic Co-operation and Development) as one of eight personnel/manpower information systems in six European countries which have been the subject of case studies in depth. The report was published by OECD in September 1973 (Hersleb and Bayhylle, 73).

2. PRISM objectives

It will be seen that what has been developed for PRISM is a very advanced data-base and information retrieval system which is expressly aimed at providing precise answers to an unlimited range of questions in the shortest possible response time. This should be the primary objective of any information system, personnel or otherwise. But information is, of course, not an end in itself. It is made available to human beings to assist them in solving the problems with which they are faced.

Civil Service personnel information is available to those who, both centrally and in Departments, are dealing with a whole range of problems within the framework of manpower planning and personnel management. It is generally the case at the present time that the personnel manager – like it or not – has to do his job mainly with short-term objectives in mind. He is concerned with taking (and subsequently implementing) decisions relating to such functions as selection, recruitment, redundancy, retirement, transfer, promotion, training, and management development. These functions are carried out to meet the operational needs of the organisation which may fluctuate and change at very short notice. The emphasis of personnel management consequently also tends to be on practical expedients in the short term.

Many organisations, however, attempt to plan their long term corporate strategy, having realised that without such a plan it is becoming increasingly difficult to remain profitable (in the case of a business) or to carry out its duties efficiently (in the case of non-profit making concerns). Long term planning normally embraces such factors as Design, Production, Sales, R & D, Capital Resources and so on, but only recently has it been realised that, to be comprehensive, it must also include manpower.

Manpower planning comprises, first, estimating (in relation to overall corporate strategic objectives) the numbers and skills of people needed in the years ahead, i.e., Demand Forecasting. Next, in estimating the future development of the work force, again in terms of numbers and skills, i.e., Supply Forecasting. The probable lack of balance between supply and demand forecasts should then lead to changes in policy, say, for example, with regard to recruitment, which will tend towards equilibrium.

When fairly well balanced forecasts are achieved a set of personnel policy guide-lines can be laid down for the personnel manager, which, whilst not superseding his essential short-term targets, will enable him to help to satisfy the long-term aims of the organisation. Manpower planning and personnel management are thus not two separate things (as they are so often regarded to-day) but are firmly locked one with the other. This concept of manpower planning is illustrated in Appendix A. Development of manpower models with the object of providing practical assistance to the personnel manager is progressing rapidly in the UK Civil Service, but this is not the place to begin to describe it. (Those interested are referred to Smith (70), Bartholomew and Smith (70) and Hopes (73).) But the new approaches which are starting to be developed depend utterly on being able to get accurate and immediate information out of a vast mass of data. This is what PRISM is all about.

But even personnel management is not an end in itself. Its primary objective is to achieve overall effectiveness in the use of manpower resources, that is to say people: to treat manpower as perhaps the most precious of resources in a way that has previously been restricted to the handling of money and physical assets. Certainly this is very much in the interests of the organisation employing people, but to a very large extent it is also in the interests of the individual if personnel management has a sensible and fair basis. It must be more satisfactory if day-to-day operational decisions are made not just in the light of short term requirements but also in the light of what is likely to develop over a fairly extended period. Clearly it is highly unsatisfactory, for example, to be recruiting peopie to-day only to be making them redundant in a year or two's time: it makes no sense to recruit high grade graduates if in 10 years' time there is likely to be no opening for their ability: it is sheer waste to train people in particular skills if those skills are not going to be utilised. It is also a requirement of personnel management to see that the requirements of the job match the skills of the individual and to see that the individual is developed so as to fulfil his potential. To the extent that PRISM provides the foundation on which effective manpower planning and personnel management can be based, I think it can fairly be stated that PRISM is in the direct interest of the individual.

3. Dangers to the individual

The ready availability of information in the way that has earlier been postulated does, however, put the individual in some jeopardy. The greatest danger is, I think, that inaccurate data will have been recorded and may be used against his interests. And this includes lack of data, which can be just as harmful: if it is not recorded, for example, that a man speaks French, he may not be considered for a particular post. In the PRISM system our first safeguard is to "lock" into the payroll system. Much of the data recorded for pay purposes is applicable to personnel use: it is usually of a high level of accuracy and is checked by a powerful audit system. It is not comprehensive, of course, but by "stretching" the set of pay data to include non-pay personal details, a very sound personnel record can be created.

The next safeguard is to ensure that a copy of the individual's record, as stored in the data-base, is fed back to the individual regularly (say no less frequently than once a year) so that he can have the opportunity to check it and bring it up to date. Arrangements have also to be made to "cycle" the corrections so that a new print is prepared and sent to the individual for rechecking. This process should continue until the entry is clear. Besides enabling the individual to correct his record, a checkprint also provides an essential service in letting the man know what the computer has on file about him.

The next danger is that the record may hold correct information, but of a kind which may be used directly against the man. For instance, a record of criminal convictions or of moral defects. In the case of a State service it may be quite reasonable to hold such details of staff in confidential files and to rely on the personnel managers who have access to them using discretion and applying a sense of perspective, e.g. when to "forgive and forget". Quite a new dimension, however, seems to be imposed when this type of information is recorded on a computer, even assuming that access to this aspect of the record is severely restricted. Accordingly, in PRISM no information of this kind is to be recorded.

Another area which is sensitive, but not to quite the same extent, relates to assessments of ability, performance and potential. The problem here is to record the information in sufficient depth to enable it to be applied in a reasonable way. This information is at present recorded on paper and again we rely on personnel managers using a great deal of sense and perspective in their perception of a man's ability from what is recorded. Of course it is simple to record a man's overall ability on, say, a five point scale ranging from "terrible" to "brilliant" but this is really of very limited practical use. To take the next step, however, which is to attempt to analyse the elements which contribute towards a man's ability and potential and to try, by applying weights to these elements, to arrive at an overall weighted index, is extremely dangerous. It is a most difficult task and it would require a great deal of proving before, in my view, such a process could be used on an automatic basis. Accordingly, no such elements are included in the PRISM Central Personal Record.

The next danger is that a personnel record could be linked to, for example, police records, or driving licence/vehicle registration records, or medical records, to provide a more complete picture of the individual. This is merely an extension of the danger which is present if sensitive items are included in the actual personnel record. Again, in PRISM categorical assurances have been given that no linking information will be obtained from other computerised records. It may be said, however, that such assurances depend on the good faith of the Administration and this is, of course, to some extent true. However, if the Administration puts the system openly on view to the Trade Unions (or Staff Associations) concerned, the latter can satisfy themselves as to the reality of the situation.

4. Vigilance by Trade Unions

This may be a good point at which to deal with the role of the Trade Unions and first it should be mentioned that in the UK Civil Service there is a history of more than 50 years of consultation and co-operation between management and unions. This is the Whitley system with its so-called Official and Staff Sides, recently surveyed by Parris (73). From the very earliest stages of PRISM – going back to 1968, even before the Feasibility Report for PRISM was produced – the National Staff Side was consulted about the project and ever since has been kept informed in detail as the systems design has evolved. The principal dangers touched on in the previous section of this paper are dangers which they have recognised and on which they have sought and obtained assurances from management. In my view no sophisticated information system can be designed if staff views are not taken fully into account during the design stage and if there is not close and genuine co-operation between management and the unions. It is to be emphasised that absolutely no detail of PRISM has been withheld from the knowledge of Staff Associations.

5. Privacy – Principles

A great deal has been written lately about the threat to privacy, to an extent, perhaps, which tends to over-emphasise its danger to the individual as against the principal risks which have already been dealt with. But Westin and Baker (72) provide a much clearer perspective for viewing the problems of intrusions into privacy. They find that, in general, existing systems are not abusing human rights, but that society should nevertheless always be vigilant because of potential dangers. It is necessary, therefore, that government, management and trade unions should keep the problems under review.

In the UK a parliamentary committee looked into the whole subject of privacy and reported (Younger, 72). The committee had some difficulty in defining privacy and, indeed, gave several definitions (pp. 327–328). Those most appropriate in this context seem to be Westin's "second 1967" definition:

> Privacy is the claim of individuals, groups or institutions to determine for themselves when, how and to what extent information about them is communicated to others.

And Judge Cooley's definition of 1888:

> The right to be let alone.

Younger (pp. 591–600) put forward ten basic principles which it was thought should apply to the handling of personal information by computer, as follows:

(1) Information should be regarded as held for a specific purpose and not be used, without appropriate authorization, for other purposes.

(2) Access to information should be confined to those authorized to have it for the purpose for which it was supplied.

(3) The amount of information collected and held should be the minimum necessary for the achievement of the specified purpose.

(4) In computerised systems handling information for statistical purposes, adequate provision should be made in their design and programs for separating identities from the rest of the data.

(5) There should be arrangements whereby the subject could be told about the information held concerning him.

(6) The level of security to be achieved by a system should be specified in advance by the user and should include precautions against the deliberate abuse or misuse of information.

(7) A monitoring system should be provided to facilitate the detection of any violation of the security system.

(8) In the design of information systems, periods should be specified beyond which the information should not be retained.

(9) Data held should be accurate. There should be machinery for the correction of inaccuracy and the updating of information.

(10) Care should be taken in coding value judgements.

Although the UK Government has not yet (November 1973) made any statement about its general policy in relation to the application of Younger in the public sector, it has, without prejudice to its eventual conclusions on the report generally, decided that the above principles should apply to PRISM, subject only to a minor reservation on (8), to the effect that the length of time historical information might be retained could not be defined in advance.

6. Security – Principles

Making the system secure, that is to say preventing unauthorised use, minimising errors and maintaining a high standard of accuracy and effectiveness, is an important design objective. The aims are in many respects very similar to those for the protection of privacy: accordingly, in implementing the principles for protecting both privacy and security, a single integrated plan should be adopted. What follows, therefore, covers both aspects of the problem.

The first thing to be said is that no system can be absolutely secure. To obtain a high degree of protection in, say, a defence application where secret information is involved requires a high overhead expense and may severely limit the ways in which terminal access can be made. Rigid control over who is allowed to operate access devices, physical security, electronic protection, enciphering and deciphering may all be involved. Even then, if an "attacker" has unlimited resources and expertise, such a system may not be absolutely safe.

The key factors to be considered are the value of the information to an outsider and what the loss to the "holder" of the information would be if it were to get out. If both these values are large, then correspondingly large sums must be spent on protection: if they are small, great expense on protection cannot be justified.

In the case of personnel records the value to an outsider is not great and he cannot reasonably be expected to spend a large amount of money in trying to crack the system. Accordingly, in PRISM we have attempted to provide safeguards which are reasonably stringent at a reasonable cost; broadly equivalent, in fact, to the protection given at the moment to confidential staff "paper" records. (Incidentally, at this point one should perhaps mention that the keeping of confidential personal information on computers is not new. Detailed pay data has been kept on computers in the UK Civil Service since 1957 and this sort of information needs careful protection both from a security aspect – fraud is an everpresent worry – and from the point of view of the individual's private affairs.)

7. Security – Implementation

One major design feature which greatly reduces the danger of the data-base being corrupted, either intentionally or accidentally, is that no on-line updating takes place. This is done in batch mode under strict controls. Whilst the system is on-line to users the data-base is in "read only" mode and is protected by a combination of the operating system (ICL's George III) and the application software.

General systems security has been described by Bridle (73). Unauthorised access to the data-base is prevented by a combination of hardware and software. The main hardware protection is a physical lock on each VDU with keys issued only to authorised users. In addition leased telephone lines are used to connect terminals with the computer, although "dial-up" is used in an emergency.

The main protection is by software and comprises:

(a) a user authorisation, or password, system;

(b) a system of privacy safeguards, or access restrictions, applied through the retrieval language PIRL.

Authorisation of users is controlled through the PRISM password system. This allows three unsuccessful attempts after which a warning message is sent to the computer centre VDU controller. The user is "locked out" from the system. Passwords are kept on User Records which are held on a specially created file of PRISM users. The user file is protected, as is PRISM's main file, from illegal access. In addition to the password each user record contains a user identity number and any access restrictions which may be appropriate (see below). A new user's password is first allocated to him by the PRISM Administration Officer and thereafter may be changed by the user through the VDU as frequently as circumstances dictate. If a user forgets his password a new one is allocated to him and his original User Record is deleted. Strict control is exercised over the running of the program which sets up or deletes user file entries.

Access restrictions are applied in three ways:

(1) Access to some records may be barred.

(2) Access to, or printing from, parts of records may be barred.

(3) Some or all records may be barred for personal print-out purposes, but not for de-personalised numerical analysis.

Since most PRISM access restrictions can be expressed in terms of PRISM elements and element values, it was decided to build access restrictions into the retrieval language (PIRL) program, as opposed to the data base handler routines. The PIRL language consists of PRISM element expressions linked together to identify sub-sets of the PRISM population required by users and it became apparent that the most frequently required access restrictions could be imposed through the language. Thus implementation was simplified and costs reduced.

Three methods of restricting access were eventually defined. The first limits the population by means of access restrictions stored as PIRL expressions on a user's record. These stored expressions are added by the retrieval program to each question a user inputs through his VDU. The effect is arbitrarily to limit the population the user may select. For example, management may decide that the duties of a particular user do not require him to access records of civil servants outside his own Department. That user's record would, for example, contain the entry DEPT(XYZ). This expression would be applied to each question input by that user so that whatever the nature of the enquiry the starting population would be limited to people in Department

"XYZ". Stored expressions of this kind are set up when a user is first accepted into PRISM, the user being told what restrictions have been applied to him. Processing is straightforward: any "restriction" is taken from the User Record at the initial check stage and then combined with the enquiry expression using the Boolean "AND" operator. Thereafter retrieval processing is normal.

The second method vets each PIRL expression in an enquiry. A question is rejected if it contains elements which the user is not permitted to use in defining a population. For example, one user may not be permitted to select populations on the basis of PRISM element "grade". The user's record would contain "GRD"; any attempt to select a population using "GRD" in a PIRL expression would cause the enquiry to be rejected. A similar check can be applied on PIRL expressions used to define PRISM output so that control can be exercised upon the contents of personal prints, lists and tables.

The third control operates at the output stage to prevent personal records being supplied to someone who is not authorised to see them, although he may be using the relevant data in a de-personalised sense. There is a relatively high processing overhead when this restriction is applied, because each record to be output for a list or personal print is checked to see whether or not it is of a type which should be output. If a whole record is not to be printed, the user is told of the discrepancy between record "counts" and the number of detailed records actually produced.

PRISM access restrictions are written into half a dozen modules out of a total of over 100. Clearly, if new types of restriction are called for then some or all of these modules, and possibly others, will require amendment. On the other hand there is a good chance that the types of access restriction so far specified will meet privacy requirements for some time to come. Certainly within the access restriction methods now defined the system is flexible, because any PRISM element may be specified, singly, or in combination with other elements and access restrictions. As has already been said, it is recognised that, despite these access restrictions, a person utterly determined to "break" the PRISM privacy system might do so, given unlimited time and resources. Short of this type of attack, however, the protection provided by the PRISM system is considered adequate to prevent unauthorised and inappropriate access.

8. Conclusion

It is hoped that this paper will have shown that, on the one hand, there can be no absolute freedom of information in a personnel information system and that, on the other, absolute security and protection of privacy is not possible. There has to be a compromise between the two extremes and in PRISM we have attempted to find a balance point which in all the circumstances is fair and reasonable. This idea of a balance between provision of information and its restriction is not confined to personnel information systems, but has its application in other areas. It is true, for instance, in the medical field, where one has to balance the advantage of having immediate availability of a person's record if he should suddenly become seriously ill or involved in an accident, against making it too readily available to a casual enquirer. It is also true in the criminal field, where the advantage of having comprehensive records to assist in quickly apprehending a suspect has to be balanced against the undesirability of keeping old and minor offences fresh and alive with the risk that the information could be used against the interests of a decent citizen.

It is not claimed that in PRISM we have the perfect balance and probably our ideas will have to be modified in the light of experience, but the important thing to observe is that, in any information system, the factors relating to security and privacy must be brought out into the open and a conscious decision taken as to the balance between provision and restriction of information. And, of course, this decision must reflect the views of those who represent the staff.

I cannot do better than to conclude this paper by quoting verbatim from Westin and Baker (72, p. 405), adding the rider that these comments apply world-wide, not just in an American context:

> If our empirical findings showed anything, they indicate that man is still in charge of the machines. What is collected, for what purposes, with whom information is shared, and what opportunities individuals have to see and contest records are all matters of policy choice, not technological determinism. Man cannot escape his social or moral responsibilities by murmuring feebly that "the Machine made me do it".
>
> There is also a powerful tendency to romanticize the precomputer era as a time of robust privacy, respect for individuality in organizations, and "face-to-face" relations in decision making. Such Arcadian notions delude us. In every age, limiting the arbitrary use of power, applying broad principles of civil liberties to the troubles and challenges of that time, and using technology to advance the social well-being of the nation represent terribly hard questions of public policy, and always will. We do not help resolve our current dilemma by thinking that earlier ages had magic answers.
>
> Computers are here to stay. So are large organizations and the need for data. So is the American commitment to civil liberties. Equally real are the social

cleavages and cultural reassessments that mark our era. Our task is to see that appropriate safeguards for the individual's rights to privacy, confidentiality, and due process are embedded in every major record system in the nation, particularly the computerizing systems that promise to be the setting for most important organizational uses of information affecting individuals in the coming decades.

References

Batholomew, D.J. and Smith, A.R. (eds.) (1970). *Manpower and Management Science*, London: The English Universities Press Ltd.

Bellerby, P.A. (1973). PRISM – Countflow – A date sensitive inverted file, Paper presented at Datafair. London; Obtainable from Civil Service Department.

Bridle, J.W. and Gregersen, R.J. (1971a). The central management staff record – A personnel information retrieval system, *O and M Bulletin* 26 (2) pp. 93–104.

Bridle, J.W. and Gregersen, R.J. (1971b). CMSR - A Personnel Information System, *The Computer Journal* 14 (4) pp. 338–343.

Bridle, J.W. (1973). PRISM's use in privacy systems, *Computing* 29/11/73, p. 14.

Fulton, Lord (1968). *The Civil Service: Report of the Fulton Committee*, London: Her Majesty's Stationery Office.

Hersleb, A. and Bayhylle, J.E. (1973). *The Development of EDP in Manpower Areas*, Paris: Organisation for Economic Co-operation and Development.

Hopes, R.F.A. (1973). Some statistical aspects of manpower planning in the civil service, *Omega, The International Journal of Management Science* 1 (2) pp. 165–180.

Parris, H. (1973). *Staff Relations in the Civil Service – Fifty Years of Whitleyism*, London: Allen and Unwin.

Smith, A.R. (ed.) (1970). *Models of Manpower Systems*, London: The English Universities Press Ltd.

Westin, A.F. and Baker, M.A. (1972). *Databanks in a Free Society – Computers, Record-Keeping and Privacy*, New York: Quadrangle Books.

Younger, K. (1972). *Report of the Committee on Privacy*, Cmnd 5012, London: Her Majesty's Stationery Office.

Appendix A. A concept of manpower planning

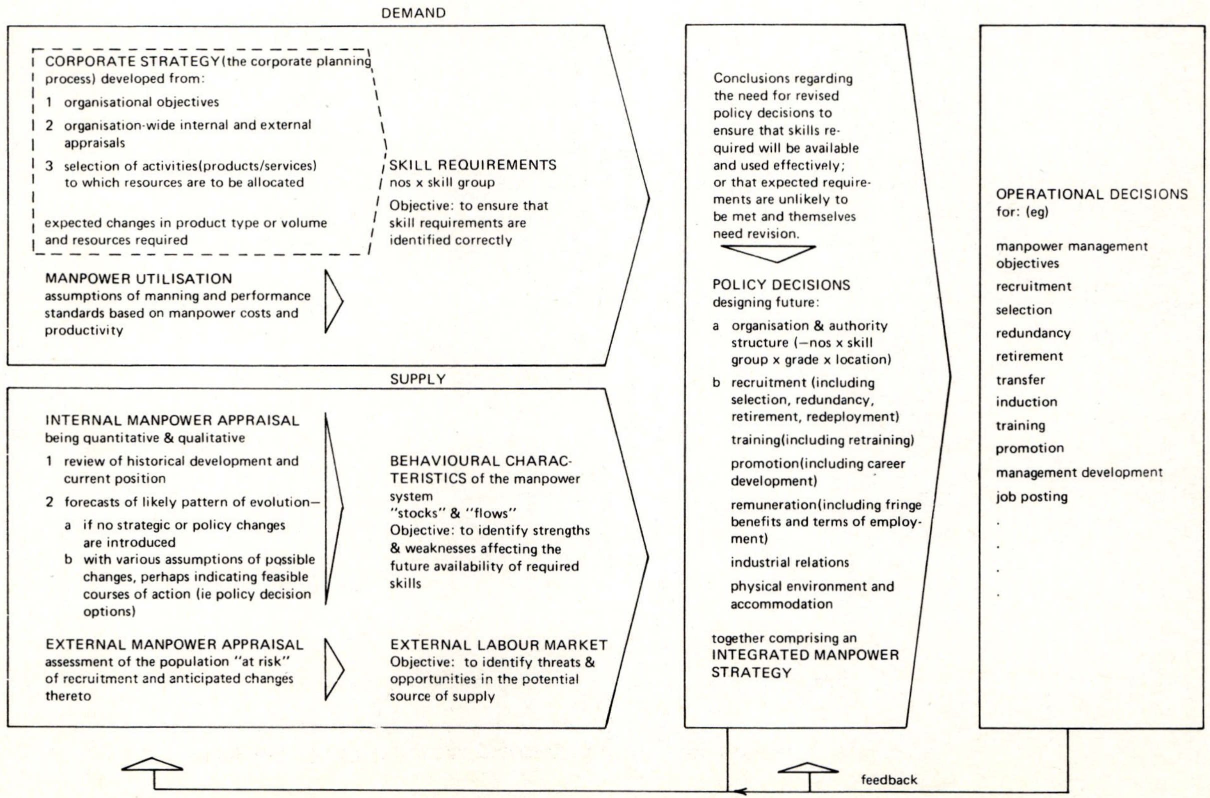

Appendix B. Civil Service personnel information system

Schematic Diagram of Information Flow for Network System

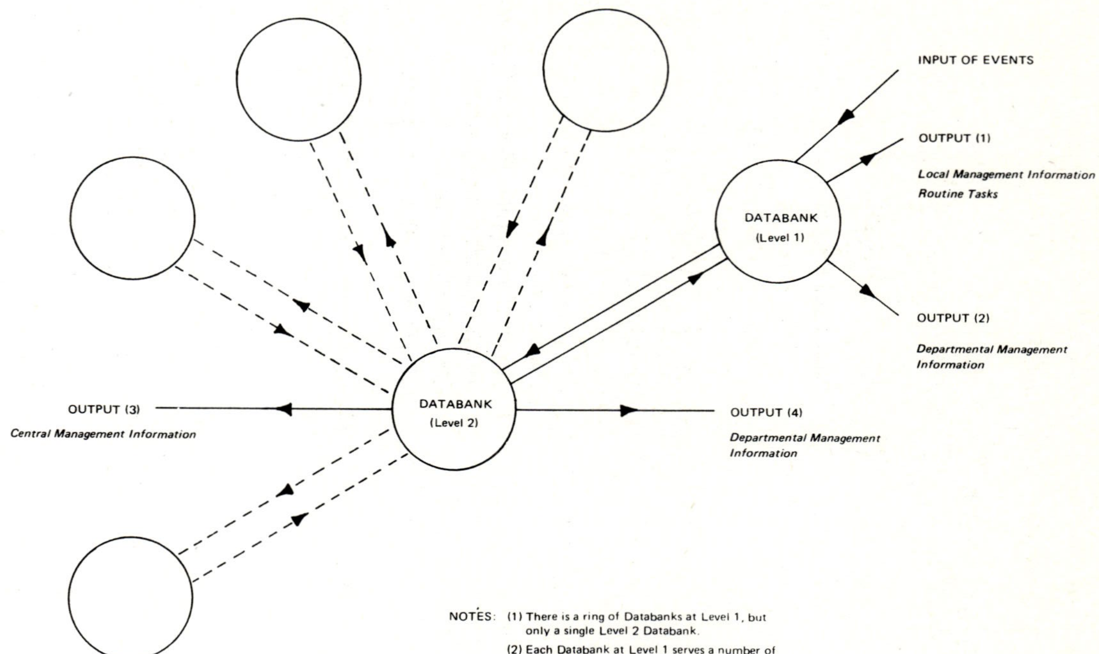

NOTES: (1) There is a ring of Databanks at Level 1, but only a single Level 2 Databank.

(2) Each Databank at Level 1 serves a number of peripheral points.

Appendix C

PRISM PHASE I

CENTRAL PERSONAL RECORD

PRISM STANDARD ELEMENT No.	ELEMENT NAME
	BASIC DETAILS
100	National Insurance number/Civil Service identity number
101	Surname – recorded date
102	Surname
103	Initials – recorded date
104	Initials
105	Date of birth
106	Sex
107	Marital status – recorded date
108	Marital status
112	Hours of work (part-time staff) – date
113	Hours of work (part-time staff)
114	Registered disabled
115	Employment status or type of appointment – date
116	Employment status or type of appointment
	CIVIL SERVICE CAREER
200	Civil Service – date of entry
201	Civil Service – grade on entry
202	Civil Service – method of entry
203	Civil Service – source of entry
204	Department – date of entry
205	Department
206	Department – method of entry
207	Grade – date of entry
208	Grade
209	Grade – method of entry
210	Grade – seniority date
211	Professional/scientific discipline – date of entry
212	Professional/scientific discipline

Appendix C. (continued)

PRISM STANDARD ELEMENT No.	ELEMENT NAME
	CIVIL SERVICE CAREER
213	Occupational group or class – method of entry
214	Temporary promotion – date
215	Temporary promotion – grade
216	Responsibility allowance – date
217	Responsibility allowance – amount
	ACADEMIC AND PROFESSIONAL QUALIFICATIONS
300	Qualification – type
301	Qualification – awarding institution
302	Qualification – level of attainment – overall
303	Qualification – subject
304	Qualification – year of award, or year of cessation/reinstatement of membership of a professional institution
	TYPE OF OFFICE/LOCATION
402	Type of office – date of entry
403	Type of office
404	Location area – date of entry
405	Location area
	BORROWED/LOANED
500	Borrowed staff – date of return
501	Borrowed staff – parent department
502	Temporary absence from Civil Service – date started
503	Temporary absence from Civil Service – date of return
504	Temporary absence from Civil Service – category
505	Temporary absence from Civil Service – type of outside employment or occupation

Appendix C. (continued)

PRISM STANDARD ELEMENT No.	ELEMENT NAME
	PAY
600	Pay (national rate) – date of effect
601	Pay – national rate
605	Estains option
	SUPERANNUATION/GRATUITY
700	Superannuation/gratuity scheme – date of entry
701	Superannuation/gratuity scheme
702	Re-employed Civil Servant – date
703	Re-employed Civil Servant
704	Superannuation/gratuity emoluments – date
705	Total emoluments reckonable for superannuation or gratuity
706	Notional date of entry to service reckonable for superannuation or gratuity
707	Balance of unestablished service prior to 14 July 1949 not reckonable for superannuation purposes
708	Reckonable unestablished service prior to 14 July 1949 – date
709	Date of entry to service reckonable for superannuation or gratuity
710	Established service – grade on entry
711	Established service – method of entry
712	Widow's pension – recorded date
713	Widow's pension option and the rate of contribution
714	Pension for an adult dependant – recorded date
715	Pension for an adult dependant – option
718	Invalidity pension – recorded date
719	Invalidity pension – option
720	Purchase of added years for superannuation purposes – recorded date
721	Purchase of added years for superannuation purposes – number
722	Purchase of added years for superannuation purposes – method

Appendix C. (continued)

PRISM STANDARD ELEMENT No..	ELEMENT NAME
	LEAVING
900	Leaving – date
901	Leaving – cause
902	Leaving – nature of award
903	Leaving – type of new employment or occupation

TRADE UNION CHOICE AND COMPUTERS

E. Mumford and H. Sackman, eds., Human Choice and Computers
North-Holland Publishing Company (1975)

TRADE UNION STRATEGIES FOR THE HUMANISATION OF WORK IN THE FRG

Gerhard LEMINSKY

Institute for Economic and Social Research of the German Trade Unions Federation, Düsseldorf, Federal Republic of Germany

The trade unions in the FRG have started to discuss strategies for the humanisation of work* as an overall policy to enable the worker to control his work situation. FRG unions have no "computer policy"; they are only interested in computers as instruments and they seek to identify the implications of this machinery for employment, income or content of work.

The *main thesis* of the author is, that real humanisation of work is only possible if all factors affecting industrial work can be influenced by the interests of the workers. The relation of humanisation to productivity is an open one but many experiments with new forms of work have led to a considerable increase in productivity. However, it is too narrow to relate humanisation only to the single private firm concerned; social criteria affecting communities as a whole must also be considered.

In the early days of industrialization paternalism and the strict rules of discipline of the armed forces constituted the main pattern of cooperation in factories, where the worker was seen by management only as a factor of production. This pattern was modified by Taylor and Mayo. In Taylor's view, the workers wanted only high wages and these could be provided through the

* In May 1974 the first DGB-Congress "Humanisierung der Arbeit als gewerkschaftspolitische und gesellschaftspolitische Aufgabe" was held. Papers and the discussions of working groups at this conference were published at the end of 1974 by Europäische Verlagsanstalt, Frankfurt a.M.

The monthly review of the DGB "Gewerkschaftliche Monatshefte" has already published in No. 1/73 a number of articles dealing with new approaches to humanisation.

extreme division of labour. Mayo wished to solve the problems of industrial work through a human relations approach of trying to motivate people through factors other than money.

1. New factors

Since the end of the Second World War new ideas have emerged, which have been directed at the elimination of alienation in work but which have not fundamentally changed the old structures of work.

(1) *A reduction in the hours of work* led to the idea that alienation in work could be compensated by self fulfillment outside work. However, from todays perspective, alienation within work leads also to alienation outside work. More stress and an increased repetitiveness in job content; more overtime and shift work, together with increasing urbanization with long journeys from and to the work place, have led to more accidents and more early retirements than before (Kern and Schumann, 70).

(2) There is no valid test for the hypothesis that automation will lead to more autonomy for the workers. On the contrary: empirical studies in the FRG indicate a "polarization" of the labour force in automated plants; the majority of workers are in repetitive work situations and only a small minority has jobs with high qualifications.*

(3) As a result of the process of *technological rationalization* by computers work now is less dependent on personal control and more dependent on impersonal control factors in the same way as the assembly line or the wage system. Organizational changes go in the same direction. Work is more repetitive, isolated and provides fewer chances for learning. New management techniques, which aim to increase productivity through increased motivation to work, only affect a minority of employees.

(4) The growing number of *foreign workers* is characterized by high mobility, a willingness to work for low wages and a reluctance to press hard for new conditions of work; although since last year there have been some changed attitudes. Most of the 2.5 million foreign workers are employed in jobs requiring only the lowest qualifications. In automobile plants more than 80% working on assembly lines are foreign workers. However, in some spontaneous strikes they have claimed not only more money but also a change in working conditions.

* See special number 7/74 of "Gewerkschaftliche Monatshefte" on the flexibility of working time.

(5) The main factors which explain progress in the humanisation of work are the pressures of *unions* and the *works councils*. Although, up to now, no complete concept has been elaborated, minimum standards and controls concerning safety and health have been introduced and the workers' representatives have succeeded in obtaining compensation for specific undesirable conditions of work in terms of money. A new slogan is: "no financial compensation for unhealthy work, but a new structure for the job."

2. A concept of humanisation of work

The concept of humanisation of work, discussed here, implies that work is of central importance for satisfactory human existence. It is no solution merely to reduce working hours; opportunities for autonomy, freedom and choice have to be brought into the work situation. This cannot be achieved solely through new institutions, through countervailing powers, or through monetary compensation, the content and the structure of work must be changed in itself. Even age is a social category dependent on the work a man is doing: a manager of 50 is a young man, an assembly line worker of 50 is an old man.

Only a structure of work which gives autonomy and qualifications and the possibility of identification with a job can be called humanised. Norwegian researchers have listed some of these basic requirements of work, and these provide a good example of the direction which the humanisation of work should take for each job and not merely for managers or some white collar-workers (Thorsrud, 72).

(1) The need for the content of a job to be reasonably demanding in terms other than sheer endurance, and yet to provide a minimum of variety (not necessarily novelty).

(2) The need for being able to learn on the job (which implies standards and knowledge of results) and to go on learning.

(3) The need for some minimal area of decision-making that the individual can call his own.

(4) The need for some minimal degree of social support and recognition in the workplace.

(5) The need to be able to relate what he does and what he produces to his social life.

(6) The need to feel that the job leads to some sort of desirable future.

These requirements are obviously not confined to any one level of employment. Nor is it possible to meet them in the same way in all work settings or for all kinds of people.

In such a concept, which has been empirically tested in Great Britain and Norway, technique, organization and the wage system are variables for a new work situation.

3. Main elements of the new concept

Flexibility and autonomy often require the organization of work around groups. A new work structure requires different instruments: better training, job enrichment, job enlargement, job rotation. Production, repair and production control are now done by the same group of workers. The technique of production has to be changed to some extent, organizational changes will certainly be required. Some of the functions of the foreman are taken over by the group, information and communication have to be adapted to the new structure. The wage system has to fit into the requirements of group work. The introduction of new work elements becomes dependent on the approval of those involved. It involves both a learning process and a bargaining process which affects the level of earnings. It is important to realize that humanisation in this sense cannot be brought about by a specific technique but only through a new view of the problem.

4. Resistance to such a new concept

The main problem here lies in the fact that man in production has been seen only as a factor of production. Because of this, science has been directed only to factors which could be measured and not to the development of new structures of work.

In the science of *ergonomics* technique and organization are given and human work has to be adapted to a set of given conditions. In addition, ergonomics is focussed on the technical organization of the isolated working place. Ergonomics is taught at technical universities and practiced by engineers who neglect social factors such as team- or group work, flexibility, reliability, polyvalence, responsibility, the capacity to solve conflicts, etc.

Organizational changes are generally planned in an isolated way, directed only at increasing productivity and including only people with management functions. The interdependence between wage systems, group work, communication systems, organizational and technical change is not understood. The distrust of unions and works councils with these organizational changes can be explained as a product of experience that such innovations are not in the interests of workers and have not led to a better work situation for the majority of workers.

Technology is also an important variable. However, in reality, new technologies are introduced without any recognition of the problems of those who have to work with them. Technicians exclude all social factors which cannot be strictly controlled in the same way as engineering factors. An example of the impact of technology might be the introduction of computers which could, if no social factors are considered, prevent the decentralisation of work. But, if used to achieve human objectives EDP could help to establish opportunities for a decentralisation of enterprise planning; it could offer techniques to integrate personnel and investment planning, it could assist a choice of working hours; it could help a group to control its own work and to communicate with each other.

All techniques and technologies have an instrumental character. Those who have the power to guide the use of these instruments will determine the direction and for what purpose they are developed.

5. Outlines for trade union strategies

In different countries trade unions take different approaches to the development of a strategy for the humanisation of work. New structures of work can be introduced through confrontation, collective bargaining and strikes, as in Italy and France, or through consensus between unions and employers as in Norway, or with the active help of government as is now beginning in the FRG. But, in the long term, new methods of work cannot be defined solely in terms of conflict or integration, they must contain both elements as does every reformist strategy.

(a) As a result of the activities of *parliament and government* in the FRG the need for a greater humanisation of work has been recognized through the introduction of some minimum standards for the industrial environment and by procedures which subject changes of work and work organization to the influence of the workers concerned and of their representatives.

The Government established a Federal Institute for Accident Protection and Accident Research (Bundesanstalt für Unfallschutz und Unfallforschung) at Dortmund in 1972. Since 1974 employers are obliged by law to employ occupational health physicians, safety engineers and other specialists concerned with safety at work (Gesetz über Betriebsärzte, Sicherheitsingenieure und andere Fachkräfte für Arbeitssicherheit). In the Federal Ministry of Labour an administrative decree is under consideration regulating minimum conditions of the industrial environment at the work place, e.g. air conditioning and temperature, protection against noise, minimum standards for washing rooms and toilets, rooms for recreation and communication. There are some further activities, e.g. for young workers protection. Of particular importance is a research program of the federal ministries of labour and of science and technology for the humanisation of work, beginning May 1974 (Forschung zur Humanisierung des Arbeitslebens).*

This program has three main components: first, the collection of data and the development of standards and minimum requirements for machines, technical plants and work places; second, the development of technologies to meet human requirements ("menschengerechte Arbeitstechnologien"). This includes new machinery, new systems for control and transport, and computers may play an important role in this field; third, case studies and models for the organization of work (as developed using socio-technical analysis in Britain and Norway). Firms which are willing to introduce new forms of group work which include more job variety will receive subsidies to meet part of the costs of such experiments, provided they permit researchers to follow through the change process and to publish their findings so that there can be a transfer of methods and results to other firms.

These tendencies towards greater humanisation of work have to be viewed in the context of the new Works Constitution Law of 1972 and of the system of workers' influence at the level of work place, plant and enterprise, as this is partly regulated by law. These laws have to some extent fixed the procedures and the rights of workers to exercise influence over plant and company policy, especially in the field of conditions of work. One of the most discussed innovations of the new Works Constitution Law is division IV on "structuring, organization and design of jobs, operations and the working environment".

§ 90 provides for the giving of information to the works council by the employer of any plans concerning the construction, alteration or extension of works, or offices in the establishment, of technical plant, of working process and operations, and of jobs. "In their consultations the employer and the works council shall take into consideration the established findings of ergonomics concerning the tailoring of jobs to meet human requirements."

And § 91 says: "Where a special burden is imposed on the employees as a result of changes in jobs, operations or the working environment that are in

* Aktionsprogramm des Bundesministers für Arbeit und Sozialordnung und des Bundesministers für Forschung und Technologie, in: Sozialpolitische Informationen, Sonderausgabe vom 8. Mai 1974, herausgegeben vom Bundesministerium für Arbeit, Bonn.

obvious contradiction to the established findings of ergonomics . . the works council may request appropriate action to obviate, relieve or compensate for the additional stress thus imposed." A crucial point here is that nobody knows what are the "established findings of ergonomics", nevertheless these provisions have opened a broad public discussion in the field. Within ergonomics there are tendencies towards a redefination of work including social factors.* The unions have started extensive activities to train works council members and shop stewards in these new tasks. Proposals are made on how to establish new procedures to influence plant policy; check lists are provided in which essential points of humanisation are summarised and new perspectives are developed.**

In the long run "Mitbestimmung" at enterprise level may play an important role, too, for the humanisation of work.† All experiments have shown that a real humanisation cannot be realized at the level of the individual work place: the structure of individual development is decided by policy at shop level, by decisions on technical equipment, by investment and personnel planning. Therefore it is necessary to seek at *all* levels of plant and enterprise for an overall policy which guarantees equal influence on the problems of labour. The system of Mitbestimmung claimed by the unions (equal representation of labour on supervisory boards and labour directors on executive boards, up to now only practiced in coal and steel) takes account of the fact that the humanisation of work is not only a psychological problem of the individual but a structural problem determined by conflicting interests. Mitbestimmung at enterprise level makes it possible to integrate humanisation into a firms' policy by exercising countervailing power.††

* Memorandum der Gesellschaft für Arbeitswissenschaft e.V. "Arbeitswissenschaft in der Gesetzgebung". In: afa-Informationen, Hrsg. Deutscher Gewerkschaftsbund, 1972, H. 6, S. 75ff.

** See e.g. special number of the monthly review "Das Mitbestimmungsgespräch" 1974, H. 5/6, to the § § 90/91 of the Works Constitution Law to legal, practical and trade union aspects of humanisation of work.

† See articles in special number "Gewerkschaftliche Monatshefte", 1974, H. 10.

†† It is not possible here to give an overview of the legal and practical problems of Mitbestimmung. The fundamental relationship between Mitbestimmung and humanisation has been already defined in 1973 by Heinz O. Vetter, President of the DGB "Humanisierung der Arbeitswelt als gewerkschaftliche Aufgabe", in "Gewerkschaftliche Monatshefte" 1973, H. 1. See also Werner Vitt "Mitbestimmung und Humanisierung der Arbeit", Munich Conference, May 1974.

It is not by chance that firms in coal and steel where the "qualifizierte Mitbestimmung" (not only works council but also labour directors and equal representation of labour on the Board) is practiced, are among the first to have experimented with personnel and social planning.

Some firms have established a group which might be called an "ergonomic team" consisting of technicians, ergonomists, safety engineers, and industrial relations experts who examine each investment program of the firm before it is accepted. These firms are also now commencing new forms of personnel planning including career planning (Schweres, 74).

(b) The unions realize that a complete humanisation of work requires an elaborate structure on all levels of the plant and enterprise. But they stress more and more, and their Conference on Humanisation at Munich in May 1974 emphasized this, that a better work situation cannot be reached by law alone. Only the power of union solidarity through collective bargaining can enforce a real change. The provisions of collective agreements should indicate the direction which humanisation should take; through the procedures and the institutions of Mitbestimmung it has to be adapted to the specific situations of the different firms and plants. Both elements, Mitbestimmung and collective agreements have to be seen as interdependent.

The Munich Conference stated that any further reduction of job content and increased intensification of work must not be accepted. Unions should realize the importance of wage differentiation and wage structure for the organisation and the content of work. Monotonous, repetitive and restrictive jobs should not be legitimized through collective bargaining. Also, financial compensation should not be accepted for such jobs; unions must press for a restructuring of the job itself.

During the discussion the point was made that a strategy of humanisation needs additional activities in other fields, e.g. protection against dismissals, provisions for the employment of older workers or facilities for further learning and training. The technological problems, the organisational implications, the possibilities of variations in the working time structures and the role of collective bargaining were discussed and many detailed recommendations were given.*

A first step towards a better quality of working life has come about through a collective agreement made in October 1973 by the metal worker's union in Baden-Württemberg. This agreement was reached after a strike** and

* As already mentioned the results of the conference were published by the DGB at the end of 1974 (Europäische Verlagsanstalt, Frankfurt).

** 55 Punkte, die für IG Metall sprechen, in: Metall-Pressedienst vom 23. Oktober 1973.

was called a "mile stone" by the mass media and the general public. It lays down provisions in five fields: collection of data; organisation of work; stabilisation of employment; information on conditions of work; wage principles.

The collection of data relevant to wages and working conditions has to follow an agreed procedure. In the field of organisation of work all workers on assembly lines or paid by piece rates now have a minimum recreation time (Erholungszeit) of 5 minutes and a minimum time of 3 minutes for their personal needs per hour. In restrictive work situations, particularly assembly line work where an individual has to repeat the same functions within 1.5 minutes, employers and works councils have to use the techniques of job enrichment and job enlargement. Group work can only be introduced by agreement between works councils and employers on such things as the task of the group, the members of the group, information to be given to the group.

The provisions concerning the stabilisation of employment give a guarantee of income for piece workers of at least 125% of the average sum of piece work paid by the plant by collective agreement.

This was one of the points which the employers strongly opposed because they said it was against the "Leistungsprinzip" (principle of achievement). The protection against dismissals was enlarged, especially for workers older than 55, who normally cannot be dismissed if they have been in the same firm for at least 3 years.

The next section deals with information related to working conditions and puts an obligation on the employer to give the worker, when he starts work, written information on his task, work place, wage principles etc.

6. Specific implications of computerisation for the humanisation of work*

If it is accepted that humanisation as an opportunity for selffullfilment requires a structuring of work along these lines, then this means that the introduction of computers is not merely a technological problem without relevance for the social context of work. The design and functions of control systems are of great importance for the work of men.

* The following outline is related to discussions the author was involved in at IFAC Workshop on Productivity and Man, Bad Boll, FRG, January 21–25, 1974, sponsored by the International Federation of Automatic Control, IFAC-Committee on Social Effects of Automation.

Therefore unions should exert influence to ensure that the *curricula and professional* training of control engineers deals with social problems, not in a form of isolated information on social theories or industrial relations, but starting from concrete problems which emphasise the interdependence of organization, technology and wages with the design of computer systems.

The *process of designing a computer system* is as important as the result of such activities. The problems of men who have to work with the system should be taken into full consideration through consultation with them and their representatives (unions, works councils, shop stewards, etc.) at all stages of the planning process. The final design should be made with the users and with their approval, recognizing that success depends not only on the structure of hardware but also on changes in information and communication, new roles of foremen, an accepted new structure of tasks, etc.

This requires a *new definition of the role of control engineers and computer specialists in the planning structure of an enterprise*. They should be involved in the overall planning process of a firm from the beginning and not merely "transfer" given decisions in computerisation under extreme time pressure, as now frequently happens, without any possibility of evaluating the social problems involved.

Last but not least the computer specialist has the chance of *autonomous action* in the field of humanisation. He can offer his professional knowledge to assist the collection of data and correlations related to humanisation – for example, figures on sickness, absenteeism, accidents, turnover, low quality work. He can design systems which give man the opportunity to intervene and he can offer alternatives to men through simulations or games. By his ability to combine man and machine in a system, he can press for short/long term personnel and social planning as an integrated part of managerial philosophy. But he can do this only when human problems are given the same weight as problems of capital in the philosophy of the enterprise. This is why unions press for what is called codetermination.

Experiments already published indicate that there is a real chance to reconcile computerisation with humanisation if commitment and knowledge are directed this way. Computer experts have not been ignorant people, but they have not recognized these human problems when designing systems. They have a technical education and they work in a industrial structure where they have to behave in a certain way. If we can change this structure/environment the computer can be adapted to humanisation, too.

References

Kern, A. and Schumann, B. (1970). *Industriearbeit und Arbeiterbewusstsein*, 2. Bde. Frankfurt a.M.

Schweres, M. (1974). Die Verwirklichung der § § 90 und 91 im Betrieb. Praktische und organisatorische Aspekte und Beispiele, in: Das Mitbestimmungsgespräch H. 5/6, S. 103 ff.

Thorsrud, E. (1972). Policy-making as a learning process, in: Cherns, Sinclair and Jenkins (eds.) *Social Sciences and Government: Policies and Problems*, London.

E. Mumford and H. Sackman, eds., Human Choice and Computers
North-Holland Publishing Company (1975)

THE ROLE OF INFORMATION PROCESSING SYSTEMS IN EMPLOYEE PARTICIPATION IN MANAGERIAL DECISION-MAKING

Ulrich BRIEFS

Institute for Economic and Social Research of the German Trade Unions Federation, Düsseldorf, Federal Republic of Germany

1. Business objectives as determinants of information processing systems

Information systems based on electronic data processing (EDP) increasingly support the processes of planning, execution, and control in business organizations. These systems are designed and implemented to support the functions of the management of the different levels. Managers' needs in information derive from their functions and the objectives they are given. The latter normally describe expected results of the execution of managers' functions and are in the typical capitalist business organization derived from the pursuit of interests of the capital owners. These interests again can be summarized essentially by "return on investment and capital growth", notwithstanding the observable differentiations of business objectives systems (Ansoff, 65; Starbuck, 65; WSI-Projektgruppe, 73) and leaving aside the maximizing-satisficing debate (Simon, 64).

New needs in information, however, are emerging if employees and their representatives – the trade unions – are given the right to participate in managerial decision-making thus enabling them to formulate their own objectives with respect to the relevant business organization. In some countries indeed, certain forms of participation in management decisions have already been provided for by legislation, in other countries the demand for participation is part of the propositions made by trade unions in order to establish economic democracy.

The concept of employee participation in managerial decision-making is, however, not unanimously accepted by trade union organizations as a suitable strategy for the achievement of economic democracy. One of the basic problems of the long-range strategy of trade unions – which will not be discussed here – is whether it is better to fight for an improvement of the situation of employees from a strictly outside position with no involvement in management decisions, or whether it is more advantageous to participate actively and cooperatively in the decision-making within business organizations thereby gradually changing the conditions of salaried work.

If, however, such a system of employee participation in managerial decision-making is accepted and promoted by trade unions, how efficiently these participation rights can be used depends to a considerable degree on the information available about the planning, execution, and auditing of management's decisions in the business organization.

From this fact the interest of employees and their representatives in the spreading of modern information technology and especially in EDP supported information systems in business organizations becomes obvious. One of the effects of the implementation of EDP based information systems may indeed be the provision of more and better information for the pursuit of employees' objectives in business organizations. However, we must stress that this may be one of the effects, because an efficient use of EDP information systems by employees and trade unions presupposes that these systems are accessible to them. Only too often do we observe instead that managements withhold or manipulate information to which employees' representatives are entitled. Securing the access to information necessary for an efficient use of participation rights must therefore remain one of the targets of the further legal corroboration of participation rights, and will be central to the day-to-day controversies between employees and trade union officials on one side and managements on the other.

But there is one other problem which arises out of the matching of participation requirements and the application of information technology: the design and implementation of EDP based information systems in a way which makes them useful also for employees and trade union officials as their representatives. If computer scientists' prognostics about the spreading of information technology and its impact on business organizations are to become true, the growing tendency for employee participation in business decisions should be accounted for in the design and implementation of EDP based information systems, too.

To illustrate this proposition we will first give a short description of employee participation rights in management decisions which are in operation in West Germany. Then, in the following paragraphs an attempt will be made to outline some perspectives for the adaptation of business information systems to a pursuit of employee objectives under participation conditions.

2. Forms of participation and information needs: the West German example

Participation by employees and trade unions in West Germany is in operation on two levels of the business organization:

(a) on the enterprise level,

(b) on the plant level.

On the enterprise level the main participation instrument is employee representation on the board of directors whose main duty is the control of the management board and its business policy. According to articles 90 and 111 of the Joint Stock Company Law the board of directors is entitled to any information necessary for this function and especially to any information concerning the planning of business policy.

For the moment, however, employee participation is restricted by the fact that in joint stock companies outside the iron and steel and the coal mining industries employees and trade unions nominate only one third of the members of the board of directors. In the iron and steel industry and in coal mining, however, half of the members of the board of directors are nominated by them and also one of the top managers, who is responsible for personnel and social administration in the organization, is nominated by the trade union.

This latter form of participation – one half of the members on the board of directors and one member on the management board are delegated by employees and trade unions – is the so-called co-determination on a parity basis.

According to the propositions of the German Trade Union Confederation this form of participation should be extended to all joint capital firms above a certain size measured in number of employees, value of assets and turn-over (DGB-Bundesvorstand, 71).*

Co-determination on a parity basis is likewise demanded by the European Trade Union Confederation for the European joint stock company the statutes

* In the meantime the project of a law on enlarged co-determination in the industries which so far have not been subject to the co-determination regulations on a parity basis has been elaborated by the two partners in the present government in the Federal Republic. This law does not provide for participation on a parity basis but it nevertheless will advance participation beyond the one-third participation on the board of directors in about 500 enterprises. Besides this the project of the law contains several points which remain substantially behind the propositions of the trade unions. Interestingly enough the problem of the information gap between the two sides of the industrial relation system is more urgent the more the participation regulation deviates from the parity pattern.

of which are still discussed in the European Community's administration (DGB-Bundesvorstand, 72).

An extension of participation rights on the enterprise level is also demanded for multinational corporations (DGB-Bundesvorstand, no year).

If employee participation in management decisions in this or in any other form of co-determination is to be efficient in terms of employee objectives, the representatives of employees on the board of directors must be given information that is comparable to that of the representatives of the capital side. Furthermore the board of directors as a whole must be in a position to get the information which it needs for its function of controlling business policy.

Since the planning and execution of business policy by management is more and more supported by information processing systems, the support by these systems may indeed become a crucial point for the efficient use of participation rights.

A second form of participation* has been established at the plant level. The Works Constitution Act of 1972 prescribes the establishment of works councils at the plant level. These works councils in most cases do not participate in general top management decision-making, though in smaller firms, where plant and enterprise level often coincide, the involvement of the works councils in top management decisions is often more direct.

The works councils, too, have extended rights to information about business plans and activities at the plant level. Article 106 of the Works Constitution Act gives the following list of information the works councils are entitled to:

(1) the economic and financial situation of the company;
(2) the production and marketing situation;

* In order to roughly depict the importance of the different approaches to participation the number of employees working under the (existing or proposed) regulations can provide an indication:

co-determination on a parity basis in steel and iron resp. coal-mining – 0.6 million employees.

co-determination as presently proposed by government regulation for large-scale enterprises (about 500 enterprises, cf. footnote on page 171) – 4.0 million employees.

one-third participation on board of directors according to the Works Constitution Act – 1.0 million employees.

participation according to the Works Constitution Act in enterprises not having a board of directors – 10.3 million employees.

special regulations, which are not as far reaching as the Works Constitution Act's regulations, in the public services – 3.4 million employees.

no participation – 3.2 million employees.

(3) the production and investment programmes;

(4) rationalisation plans;

(5) production techniques and work methods, especially the introduction of new work methods;

(6) the reduction of operations in or closure of establishments or parts of establishments;

(7) the transfer of establishments or parts of establishments;

(8) the amalgamation of establishments;

(9) changes in the organization or objectives of establishments; and

(10) any other circumstances and projects that may materially affect the interests of the employees of the company.

This list additionally illustrates to what extent employee representatives have to take an interest in the amount and quality of information which is supplied to them by the business organization.

It would be highly interesting to go further from this outlining of the legal content of the participation system and its quantitative structure by adding material elaborated on the basis of empirical studies on the factual outcomes of co-determination. This material, however, is almost entirely lacking* – a fact that is the more astonishing the more distinct the all-embracing character of co-determination becomes. The only major study attempting a review of the observable results of the German co-determination regulation is not a study relying on the methodology of social research but an enquiry which evaluates co-determination against the requirements of a market economy (Sachverständigenkommission, 70). It is worth noting that this study was initiated and conducted by the Christian Democrats, who firmly oppose an extension of co-determination on a parity basis, and that the leader of the group conducting this enquiry is now one of the top representatives of the Christian Democratic opposition. However, it must be stressed that the factual findings of the enquiry were largely in favour of the co-determination system. Nevertheless the problem of the information needs of employee representatives was not dealt with in the sense it is exposed here, i.e. a screening

* Two other references to empirical material must not be omitted. One is a study of the effects of the distribution of expert knowledge on the power structure in participation systems (Mulder, 70), which shows that participation systems operate efficiently only if there is sufficient information and expert knowledge available to both sides of the pattern. The other one is the experience of those – among them the author – who in connection with contributions to training programs for co-determinators are confronted with the very problems caused by the information gap between management and employees' representatives thereby gaining an admittedly largely unstructured and certainly biased insight into the real structures and processes of co-determination.

of the information needs of employees' representatives against the requirement for an efficient participation in managerial decision-making, always keeping in mind that on management's side substantial change is going on due to the increased use of computers.

Since empirical findings cannot lead to conclusions with regard to the relationship between the spreading of participation regulations and the process of computerization of managerial decision-making one has to start from theoretical assumptions. One of these assumptions is that for an active participation in the planning, execution, and control of business activities by employees it is not sufficient to give employee representatives the same information which management receives. What the representatives of employees need in addition is information which is specific to the needs and objectives of the individual employees and of the work force as a whole. This again implies that in the design of information systems based on EDP a check has to be made on the degree to which these systems are to be tailored to the information needs of employee representatives.

This requirement concerns especially the semantical scope and the internal logical structure of information processing systems. As a common label for both kinds of modifications the term "structuring" is used here. This aspect of the information problem under participation conditions is therefore called "structuring of information systems according to the needs of employees". But, since in most business organizations the basic structures of information systems are already fixed, the term "re-structuring" may be used as well.

3. Structuring of information processing systems under participation conditions

The information necessities derived from the participation rights which are given to employee representatives pertain so far primarily to the usual information about the actual and planned course of business. If employee representatives, however, endeavour to participate actively in the formulation of business policy, they need additional information which is specific to the needs and objectives of the employees as individuals and as a class.

This is illustrated by the following example: after a pay-rise the main decision for management may be how the increased costs are absorbed by the different products while the works council may be primarily interested in the new pattern of income distribution among different classes of qualification; among male and female workers, among clerical and blue-collar workers, among the different ethnic groups represented within the business organization. Information of the latter kind is needed when the works council evaluates the pay-rise and formulates its own future strategy towards management and business policy.

In more general terms: the structuring of information systems in business organizations according to the needs of employees and their representatives must make it possible to trace the impact of business policy on the different dimensions of employees needs and objectives.

Since business policy formulation essentially consists in the generation, evaluation, and choice of different patterns of allocation of the firm's resources to its objectives, employees and their representatives need more and better information relevant to both – to business objectives and to their own objectives as well as to the internal and external resources of the firm.

In a capitalist business organization, where objectives normally are determined by the firm's striving for capital return and growth, objectives are derived by fixing a goal value on an economic activity variable of the firm (sales, costs, profit, etc.). Business information systems are structured to primarily give information about these objectives, thereby neglecting some of the major variables on which employees fix their goals (salary, social benefits, intensity of work, other conditions of work, work satisfaction, self-realization and autonomy in work, etc.). Participation of employees in managerial decision-making leads to a juxtaposition of objectives expressed in these variables to the traditional objectives of business organizations. Business information systems consequently need to be re-structured so that they can also furnish information about employees' own objective variables.

More and better information, however, is not only needed with regard to the variables describing actual and possible objectives of the business organization and its subsystems but also with regard to the resources which are absorbed by activities of the business organization.

Employee representatives, for instance, cannot remain indifferent if business policy leads to increased pollution in the natural environment of the business organization, because employees' "quality of life" is much more dependent upon the environmental impact of business policy than capitalists' "quality of life" (a capital owner can more easily escape pollution by retiring to a less polluted part of his community or province than a worker).

The same holds essentially for the social environment of the business organization: employee representatives cannot be indifferent to the impact of their firm's business policy on regional employment, on the usefulness of products and services, on educational facilities, on housing and living conditions in the community, etc.

Established business information systems normally process information about those resources which are in the disposition of the firm and for which the firm has to account an equivalent in terms of costs and expenses. Beside these resources there are other resources which are absorbed as well by business decisions without appearing in the firm's accounting system. These resources are often essential to employees' "quality of life". In view of a better use of participation rights business information systems should therefore give information about these external natural and social resources as elaborately as they do about the firm's internal economic resources.*

Employee needs require that the boundary of these external resources will be drawn far enough so that all major variables of the "quality of life" of employees are accounted for. This has not necessarily to be done in financial or even numeric terms, but the relationship between variations in economic variables and in these social variables has to be singled out to the extent that it can be a matter of sensible discussion and choice among employees and their representatives.

In addition to the conclusions regarding the enlargement of the objective system of the business organization by employees' objectives, and in addition to the conclusions pertaining to accounting for the use of all resources which are essential for employees, and which are directly or indirectly disposed of by management's decisions, there is one further conclusion which indicates the direction in which computerized information systems have to be designed if employee participation in decision-making in business organizations is to be made more efficient. The internal structure of business information systems must make it possible to trace the planned impact of business policy as well as the actual impact of business policy on employee needs and objectives and on external resources.**

Employee participation in managerial decision-making requires a high degree of planning and control in the business organization, because employees and their representatives are interested in reducing the opaqueness of business decisions. Even under participation conditions employee representatives cannot be so deeply involved in the permanent decision-making in the

* Some managements are already trying to re-structure information systems in this direction. In West Germany one of the co-determined firms in coal-mining was the first to publish an additional balance sheet containing social returns. In the US some large business organizations are trying to integrate social and environmental criteria into their planning systems (information by Battelle Institute Frankfurt).

** This has to be seen against the fact that formalized planning and monitoring of business activities on the background of distinct objectives so far has not been generally accepted by management in Western Germany as a tool for conducting business.

organization, that they always have a sufficiently clear picture of the state of the business.

Plans and the information resulting from the planning activities therefore are a valuable tool for evaluating the business policy, the actual situation of the business organization, and employees' own objectives. Efficient procedures of business planning and a stable framework of planning information may furnish useful material for an open and sensible discussion among employees and their representatives about employees' own objectives and the absorption of resources as well as for negotiations with the top management about the policy of the business organization.

The conclusions so far derived from the requirements of an efficient use of participation rights roughly suggest the following guidelines for EDP systems design:

(a) Incorporation of variables which describe the dimensions of employee objectives into the planning and control models and the corresponding data bases on the enterprise and plant level.

(b) Extension of planning and control models to information on resources which up to now are not accounted for but which are essential for employees' interests.

(c) Use of EDP systems for a permanent monitoring and control of predefined objectives for the business organization as a whole and for its major subsystems.

(d) Access for employee representatives to the planning models, participation from the very beginning of the planning process, access to the relevant data bases and the possibility of introducing their own objective systems into planning alternatives, which they develop themselves.

One further fact becomes clear through setting out these guidelines. The problem of a better use of EDP systems in the interests of employees is not so much a problem of EDP technology – the major changes probably having to be made in the software field – but has to be seen in the context of the structures to be shaped for an efficient use of EDP in decision-making in business organizations in general.

A few words should be added with regard to the general strategy of trade unions towards the process of spreading information systems.

Trade unions so far have been mainly concerned with three aspects of this development.

The first is privacy and the protection of personal rights. Here trade unions in West Germany hold a position in favour of a very far reaching regulation against the misuse and possible trading of personal data.

The second aspect relates to the personnel information and planning systems which are about to be developed by many firms as part of their business information systems. This is a field in which, however, very little reliable information about the extent and content and about the use of these systems is available. On the other hand the participation rights of the Works Constitution Act pertain substantially to the area of personnel planning and administration. The very idea of participation requires an access by employees and their representatives to these systems and this must be secured either by public regulations or by collective agreements.

The third aspect relates to alterations in working conditions due to computerization. This field is likely to become a major source of disturbance in industrial relations for the reason that the spreading of computerized operations may reduce a lot of activities to a status in many respects similar to unskilled work in industry.

Trade union action with respect to computerization in West Germany is therefore in several directions:

(a) creating educational facilities for computer specialists;

(b) developing concepts related to the humanization of computer based work systems;

(c) increasing TU membership among computer specialists;

(d) influencing the legislator to provide for better privacy regulations;

(e) trying to get access to and control of personnel information systems.

The problem of re-structuring information systems which are supported by EDP does not figure as a major item in this list for the reason that only a small fraction of management decision-making is supported by these systems at the present time. The picture, however, is rapidly changing and the process of computerizing managerial functions will necessitate a TU strategy in this field, too. A further problem in this context is that existing participation patterns still predominantly aim at ex-post control and not at an efficient ex-ante participation in the decision-making process. This may account for neglect of the impact of EDP on participation systems.

4. Structuring of information systems in correspondence to central planning

There is one more point which has to be taken into account when the adaptation of business information systems to employees' needs is being considered. Employees have not only individual but also collective needs and objectives. Solidarity amongst the employees of the same business organization certainly requires an open and sensible discussion among the employees and their representatives within the firm, but what happens about the needs of all employees in the province or in the country?

This is a problem the solution of which is likely to affect the internal structures of business organizations and of information systems even more deeply than the re-structuring mentioned above. It is basically the problem of the relationship between the autonomous capitalist enterprise and social objectives expressed by central planning.

The trade union view in West Germany is that in the long run private autonomy in economic decisions must be reduced in favour of central planning which takes account of the collective needs of the population and of employees as a class.

The reduction of the autonomy of private enterprise implies also a reduction of the social impact of co-determination rights at the enterprise and plant level. Consequently the DGB is proposing to subject the central planning bodies likewise to the principle of co-determination on a parity basis.

Furthermore central planning requires the creation of an economy-wide information and planning system with information flowing between the central planning agencies and the individual business organizations in both directions. This again requires a high degree of interfirm standardization of information system structures. If central planning and control is pushed very far this could lead to a nearly complete re-structuring of many information systems being designed or in operation.

5. Summary and outlook

Summarizing these rather sketchy remarks about the directions in which information systems are to be adapted with regard to the needs of employees, the following requirements have to be kept in view:

(a) Employees are interested in more and better information about actual and possible non-economic objectives and consequences of business activities.

(b) Employee needs require more and better information about the absorption of resources in the natural and social environment of the business organization induced by its business policy.

(c) Employee objectives can be better pursued if there is a stable framework of planning information in addition to actual information.

(d) Employee collective needs probably require a reduction of private autonomy in economic decisions and consequently in the design and implementation of business information systems.

Checking former and present concepts of information processing systems against these requirements shows up some of the defects of these concepts:

(1) Traditional business information systems (Sizer, 69) primarily proc-

essed actual economic information neglecting non-economic (social), external (environmental), and planning data.

(2) The concepts of the so-called "Management-Informations-Systems" (Wahl, 69) concentrated too much on the interaction between actual and planned forecast data, leaving aside non-economic and external data.

(3) The concept of business strategy (Ansoff, 65) stresses the feed-back between external and internal information, but does not account for the role of the social objectives of employees in the heuristic processes of business planning.

(4) The concept of social accounting takes account of social variables but omits to consider that social objectives must be formulated by employees themselves and that their place in business planning must be co-determined by employees (WSI-Projektgruppe, 73).

After considering the numerous very misleading practical approaches to MIS it seems that the pretended intrinsic advantages of MIS (speed, cost efficiency, ubiquity of information, etc.) are far from being reached. Perhaps an interesting object of study could be to trace whether MIS originated in the sales or in the research and development departments of computer firms.

It is not the place here to discuss in length the fundamental criticisms of the development of EDP technology under capitalist conditions (Quiniou, 71). This development, so far as the building-up of complex business information systems based on EDP is concerned, seems to be characterised by an exclusive concentration on the information needs of management and by a complete disregard of employee striving for participation and for more autonomy. In West Germany there is a tremendous disbalance between the effort put into information systems, which are to support management planning and control functions, on the one side, and the needs of employees and their representatives for reliable information about the actual business as well as about alternative business policies, on the other side. The re-structuring of EDP based information systems in the directions sketched above could certainly contribute to closing the information gap between managers and their counterparts in co-determination.

Some managements, and this is a practical experience, try to make co-determination rights void by withholding and manipulating information, some even try to control employee and trade union actions by the use of modern information technology, e.g. by storing and processing data about trade union membership in personnel information systems. This strategy may be successful in the short term but it arouses and reinforces the resistance of employees and their organizations, and will lead to a greater readiness to fight for more legitimation of participation in managerial decision-making as well as for better technical aid in the use of these rights.

At the same time, the growing tendency for more participation in economic decisions by employees provides the opportunity for transforming the most efficient new productive force of our time into an instrument contributing to greater self-determination by employees and to a sensible discussion about common objectives among all those who cooperate in business organizations.

References

Ansoff, H.I. (1965). *Corporate Strategy*, New York: McGraw-Hill.

DGB-Bundesvorstand (ed.) (1971). *Mitbestimmung – eine Forderung unserer Zeit*, Düsseldorf.

DGB-Bundesverstand (ed.) (1972). *Europäische Aktiengesellschaft*, Düsseldorf.

DGB-Bundesvorstand (ed.) (no year). *Protokoll des 9. Ordentlichen Bundeskongresses in Berlin vom 25. - 30. Juni 1972:* Anträge und Entschliessungen, Düsseldorf, S. 14.

Mulder, M. (1970). Participation and power equalization, *The Journal of Organizational Behaviour and Human Performance* 5.

Quiniou, J.C. (1971). *Marxisme et informatique*, Paris: Editions Sociales.

Sachverständigenkommission zur Auswertung der bisherigen Erfahrungen bei der Mitbestimmung (1970). *Mitbestimmung im Unternehmen*, Stuttgart: Kohlhammer.

Simon, H.A. (1964). On the concept of organizational goal, *Administrative Science Quarterly* 9 (1) pp. 1–22.

Sizer, J. (1969). *An Insight into Management Accounting,* Harmondsworth: Penguin.

Starbuck, W.H. (1965). Organizational Growth and Development, in: W.H. Starbuck (ed.), *Organizational growth and development*, Harmondsworth: Penguin, pp. 11 – 141.

Vetter, H.O. (1971). Mitbestimmung in der Europäischen Aktiengesellschaft, *Europäische Schriften* 31.

Wahl, M.P. (1969). *Grundlagen eines Management-Informations-Systems*, Neuwied: Luchterhand.

WSI-Projektgruppe (1973). *Grundelemente einer Arbeitsorientierten Einzelwirtschaftslehre*, Köln: Bundverlag.

E. Mumford and H. Sackman, eds., Human Choice and Computers
North-Holland Publishing Company (1975)

TRADE UNIONS AND COMPUTERS: A SURVEY OF BRITISH EXPERIENCE

Patrick FISHER

Trade Union Congress, Great Russell Street, London, England

1. Introduction

It is only twenty-five years ago that the computer was a rarity, and its potential implications for industry and society were debated, sometimes with hope and often with fear. Since then, even in comparison with many other examples of rapid technological changes, the development of the computer has been remarkable. For example, the famous pioneer LEO computer built and operated in Britain by a catering firm was the subject of widespread interest as a result of its ability to compile the wages sheets of all the firm's employees in part of a single afternoon! The computer was out-of-date within a few years and is now like Babbage's mechanical calculating machine that had been designed well over a century earlier, merely of historic interest. Minaturisation, printed circuits, transistors and other developments in both the hardware and the software have brought about enormous advances in the capabilities of computers, and the differences between Babbage's machine and the earlier computers were probably less great than exist between the first generation of computers and computers now available to the modern firm.

Although the debates about the future implications of computer developments go on unabated they are better informed now. We have considerable experience of the use of computers, and this experience helps trade unions in formulating their policies and views. Broadly speaking the principal trade union interest in computers is in five areas. These are (a) the effect of computers on employment, pay, and condition of work for trade unionists generally; (b) the effect of computers on staff directly employed in their use, including training; (c) the use of computers by trade unions themselves; (d) the significance of maintaining a national computer industry; (e) longer term possibilities arising from computer developments. It is with these issues rather than with technical complexities of computer systems that this note is principally concerned; and inevitably it draws chiefly from British trade union experience.

2. General effects

The effects of a particular development like computerisation are difficult to isolate from the developments inter-related to it or coinciding with it. In the early 1950's a good deal of time and effort was spent in seeking agreement on a precise definition of the term automation. Probably the best result was achieved by the Department of Scientific and Industrial Research in 1955. In the DSIR's view, automation represented the confluence of three existing trends of development. These were automatic machining, automatic control, and the automatic processing of data. The TUC used this concept in their own first publication on automation (*Trade Unions and Automation*, 1956) but later a TUC publication, (*Automation and Technological Change*, 1965, revised 1970) took a broader perspective. What came to be seen as most important was the overall situation – the totality of technological change. Workers were concerned about the consequences, or the possible consequences, of all the various forms of technological change rather than about the niceties of arguments as to the exact kind of change that affected or threatened their interests. Thus the general attitude of the Movement to technological change incorporated its particular attitudes to the consequences of computers.

The British Trade Union Movement has long recognised that in the circumstances of the post-war British economy, the interests of workers and their families could more easily be advanced by co-operating in raising industrial efficiency and sustaining economic growth than by possible alternative policies. However, this overall support was and is subject to conditions.

The principal condition has been that Government should follow policies that would maintain the overall level of employment in the economy. This has been an essential pre-requisite without which any more detailed measures to safeguard workers' interests would be largely meaningless. It is remarkable that in general little or no hostility developed among trade unions towards the policy or accepting technological change despite the worsening unemployment situation in the United Kingdom during the 1960's and especially towards the end of the decade. It indicated perhaps a belief by trade unionists that technological change was not the main problem in the British economy.

It has been accepted by the Movement that major changes would come about in the pattern of employment as technological and other factors led to the contraction of some categories of employment and to the expansion of others. The TUC said that the effects of this process should be minimised by the efficient transfer of redundant workers into new forms of employment. These arrangements would need to be associated with adequate compensation from the state, or the employer, or both, to mitigate any hardship caused by any period of unemployment due to redemployment problems, in conformity with the general principle that workers' living standards should be protected against the consequences of technological change.

In this approach the Movement emphasised the important fact that the speed and extent of technological change represented a significant difference from earlier periods of technological change. It was critically important, if unacceptably heavy unemployment for protracted periods was to be avoided, that action should be taken to anticipate and avoid the harmful consequences of technological change including automation. It was not acceptable to wait for problems to manifest themselves before seeking to solve them. This meant that there had to be more sophisticated and accurate means of forecasting probable changes in employment, together with more adequate training provisions, and more effective regional policy. In short, we needed an "active manpower policy" and greater intervention by Government to reconcile technological change with human interests. Nonetheless, despite some Governmental action especially as regards training, it cannot be claimed that Britain yet has an "active manpower policy" or that, despite much talk within industry, many employers have given attention to manpower budgeting.

As to pay, trade unions were determined to ensure that the benefits derived from technological change were more equitably shared than in the past. This involved action to ensure that pay structures and the basis of pay was kept firmly in the control of free collective bargaining, and that the Government should do its part to ensure that effective steps were taken to bring about the redistribution of wealth and income more equitably. It would not be good enough for workers to pay the price of technological change while their employers reaped the benefits. It is for this reason also that the Movement resisted, and still resists, attempts by Governments to diminish the unions' capacity to negotiate on behalf of their members.

As with employment and pay, so too with conditions of work. The Trade Union Movement is resolved that technological change shall enhance and not worsen the conditions in which the members are employed, being fully conscious that in some cases the nature of the problems with which they have to deal may be altered by technological innovations, e.g., they may be more "psychological" than "physical".

In addition to these matters, British trade unions have become more insistent in claiming that decision-making and its implementation shall cease to be the unilateral prerogative of employers and their managers. And there is a steadily increasing interest by trade unionists in extending their traditional concern with the wellbeing of the general community to include such issues as the environment. Technological change should be in the interest of the community as a whole and not for the enrichment of the few.

To sum up this section, the situation in 1974 is that substantial technological change has taken place in British industry and that computers have made a major contribution in this process. The worse fears of the trade union Movement have not been realised but this is as likely to be a reflection of inefficient use of manpower as success in taking positive action to mitigate the human and social problems of technological change. The problems of ensuring the maximum efficient use of computers and other forms of technological innovation might well be at the heart of Britain's economic difficulties, but it would be beyond the scope of this paper to attempt to discuss this matter.

3. Computers in the office

The impact of technological change has been especially dramatic in the general field of office employment, and this aspect was the subject of a special report "In the Automated Office" which the TUC published in 1964. The Advisory Committee's concern arose largely from the fact that computer installations had increased to 750 in September 1963 which was a 30 per cent increase in one year. More recently the TUC published in 1969, a survey which their Non-manual Workers' Advisory Committee had conducted that year among their unions of the ways by which computers and other forms of mechanised equipment affect employment in offices. Although the number of computer installations costing £20 000 or more was over 3 500 at the beginning of 1972 and the Department of Employment expected that figure to rise to 7 000 by 1979, it has to be remembered that effects of computers were relatively unknown until the late 1960's and the Advisory Committee were reacting to a relatively new and unknown situation. The 1969 survey helped to identify more precisely the effects of computers on clerical staffs and enabled a clearer evaluation to be made in place of guesswork due to the lack of hard evidence.

Unions representing 0.9 million non-manual workers took part in the survey which sought information about the details of computer installations, types of work for which the computer was used, number of staff employed *before* and *after* the installation, details such as age and length of service of any displaced staff, any training offered and given to staff already employed before the computer was installed; and practical problems arising and unions' success in solving them. Replies to these questions showed that computers were already being used for almost every type of clerical work in a wide range of public and private employment, mainly in large enterprises. Information about 29 individual case histories was derived from the survey.

A notable result of this survey was that unions appeared to accept the increasing use of computers and practically no reference had been made in the Unions' replies to problems arising from the introduction of computers for older workers who might have been displaced. There are several possible reasons for this result. Despite the upwards trend of unemployment during the later 1960's, the period was still one of relatively high employment. The unions' replies could be expected to deal mainly with cases in which they had agreements; and these did not include all computer installations (or even most of them). Moreover the reported cases were likely to relate to installations that had taken place perhaps several years previously. And they would relate mainly to large offices in major conurbations. In addition, it would be difficult in many cases to separate the particular effects of computers from the general effects of changes including the installation of a computer. Thus the results of the survey were indicative only of a general situation, which although it appeared not to be as threatening as might have been expected, did not justify complacency.

Since 1969 there has been little evidence that results of the survey had been misleading. Indeed it is apparent that the effects of increasing efficiency in offices due to computerisation and allied techniques have been offset by major changes in the pattern of employment. This had resulted in a substantial increase relatively and absolutely in office employment, estimated by the Department of Employment to be 250 000 jobs between 1972 and 1975, of which 175 000 are likely to be filled by additional staff. However, the changes in the pattern of employment have been taking place within sectors as well as between sectors of employment, and also the nature of many office jobs undoubtedly had changed very much as a result of using computers.

4. Computers in the factory

A comprehensive list of the uses to which computers can be put would be long. Even that section of the list dealing with the factory would be considerable in length, and range from design to the dispatch of goods and "after sales" service.

One of the most significant things about automation is that it frees the production engineer from constraints imposed by limitations on the human-being's physical strength, and on his capacity to exercise direct control of complex processes in organising production. By means of automation, materials can be processed in the way most appropriate to the needs of the production engineer. Machines do not need to conform to the ability of the human-being to operate and control them. Computers make it possible for machines and materials-handling equipment to now be conceived as an integrated production system. All this (and much more) has largely been made possibly by the computer. With such an instrument, a production system that incorporates automatic operation, automatic control, and, the automatic processing of data becomes possible. Moreover, the specialised uses of computers, e.g. for designing and translating design specifications into actual operation are also very significant (see *Computer Aided Design*, M. Cooley, Amalgamated Union of Engineering Workers (Technical and Supervisory Section), London, 1972).

All these possibilities have been appreciated for many years and were described in papers delivered to the British Institution of Production Engineers' Conference in 1955. However, although the use of the computer has increased rapidly in the period since 1955, the fully "automatic factory" has yet to make its appearance as an operating unit. Rather the computer has been used in many cases to improve, instead of revolutionise, conventional methods of production. In Britain, as in most countries, factories represent a spectrum of technological development from those wholly or mainly using older machines to those that employ some machines and plant that are as modern as anywhere in the world. While it probably is true that the range of difference between the less advanced and the most modern factories has widened in the last 20 years, it probably is true also that the average factory has become significantly more modern. Progress has been conditioned largely by the state of managerial and technical competence, relative capital costs, and the availability of suitable education and training. Strange as the truth may sound by contrast with some popular myths, there has been very little resistance by workers to technological change in British industry. Nevertheless it would be misleading to pretend that British managers and workers were enthusiastic about technological change. There have been major changes in the structure of employment in Britain especially in the last 25 years and reference has already been made to this fact. The most dramatic falls in the number employed, have been in such sectors of the economy as agriculture, coalmining, railways, shipbuilding, and heavy engineering, with large increases taking place in services, including retail distribution, entertainment, and central and local government. Within the manufacturing industries the situation is more difficult to analyse because this sector is ill delineated. Nevertheless it is clear that within the sector much concentration of ownership has taken place. In many cases technological changes have been among the important factors in this process, although not by any means in all cases. And not in all cases has technological change led to concentration of production into fewer units. However, the steadily increasing unemployment that was a feature of the decade up to 1973, and the improvements since the early part of 1973, probably is indicative as much of change in the pattern of employment within the manufacturing sector as between manufacturing and other sectors. Whatever the exact situation, there has been little evidence of major unemployment arising solely or mainly because of technological change and still less to show that computers have been a major cause. The causes of changes in the pattern and level of employment have been altogether more complex involving political and economic factors as well as technological developments, but (in this context) the effects of technological change including automation no doubt have had an effect. However, although computers in some circumstances, may have exacerbated the ill effects of other factors, their overall effects have not been wholly disadvantageous. Indeed it is easy to demonstrate that in some instances unemployment would have been higher and the general standard of living would have been lower but for these effects. Some industries (e.g., oil refining, chemicals, tele-communications, man-made fibres) could hardly have developed at all without the computer.

Some of the major problems become manifest when consideration is given to the impact of computers on employment rather than on unemployment. In this respect there can be little doubt that computers (together with other forms of technological change) are tending to polarise much of the work force in large ranges of employment. The division of industrial workers into the skilled, semi-skilled, and unskilled has always been misleading, and the impact of technological change has totally destroyed any justification it may have had in the past. It is much more accurate to visualise a spectrum of skill in which the job-demands of some workers are greater than those of other workers. However, there are two tendencies that are becoming more important. First, changes in production arrangements made possible by the computer remove the need for human-beings to perform certain jobs – e.g., certain types of machine operation, and change the work-content of other jobs by altering the intensity of work or by changing its nature – e.g., when machine-operating becomes machine-monitoring. It is true that this trend has had a sharp effect on the least skilled jobs (and the potential effect on them is even greater). But the effect, especially the change in workdemand, has not been confined to this end of the spectrum, and many highly skilled jobs – e.g., aircraft pilots, have also been affected and will increasingly be so. This means that all levels of employment are subject to the possible effect of computers.

The second tendency is the compression of manual jobs into a smaller spectrum. In other words there are fewer job opportunities for the least skilled workers while the skilled jobs at the other end of spectrum tend more and more to require qualifications that normally are obtainable only as the result of full-time education beyond the normal school leaving age (16 years in the UK). This means that there is a danger that vertical job mobility is becoming more restricted. This creates an obvious need for training to enable workers to obtain the necessary qualifications, and for the appropriate authorities to critically review the relevance of formal qualifications to the actual demands of the jobs to which they relate.

There are in addition needs for facilities to enable workers to retrain for other jobs (and thus promote horizontal mobility) and to help them to keep pace with the changing work demands of their existing jobs. The situation calls for a system of education that will provide school leavers with a sufficiently broad educational base to allow flexibility in the worker's industrial career. It is the untrained worker and the narrowly trained specialist who are at most risk, whereas any worker whose basic training enables him to be both horizontally and vertically mobile is best suited to cope with a situation of rapid change. It can be argued of course, that while causing redundancy among some specialist workers, computers also create the need for new categories of specialised worker. However, this outcome does not affect the more general situation, but it does accentuate the polarisation to which reference has been made.

It is for all these reasons (and because unions believe that workers have an inviolable right to education) that the Trades Union Congress has taken a particular interest in training. The Congress took a lead in pressing for major improvements in the Industrial Training Act 1963, to recognise the need to deal with job-recreation, job-training and job-placement as closely related issues. As a result the Government have set up a Manpower Commission and associated agencies to take over from the Department of Employment much of its responsibility in this field.

For the industrial worker, like the clerical worker, the significance of the computer is due more to its indirect effect on the employment situation than to its direct impact. It raises problems about the change in the pattern of jobs and the content of individual jobs rather than the imminent danger of unemployment.

5. The computer in other areas of employment

There are few areas of employment including trade union organisations in which the computer has not entered upon the administrative and managerial scene and reference has been made earlier to use of computers for design and allied activities. The general discussion of their effects in offices and factories probably applies also other areas as well. The number of other specialised uses, in addition to their use for design, to which reference already has been made, is almost unlimited. They include research purposes in universities and other institutions and for computational and data analysis purposes of a wide variety. However, the purpose of this paper is not to give an account of the sophistication of computers over their full range of use but to concentrate attention on the implications for workers. This includes the use of computers by unions and there followes a brief account of this aspect.

6. Use of computers by unions

During 1972 the Trades Union Congress made inquiries about the use of computers by trade unions. These inquiries revealed that unions made use of computers for their own purposes. The form of computer use included the direct ownership and operation of computers by unions; the use of computers owned by unions by other unions; and the use of specialised computer bureaux by unions. In this latter category most unions had contracts with the publicly owned National Data Processing Service (who had set up arrangements specifically to service unions) although several unions had arrangements with privately owned bureaux. The unions owning computers included several of the largest affiliated to the TUC and also some in the middle range of membership. In the case of one large organisation the computer was operated in only one of its geographical regions as a pilot exercise.

The principal use of computer services in all these cases was administrative, e.g. recording membership, members' contributions and entitlement to benefit, mailing lists for various purposes, etc. Several of the unions had begun experiments in the use of computers for analysing collective agreements, company profits, economic prospects in particular sectors, or employment trends. However, in none of these directions had these uses of computers become significant.

The impact on employment within the unions was difficult to assess. In no case had redundancy occurred as a direct result of using computers. Indeed in most cases the number of people employed increased because the computer made it possible to produce data that would have been too costly to collect by other means. This additional work called also for more staff in other departments of union offices. In addition it seemed that in some cases the computer service had been grafted onto the existing administrative arrangements rather than having been preceded or accompanied by changes in structure and administrative arrangements to get the best use of the service. As a consequence elements in old arrangements tended in some cases to continue alongside the computerised arrangements to serve the same end. These situations are not peculiar of course to trade unions, but common to a large number of installations. In contrast one union took great pains to adapt its administrative arrangements as a preliminary move, to ensure that it got the optimum value from its computer. As a consequence they operated their computer on a shift basis and were able to act as a computer bureau for other unions.

The idea of a central computer bureau run for, and by, the Trade Union Movement has been put forward in general terms on several occasions, but it appears unlikely that this idea will find expression as a fact at least for some years. One reason is that the needs of individual unions differ over a wide range, and it is improbable that such a development could lead to any helpful interchange of information. Moreover, the TUC would be the obvious body to organize and run such a bureau, but the TUC does not itself have much need for a computer facility. Running a bureau as a separate activity would detract from the TUC's basic role in the Movement. The situation might be different if the TUC had much greater centralised authority within the Movement, but in fact affiliated unions are not the agents of the TUC (indeed the reverse is true). There is little evidence of any desire to radically change this situation, and certainly not merely to facilitate the establishment of a computer bureau.

In some respects the failure of trade unions to make more effective use of computers as a back-up resource for policy makers and negotiators as well as for administrative purposes is disappointing. On the other hand it should be appreciated that administrative efficiency although desirable is not the chief criterion by which unions should be judged. They are essentially democratic organisations and thus the administrative arrangements have to be amenable to a participative type of control. Moreover, outside the ranks of full time staff the administration is conducted, by lay members in their own time. This fact has to be kept in mind by the unions' professional administrators. Similarly, as to policy matters and negotiations, the plain fact is that many union members and their leaders would claim that they had "not done badly" without the masses of data and computer aids they are sometimes urged to use. They would claim that political skills plus effective organisation are more important in this sense than print-outs. However, unions are pragmatic organisations, and the extent to which computers are being used should not be ignored. It is likely to increase at a faster rate as unions themselves become more cost-concious in relation to administration, and as more comprehensive collective agreements such as those resulting from recent negotiations with the Ford (UK) and Imperial Chemicals Industries (based on analysis of the employers' position and prospects) become more typical. The change is unlikely to be dramatic, and not based on any master plan or theory, but the trend, already evident, will continue.

7. Training for computer staff

This paper has discussed so far the effect of computers, as an aspect of technological change on the interests of workers not all of whom may be employed directly on computers. It has been stated in earlier paragraphs that the indirect effects on employment, pay, and conditions of workers in general have been found by British unions to be as significant for the Movement as a whole as the immediate and direct impact on clerical workers whose jobs have been changed or replaced by computers. On the other hand it is difficult to identify the computer's effcct on the general situation apart from other types of change in technology and industry generally. Thus there are relatively few trade union activities taken to mitigate the harmful effects, that are distinct from other aspects of policy. For example policies in relation to job security and income security are general in their application and do not require special versions in respect to computers.

Nevertheless this does not mean that the relevant trade unions and the TUC are indifferent to the particular interests of computer staffs, anymore than they would ignore the needs of any other specific group of workers. Take training for example. A long period of training is often needed for computer staff and the need for it must be seen well in advance if trained and experienced staff are to be available when they are required. There certainly have been cases in the past, when the demand for computer staff was growing rapidly. Computer firms have not been alone in this respect, and there have always been employers who have relied on the training activities of the more responsible firms. It was to correct this irresponsible practice that the Industrial Training Act, since modified, was enacted in 1963. That Act provided a system of 27 Industrial Training Boards financed by means of levies which they were empowered to exact from firms operating in the areas of employment for which they were responsible.

The Boards included among their membership a substantial proportion of senior trade union officers nominated by their organisations and there is no doubt that they added greatly to the effectiveness of the system. Although there was, and is, no Training Board concerned specifically with computer staffs (because the Boards are concerned with industries, not occupations) the trade unions saw a need for liaison between interested Boards.

In this respect it is worth noting that trade union organisation among workers in clerical, administrative, technical and managerial staffs, which include computer staff, has gone ahead rapidly in the United Kingdom during the last twenty years. The unions concerned, e.g. Association of Scientific, Technical and Managerial Staffs and the Association of Professional, Executive, Clerical and Computing Staffs, APEX are two of Britain's most rapidly growing unions.

The Boards principally concerned set up a Joint Board Committee in which the union members played a leading part. It produced reports on various aspects of computer training, including the training of systems analysts (commercial), programmers, and managers, which have had considerable influence. It has worked in co-operation with the Council for Academic Awards and the City and Guilds of London Institute, both of which together with the British Computer Society and the National Computing Centre award nationally recognised qualifications for computing staff. In general, the trade unions concerned agree with the Department of Employment's official view that the need for the rapid extension of training for computer staff has subsided. This view is reinforced by evidence of slowing down in the demand for computer staff and by the absence of firm evidence of a serious lack of training facilities. Moreover, there is evidence that the results of earlier action in this field is only now beginning to make itself felt and there is some evidence also by the underuse of the extensive college facilities that were provided in the mid-1960's. Moreover there is little evidence that the worries about certification and qualifications that have been reported from the USA have had any parallel in the United Kingdom. Broadly speaking, therefore, British trade unions can claim that both in respect to the general implications for workers and in respect to the particular needs of computer staffs, the problems that worried trade unionists in prospect twenty years ago have, in their view, to a large extent been successfully tackled.

8. Government support for the computer industry

The British Trade Union Movement has long advocated the need for a strong home based computer industry and it was in harmony with this view that the then Minister of Technology (the Right Honourable Frank Cousins, on leave from his post as General Secretary of the Transport and General Workers' Union) gave high priority to sustaining a British computer industry, when the Labour Government took office in 1964.

When the Conservative administration took office in 1970 the TUC pressed them to continue and accentuate this policy, especially in the light of the increasing domination of the U.S. firms in this field. Subsequently, the House of Commons Select Committee on Science and Technology studied the matter and issued their report in 1972. This report was in line with the TUC's support for the need to maintain and sustain a British computer industry, and it accepted also the need to give the industry financial and other support comparable to that given by foreign governments to their computer industries. To this end the Government agreed to follow up the earlier support given since 1968, when several British companies agreed to merge to form International Computers Limited in which the Government had acquired a major shareholding. This support had included a £13.5 million research and development grant. The Government now agreed to provide a further £14.2 million up to September 1973 to develop, manufacture, and market computer systems. The TUC welcomed this decision and urged the Government to continue their support on a longer term basis. Further assistance was announced later in 1973 to the extent of £25.5 million for research and development in the period 1973–1976, and the Government hoped to recoup this total by means of arrangements which come into operation in 1977.

The TUC had pointed out that the computer industry includes more than the computers themselves and the Government ultimately recognised the fact, and so in response to the Select Committee's report, the Government announced measures to assist the British software industry in addition to supporting ICL. This separate aid was calculated to amount to about £6 million.

The Conservative Government and later the present Labour administration also accepted another trade union argument to the effect that the computer industry was important to the substructure of the electronics industry.

Particularly relevant to the prospects of the computer industry is the new emphasis placed on the "customer/contractor principle" that had been enunciated by the Rothschild Report and set out in a Government White Paper "A Framework for Government Research and Development" in 1972. Although there was some divergence of view among trade unions about the Rothschild Report, its main proposals received the support of the TUC. As a result of this report the Government set up a number of Requirement Boards one of which covers the field of computers and electronics with the task of helping the Department of Industry "to identify those areas of computer and related technology and those applications, whether in industry or commerce, science or government, to which research and development support should be directed with the aim of ensuring a strong and competitive industry capable of making its rightful contribution to the national economy". This view is in line with the TUCs own views.

The British Government is a major purchaser of computers, and while they agree with the unions in aknowledging the contribution made to the British economy by computer firms, whether British owned or not, they also agree that some degree of preference should be given to British firms. However, the Select Committee's belief expressed in the above report was that instead of a system of single tendering that had previously operate for certain computers, tendering in future should be based on a number of criteria aimed at enhancing the general national interest. However the Government's view was the single tender procedure was an important part of the support needed by ICL and thus they intended to continue the system "for the present". However competitive tendering would be used (as before) except for large computers available from ICL and for computers leading into these or where compatibility necessitates single tender purchase from a particular supplier, who need not necessarily be ICL.

There was Government agreement to the need for greater co-ordination in the use of computers owned by Government departments and agencies. For this reason they set up in March 1972 a Central Computer Agency to replace the three previous bodies responsible for the purchase of computers equipment and services and to develop and co-ordinate their use in Central Government.

Further support is provided by the Government for computer services by a 1971 decision that the Government would substantially increase its use of parallel external computer services while at the same time they were strengthening their own computer capability. Over 200 contracts worth £2 million were concluded in 1972/73 with outside agencies in addition to the purchase of machine time on bureaux owned computers.

The Trades Union Congress have given strong general support to the Government's policy of sustaining a British computer industry, which represented no change of principle from the attitude of the previous Labour Government, and the indicators are that its general lines will be followed by the present Government. The TUC believe that a British computer industry could and should play a major role in the economy and that the value of this role goes far beyond the direct financial contributions represented by the sale of both hardware and software at home and abroad.

9. Conclusion

No endeavour has been made in this paper to deal with the subject as an academic treatise or to propound a general theory regarding trade unionists' attitudes to the increasing use of computers of growing sophistication. Neither has any attempt been made to assess the effects of computers on society in general. While these effects have undoubtedly been considerable and are likely in the future to be far reaching, they are not the exclusive concern of trade unions. In this paper emphasis has been placed on those matters of more direct relevance to trade unionist responsibilities. The approach has been pragmatic. It seeks to summarise in highly abbreviated form the general experience of British trade unions. The author would not deny that the development and use of computers raises some highly specific and particular issues for certain categories of workers, but he would not regard himself as competent to deal with the more technical aspects of these issues – e.g., the training needs of system analysts. In the more general field it is difficult to separate and consider, in isolation, the economic from the wider technological changes of which the computer is part. As to these wider technological changes, they are distinguishable from the technological changes of the periods before say 1939 by their greater and accelerating speed and by their increasing universality. It would be a bold man who would list occupations or forms of economic activity that he could guarantee would not be affected within 10 years by technological change. He would be bold to make such attempts even if the indirect effect of technological change was discounted, but it would be absurd to make the attempt if these indirect effects were included. It is not only the speed and extent of technological change that brings about more complicated issues than before, because the newer forms of technology are qualitatively different from those introduced before 1939. The computer is a paramount example. It not merely extends the physical and mental abilities of human-beings, but insofar as it is self regulating, it can supersede the human-being in certain areas of economic activity.

E. Mumford and H. Sackman, eds., Human Choice and Computers
North-Holland Publishing Company (1975)

COMPUTERS AND EMPLOYMENT

David B. ARCHER

Ontario Federation of Labour, Don Mills, Ont., Canada

Many people are disturbed at the seeming influence of a computer society on our way of life. My paper will exploit some of these fears as they have been expressed to me by fellow unionists, officers and rank and file. Therefore what follows has a trade union bias. For this we make no apologies, we believe that this is the type of input desired from a trade union spokesman.

In analyzing the impact of the computer on employment I make a particular distinction between the short run and the long run consequences of computer technology for the worker.

I believe that in the long run the work force as a whole benefits from the use of computers which improves the productivity of labour and can raise the income and increase the leisure of the worker. Rising incomes widen the demand for goods and thereby create employment opportunities. In the long run additional jobs can be created by the employment needs of the computer industry itself and its supporting industries. This I realize is a most simplistic and easily debated conclusion.

In the short run, however, computers may displace workers by eliminating some occupations, particularly those involving routine clerical tasks and other repetitive operations. Employees affected by these developments are of particular concern and should be a prime target group of government policies and programs.

Our problem is not that computers, automation, or technological change will create unemployment. Our problem is that the legislation does not exist to adequately look after short run dislocations, and government economic and manpower policies are inadequate to cope with a constantly increasing labour force.

Our economic goals are based on a full employment policy. We still worship the Protestant ethic. If we are successful in achieving this, we will be in a better position to solve the manpower problems of plant shutdown when and if they occur, regardless of what causes them. On the issue of the necessity or desirability of full employment I have grave doubts but I do not intend to discuss them here.

Detractors of the computer and opponents of technological change base their opposition on events as they have taken place in the past. The Luddites when they smashed the machines that threatened their jobs were perhaps reacting in the only way open to them at that time.

Today the computer not only embodies a change of technology but it has within itself the means of solving some of the problems it creates.

Yes, it can take away jobs, but it can create jobs. The economy can be disrupted by the introduction of new machines that take away jobs. On the other hand, the economist is provided with the tools and the increase in data so that he can make intelligent decisions. He can analyze trends and predict events. He does not have to guess – the computer enables him to know.

Drucker (68) said that the computer makes it impossible for us to be economic innocents any longer. The new analytical concepts and tools, the data banks, give us a tremendous volume of observations, information, and facts. Our economic policies can be based on rational arguments and facts rather than on "feel". If we do desire we can plan our economy, adopt policies that will use the advances in technology to create jobs. While machines have become more sophisticated I often wonder how far men have advanced. We apparently have always been able to find the cause in advance, but have had to wait for the cruel consequences to be apparent before we applied the necessary remedial measures.

Since the invention of the wheel, improved techniques of production have made it possible for us to produce more goods and services with a smaller expenditure of labour. We welcome technological change. Not only has it raised our standard of living, but permits us to help the less developed nations to overcome hunger and want.

Besides making it possible to take some of the drudgery out of work, it makes it possible for us to have more time for leisure.

Unions are perhaps reluctantly accepting technological change, accomodating to it, but insisting that those affected adversely by the change do not carry the burden of the change and that they share in its bounty.

It has been estimated that a one per cent increase in unemployment in Canada costs us approximately one billion dollars per year in terms of GNP. This means if we can reduce unemployment by one per cent that a billion dollars will be added to the per capital worth of the country. Again using the conventional wisdom that GNP measures a nations worth or prosperity or the satisfaction of its population.

If we cannot guarantee a sufficient number of new jobs by general economic expansion and economic growth to take up the slack in jobs resulting from new technology, automation and the computer, then we must reexamine much of our preconceived ideas. Which may be a profitable exercise.

When we try to answer the question will computers and technological change create jobs or unemployment, the answer cannot be a simple "yes" or "no".

We must take for granted there will be dynamics operating in our society to see that other factors come into play which will create an environment that will take care of the economic and social problems resulting from change. Labour is committed by its philosophy and its program to see that it is so.

A number of things have to happen as technological change takes place, and as the computer enters our lives more and more.

Governments must carry on continuous research to find ways to utilize change for our benefit and buffer society from its bad effects. A proper manpower policy must be actively engaged in to meet the needs of the economy and the labour force. The government must be committed to a policy of full employment by co-ordinating its manpower policy with a proper mix of trade, investment, production, and monetary and fiscal policies to ensure stability and growth.

Speaking of my own country at the beginning of the century about half of Canada's population was involved in agriculture or related activities. Today agriculture occupies less than 10% of our population and its character has changed so that it is more mechanized and involves a more educated and technically competent participant.

As our technological society develops, the change in the composition of the work force that has been taking place in the last several decades will accelerate. The bulk of the work force will be in the white collar, technical, managerial and professional fields. These workers are likely to have more academic training, possess more skills and are therefore more adaptable to change and are more mobile.

It is also in these professions that the computer and automation have made the greatest headway, and these areas that the computer and automation will create the most jobs.

Of course, computers and automation can create jobs directly by a snowball effect. Jobs will be created in areas such as factory building, and the fabrication of computers and automated equipment. Jobs will be created in all the supporting industries from raw materials and resources to the selling of the finished machine. Always assuming that we are an employment oriented society.

The workers in these industries may be in different unions or in no union at all. That is a problem we in the labour movement will have to contend with.

I wish to differ with Sir Denis Barnes (69) who wrote "for various reasons trade unions and employers and their associations may fade away". I have heard some make that claim about employers and others make that claim about unions, but I have never before heard one person make the same statement about both.

I believe unions will have a role to play no matter what happens. Certainly they will have a role to play in protecting workers.

We in the trade union movement must have known for some time that as technological change advances employment will shift from blue collar to white collar workers.

Organization of white collar and technical workers in Canada has not kept pace with this change. There are some real reasons why organization of these workers has not taken place to the extent desired – smaller units, different attitudes, bad legislation, and so on. But some of the fault lies with organized labour itself.

The Canadian Labour Congress, the central labour body in Canada, has made a serious turn in its approach to organizing this growing section of the work force.

Considerable money and staff were allocated to this task, new organizing approaches were introduced and inroads are being made organizing the financial and insurance institutions in Canada. Perhaps as automation and the computer make headway in the office, fears of job loss due to automation may be a spur to union organization. This added to the need for unions to keep pace with the growth in the labour force, most of which is taking place in the white collar and technical field, may be what is needed to organize this new worker.

Office workers have not been hostile to the introduction of computers to the work environment. In fact, their attitude to the computer's introduction was in most cases positive. Hardin (60) reports that in a number of studies conducted in the U.S.A. insurance companies where computers were introduced, it was found that the computer had only a moderate effect upon the work environment and job satisfaction, and that it was not a radical or extensive enough change to cause a reversal or acceleration of existing trends in work or job satisfaction.

Stieber (57) claimed that the long term effects of office automation will be that clerical employment will continue to grow but that the rate of expansion will not be sustained. However, he added that there will be an upgrading of skills and a greater proportion of skilled jobs and a great elimination of repetitive operations.

Yet in another study of a different type of operation, a steel foundry, where the Electronic Data Processing system was introduced, Elizur (70) reports that there was some dissatisfaction and the system was rejected mainly on the grounds that it required additional tasks on the part of supervisors and increased the direct intervention of pressure for production by management. In this case, hostility was not related to fear of unemployment.

Trumbo (61) and Hardin (67) did some work on the worker's attitude to change. Loubser and Fullan (70) followed this up in a study for the federal government Task Force on Labour Relations. In answer to a questionnaire asking "If it would not make any difference in the pay and security of your job, would you like to see your job become more highly automated?" they found that in the six industries surveyed, generally the ratio of those welcoming technological change to those opposing it was three to one, with the highest acceptance rate in the chemical industry.

A good example of what is happening with the introduction of technology and how it affects productivity and employment is the teletype-communications industry.

According to a study by Brand (73), output per man hour in telephone communications more than tripled over the past two decades, rising at a substantially higher rate than the rate for private economy as a whole. The growth of its employment rate was less vigorous than industry as a whole, but it did continue.

The introduction of microwave transmitters has obviated the need for long distance cables, but has increased the demand for private line long distance service.

Because of high labour content of local service transmission as well as installation and maintenance, the decline in the number of telephone industry employees has slowed down in the past few years.

In the long term, telephone industry employment has grown but there has been a shift in occupations. This has taken two directions. The shift has been to more skilled workers and also away from women, although given the activities of Women's Lib and like organizations this may change. There has been an increase in craftsmen, installers, repairmen, linemen, maintenance men and other in-plant personnel.

The introduction of technological improvements in the industry certainly affected employment, but did not result in the sudden disruption that was anticipated. The main change was in the job classifications. Jobs that were created required different skills.

Jobs do disappear with the advent of technology. Although the impact is greatest in the less skilled, goods producing, industries it has had considerable effect on some traditionally skilled occupations. Mechanization has eliminated most skilled coremaking and molding jobs in gray-iron foundries. Computers linked with photo-typesetters are replacing linotype machines endangering the continued existence of the entire craft. In the insurance industry, the introduction of electronic data processing has reduced employment of tabulating machine operators and calculators.

Yet to be analyzed is the effect of the mini computer that is designed to run the factory and is only two to four years old. This is based on an hierarchical organization of a building block approach to automation, and was made possible by the recent increase in the use of lower priced semiconductor integrated circuit technology.

This kind of automation will certainly increase productivity and may drastically decrease employment since it reaches into the area of "decision making" in simple plant operations.

In the past unions did not welcome automation and technological change because the workers believed they would not share in the benefits brought about by such change. Yet, in the early fifties, when the miners in the U.S.A. were confronted with new mechanization, the United Mine Workers of America then under John L. Lewis' leadership, co-operated in the mechanization of the mines, which would cut the work force in half, on condition that the remaining workers get high wages and good fringe benefits in return.

As a result, the miners are now making a decent living, and working under safer conditions and their productivity is seven times that of their European counterparts. Coal is cheaper. However, the number of workers in the industry dropped from 419 000 in 1947 to 150 000 at the present time. The energy shortage has changed this situation considerably.

The Longshoremen's Union on the U.S. west coast is a similar example of the union recognizing that mechanization was inevitable and negotiating a guarantee of no layoffs and a share in the increased income from mechanization.

In both cases, the coal miners and the longshoremen, negotiated royalties based on tonnage produced or goods moved to be used for retiring funds.

I cite these two examples because they both point up the fact that although collective bargaining can accomplish much, it has limitations in looking after the displaced workers.

As I said in a speech to the Conference on Automation and Social Change (Archer, 63) obviously you cannot bargain for jobs that do not exist or wages for persons who are not employees. There will have to be more government intervention to create employment.

Several wars and the race to reach the moon have given a spurt to a spectacular development of computer technology. The rapidly rising use of the computer is having a tremendous effect on our social and economic life.

The computer has arrested to some extent the growth of paper pushers in government bureaucracies and in industry. Although we are for increased employment opportunities, we are against an inordinate imbalance in unproductive work as related to productive work in government and industry. In other words, the computer should help to keep the balance between the ratio of clerical and support workers and those actually engaged in the production process in any enterprise.

The Economic Council of Canada (ECC) in its annual reviews, warns us that we must sustain and improve economic growth if we are to provide jobs for the growing labour force.

In its First Annual Review (Economic Council of Canada, 64), the ECC projected a number of social and economic goals – full employment, a high rate of economic growth, reasonable stability of prices, a viable balance of payments, and an equitable distribution of rising incomes.

The possibility of achieving these goals is initially hinged on increasing productivity. We can attain a large part of this increase in productivity by an increase in the working labour force, but almost half must be achieved by improving our performance in output per person.

The computer and automation can enhance and increase our productivity. The application of science and technology to our endeavours promises even more exciting and interesting discoveries in the future.

It is taken for granted that we as individuals are working at full capacities and capabilities. How then can we increase our productivity? The same way it has been done since the wheel was invented – by ingenuity, by improvement in techniques and methods, and by the addition of new hardware. We must find ways to do many different things in varied and multiple ways. We must find ways to use our natural and human resources more efficiently. Automation and computers can help us.

Legislation will have to be improved to deal with dislocation as a result of change. Freedman (65) has set an important milestone in this in his famous report on railway run-throughs. He was specifically concerned with the railway run-throughs – a case of railways arbitrarily discontinuing servicing stops – in Wainright and Nakina, two small communities in Alberta and Ontario in Canada. Although his report referred mainly to these specific situations, his proposals were intended to be far-reaching and indeed did result in some minimal legislation for worker protection in layoffs, job terminations and plant shutdown due to technological change.

Freedman said "the institution of run-throughs should be a matter for negotiation. To treat it as a matter for an unfettered management prerogative will only promote unrest and drive the parties further apart . . ."

"By placing run-throughs, on the other hand, within the realm of negotiation, a long step will be taken toward the goal of industrial peace. More than that, such a course will help to provide safeguards against undue dislocation and hardship that often result from technological change."

". . . that obligation has its roots in the principle that, when a logical change is introduced, the cost of reasonable proposals to protect employees from its adverse consequences is a proper charge against its benefits and savings."

Various government jurisdictions have initiated such programs in an attempt to soften the hardship and disruption caused by these displacements. The Canada Manpower Training Program and the Canada Mobility Program and the sections dealing with technological change in the Canada Labour Code are to some extent directed towards reducing the adverse effects of technological advance.

In Ontario the notice of termination section of the Employment Standards Act is designed to do the same.

However, these are very minimal provisions and both levels of government are dragging their feet, and are resisting efforts to improve this legislation.

Several years ago the Ontario Federation of Labour produced a 160 page study called Shutdown (Eleen and Bernardine, 71). Ontario was the scene of a great number of plant closures during that year, many of them by multinational corporations. In addition to surveying the havoc created by plant shutdown we made some important proposals in the book and in subsequent briefs to the government on extending and improving the legislation on what is now inadequately called "notice of termination".

A shutdown during a strike or lockout in Ontario makes much legislation inoperative. It is not mandatory for the company to meet with the union and the manpower department of the government to resolve the problems attendant to a shutdown. Nor is there any provision for reopening the contract for meaningful negotiations in the case of extensive layoffs or plant shutdown. The legislation does not permit us to strike during the term of a collective agreement even on items that we could not foresee as arising after we signed the agreement.

Although we have the hardware and the computers, and although my province, Ontario, alone spends $4 943 000 on computers, we still lack detailed information on productivity, and manpower needs, particularly as related to occupations and industry.

If we are to have an efficient manpower policy, we must develop an accurate measurement of the kinds of jobs that will be needed in the future and in what parts of the country they will be.

Although this is difficult to do in an unplanned economy, unless it is done, then those who fear technological change and the disruption it may cause to jobs will have their fears well founded.

Surely if private enterprise can devise a system whereby you can get an almost instantaneous seat reservation on a plane from any part of the country for any day months ahead by telex and computers, then the public sector through its manpower agencies could surely devise a system using the same mechanical and electronic aids to permit us to know immediately what job vacancies are available and where they exist, what jobs will be needed, and when and what skills will be required so that workers could be trained for them at the appropriate time.

We believe that workers must not be the victims of technological change but where such change is for progress, then the workers should share in the proceeds.

New discoveries and technological change can be to the benefit of workers if the rewards from these discoveries and changes are distributed equitably. We in the trade union movement will attempt to see that the benefits of increased productivity, whether they come from improved technology or human ingenuity and expertise, are shared by all who participate in the enterprise.

These benefits may be in the form of increased leisure, more pay, improved working conditions, better working facilities, a better, safer and more competitive product, and a more viable economy.

The real significance of the computer, automation and technological change lies in the fact that the age of scarcity can be ended. The problems will not be in production but in distribution. To meet the needs of our own country and the two-thirds of the world living in poverty will keep us busy for a long time to come.

The first task we have is to establish a new system of income maintenance so that all who labour can share in the wealth that technology can bring. As a quid pro quo for the introduction of technological change, unions may demand a quaranteed annual income.

Technological change, automation and computers will create efficiency, but will they benefit the workers? Organized labour will attempt to see that they do. As Jacques Ellul said, "Efficiency is a fact: justice is only a slogan." Our task is to make justice a fact.

References

Archer, D.B. (1963). A union viewpoint, in *Automation and Social Change*, Conference Papers, Toronto: Ontario Government.

Barnes, Sir Denis (1969). in *The Challenge of Change: Report of a Conference on Technological Change and Human Development at Jerusalem, 1969* by Trevor Evans, London: Pergamon Press, p. 75.

Brand, H. (1973). Productivity in telephone communications, *Monthly Labour Review* 96 (11) pp. 3–9.

Drucker, P.F. (1969). *The Age of Discontinuity: Guidelines to our Changing Society*, New York: Harper and Row.

Economic Council of Canada (1964). *First Annual Review – Economic Goals for Canada to 1970* Ottawa: Queen's Printer.

Eleen, J.W. and Bernardine, A.G. (1971). *Shutdown: The Impact of Plant Shutdown, Extensive Employment Terminations and Layoffs on the Workers and the Community*, Toronto: Ontario Federation of Labour.

Elizur, D. (1970). *Adapting to Innovation: A Facet Analysis of the Case of the Computer*, Jerusalem: Jerusalem Academic Press.

Evans, T. (1970). *The Challenge of Change: Report of a Conference on Technological Change and Human Development at Jerusalem, 1969*, London: Pergamon Press.

Gotlieb, C.C. and Borodin, A. (1973). *Social Issues in Computing*, New York: Academic Press.

Hardin, E. (1967). Job satisfaction and the desire for change, *Journal of Applied Psychology* 51 (1).

Loubser, J.J. and Fullan, M. (1970). *Industrial Conversion and Workers' Attitudes to Change in Different Industries*, Task Force on Labour Relations Study No. 12, Ottawa: Queen's Printer.

Report of the Industrial Inquiry Commission on Canadian National Railways "Run-Throughs" (1965). Honourable Mr. Justice Samuel Freedman, Commissioner, Ottawa: Queen's Printer.

Stieber, J. (1957). Automation and the White-Collar Workers, *Personnel*, November-December, p. 16.

Trumbo, D. (1961). Individual and group correlates of attitudes toward work related change, *Journal of Applied Psychology* 45, pp. 338–44.

DEMOCRATIC CHOICE AND COMPUTERS

E. Mumford and H. Sackman, eds., Human Choice and Computers
North-Holland Publishing Company (1975)

COMPUTER SYSTEMS TO SUPPORT INDUSTRIAL DEMOCRACY *

Bo HEDBERG

School of Business Administration, University of Wisconsin, Milwaukee, Wis., U.S.A.

1. Introduction

The topic of this paper will be broken down into two questions which I shall try to answer. Part one of the paper is concerned with the question: "Can computer systems support industrial democracy?" Part two asks: "Have computer systems been used to support industrial democracy thus far?"

The argument in part one is the following:

(1) Information processing capacity is becoming a scarce resource in our increasingly complex, information-rich society.

(2) Possession of new information processing resources means possession of new premises of *power*.

(3) Design and development of computer systems are activities partly concerned with the distribution of power.

(4) Democratic control of systems development activities is an important target of industrial democracy efforts.

(5) The design of the *metasystem* which controls the design of computer systems should be a major concern of non-computer specialists such as employees, trade unions, and managers.

(6) Democratic bodies at the strategic level of the metasystem should transform *values* and goals into guidelines, which could be used for systems development work at administrative and operative levels.

Part two reports some data on the *fit* between various influence schemes and computerized systems which have recently been designed.

* This study was carried out while the author was a research fellow at the International Institute of Management, Berlin. The full support from the institute is gratefully acknowledged.

PART ONE: "CAN COMPUTER SYSTEMS SUPPORT INDUSTRIAL DEMOCRACY?"

2. The "mental energy" crisis

Many industries are experiencing more and more complexity today. Size increases as firms grow and merge. New interdependencies are established. The wholeness of reality becomes difficult to grasp. Even where system complexity does not grow, the increasing speed of change typically adds to the information processing demands on management. Several new interest groups arise which rightly demand an influence on company decisions. Traditional managers are requested to widen their scope of consideration to include not only the firm, but also the firm's environment; not only economic indicators of company performance, but also the quality of working life for employees and the *quality of life* for outsiders affected by company decisions. More difficult decisions seem to have to be taken more frequently by decision-making bodies representing more interests.

As society grows more complex, so our information about society also grows. The last few decades have seen a rapid move from comparatively information-poor to information-rich societies in the industrialized part of the world. Information that not long ago was a scarce resource is today normally not so scarce. Multiple sources inform us about world events. Information overlap and redundancy are growing.

This is not to say that we need no more information. Richness does not imply distributive justice, and distributive justice does not necessarily mean that what is distributed is good. Inequality is a reality also on the information market, and the quality of information varies. Some know too much about too little, and too much relevant information is concerned with irrelevant events. However, on the whole, information processing capacity is replacing information as a scarce resource of industrialized countries (cf. Simon, 71). While we may have access to abundant information from multiple sources, our ability to act on the basis of this information is typically limited.

We are approaching a "mental energy" crisis. Man's cognition puts limits on human problem-solving. When problems become complex, the human problem solving process may not be sophisticated enough to keep up. Short-run behavior and limited solutions to subproblems are consequent human responses to increased complexity in industry and politics. Problems demand more "mental energy" than is available. Like the fuel energy crisis, the "mental energy" crisis is primarily a refinery crisis. Processing capacity rather than raw material supply seems to be the current bottle-neck. But, unlike the other crisis, the "mental energy" crisis has already available a tested technology (information technology – cf. Whisler, 67) that promises to supply the badly needed information processing capacity to individuals, organizations, and societies. Computer technology, along with telecommunications and management science techniques, provides new and developing resources for collecting, storing, processing and transporting information at low cost.

Thus, information processing capacity is a scarce resource in the information-rich society. The addition of information processing capacity to a unit means the addition of potential *power* for that unit (cf. Pettigrew, 72). The design of computerized systems may affect the way power is distributed in societies and organizations. The exploitation of information technology must therefore be tied into the ongoing debate and experiments concerning improved *democracy* in industrial and public organizations. The technology provides options to support – or prohibit – industrial democracy.

3. Industrial democracy in the computer age

Among a number of foci in the industrial democracy debate two major targets can be identified: (1) One is *indirect participation* (or co-determination), i.e. employee influence on the total system in which he, his group, or his department is a subset. (2) The other is *direct participation* (or self-determination), where a group of employees can control important aspects of their own subsystem.

Computer systems, and information technology as a whole, come into the picture in two ways: (1) They form important parts of the *work environment* and influence *work design*. This is the control aspect. (2) They also affect the *basis for power and influence* by adding processing capacity and providing information to decision centers of the firm. This is the power distribution aspect. If new designs of computer systems do not take into consideration the new schemes and systems for widened influence, employees could very soon find themselves in forms without content. Instead of sharing the power of management, worker representatives with little control of the firm's information processing resources, might discover that they *share the lack of power* in traditional decision centers, or that they share power with management on unequal terms.

When *participative management* replaces traditional management, participative management information systems should replace traditional management information systems. Distributive justice with respect to decision-making and responsibilities requires distributive justice with respect to available information and processing resources. The new information technology is on its way to change organizations. It opens up possibilities for improved decision-making – but also for re-distribution of power.

4. Industrial democracy and systems design

Given the "mental energy" crisis and the rapid development of information processing equipment, it seems reasonable to assume that computer systems will form an increasing part of the future work environment in offices and factories. (Although this is *not* a deterministic process, and particular outcomes can be avoided if considered undesirable.) Computerization means the formalization of routines and procedures. Work design and job organization are decided upon at the time new systems are designed. The advent of computer technology accentuates the *trend to separate the moment in time, when decisions are made about how decisions should be made, and the later moments when decisions are made in accordance with pre-determined rules*.

Since most computer systems represent considerable investment in man-hours and equipment costs, it is reasonable to assume that organizations in the future will tend to freeze their structures for rather long intervals of time. Although most computer systems could be designed to include some flexibility and to permit the possibility of organizational re-structuring; present evidence suggests that the net result of computerization may be reduced flexibility with respect to basic structural change (Hedberg et al., 71). Information flows and processes will be defined at the time of *systems design* and may then remain virtually unchanged for a long period of time, while the investment pays off.

In order to influence systems design and job organization in computerized firms, interested parties have to exert influence during the design phase. Once the system is completed, there is typically very little that can be done about it for a period of time. If one wishes to decentralize and re-distribute decisions in an organization, this has to be done when the decisions are taken about how decisions shall be made. In the future it may be as important for workers to particiapte in systems design groups as to sit on the board of directors, or participate in management groups. As decisions gradually move from the "decision makers" to those who design decision processes, traditional locations of influence and power also shift from the formal to the informal power structure. The industrial democracy debate is shooting at a moving target. Have we realized that the target has moved?

5. Designing the metasystem

Worker representatives in systems design groups at present would be likely to find themselves in one of two equally impossible situations:

(1) *The hostage alternative*: With a limited background in computer technology, management science, system analysis etc., employee representatives in design groups may choose to avoid embarrassing scenes and refrain from asking "silly questions". In selecting this strategy they are also likely to exert little influence on the system they are supposed to design. The professional systems designers and the potential users can in this way remain in a relationship of mutual esteem and disregard the fact that no essential communication and problem-solving has taken place within the group.

(2) *The indoctrination alternative*: If on the other hand the employee representatives start asking "silly questions", or if the computer experts from the start anticipate that "silly questions" will be asked, the representatives will in most cases be exposed to some introductory short course on computer issues. However, if the course is "successful", these representatives will no longer be representative of their respective groups. They will be able to com-

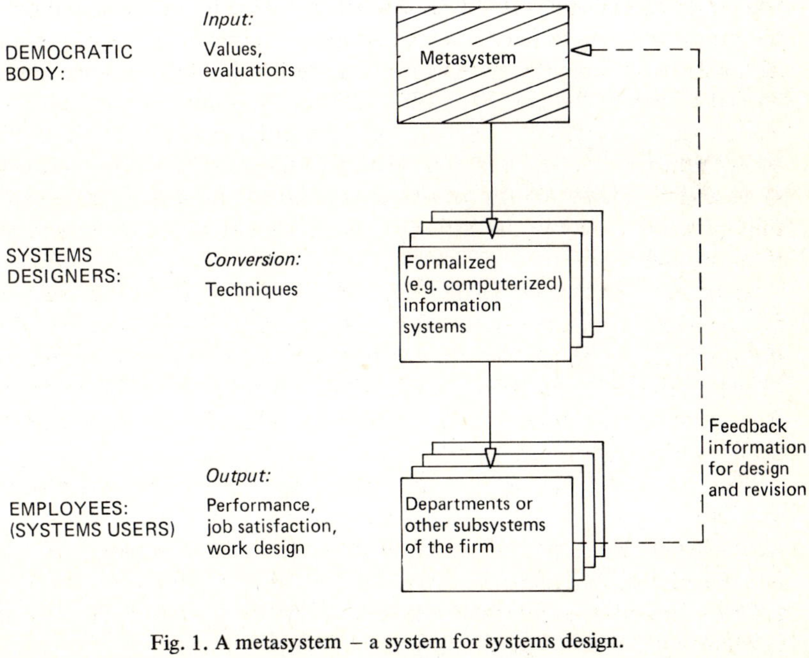

Fig. 1. A metasystem – a system for systems design.

municate with systems analysts and will see their problems in their way. (It is not uncommon for employee representatives in system design groups to end up as system designers and leave their earlier jobs.) If the course is not "successful", the employees are likely to end up with an impression that there is something mysterious about computers, and they may then act according to the hostage strategy.

The extreme cases quoted above should not conceal the message; it is not enough to influence systems which are already designed and implemented. These can only marginally be changed. It is also not enough merely to participate in the systems design process. The evidence is that, to date, employee representatives have not been successful in exerting influence in such situations. *Trade unions* and other groups, which want to control and influence the utilization of information technology in organizations, have to take measures, it seems, to *design the system which designs computer systems* (= *metasystem*). Procedures have to be set up which permit co-determination and repeated system revisions to take place. To "play the metagame" (Starbuck, 73) seems to be a more promising strategy for democratic bodies than to become involved in computer systems design. Industrial democracy in computerized firms calls for the design and implementation of workable, democratic metasystems for the production of *information systems* (Fig. 1).

6. Alternative systems – An alternative view

There are alternative computer systems. Systems design means making a number of choices between design alternatives. This has been an underlying assumption of this paper so far. Information technology should be seen as one variable in the multivariate systems we call organizations. Leavitt (64) has captured this view in his simple but powerful model of the organization (Fig. 2). In Leavitt's terms the major variables "technology", "people", "task" and "structure" constitute the basis of an organization. The interrelationship is complex. A change in one variable may affect all the other variables, if the system changes at all. Technical change may lead to alternative new system states.

Accepting Leavitt's model of the organization it seems reasonable to assume that:

(1) Technology design cannot be isolated from *organizational design*. In other words; computer systems design has to be understood within its organizational framework. The complexity of the task is considerable and the full consequences of design alternatives are seldom understood.

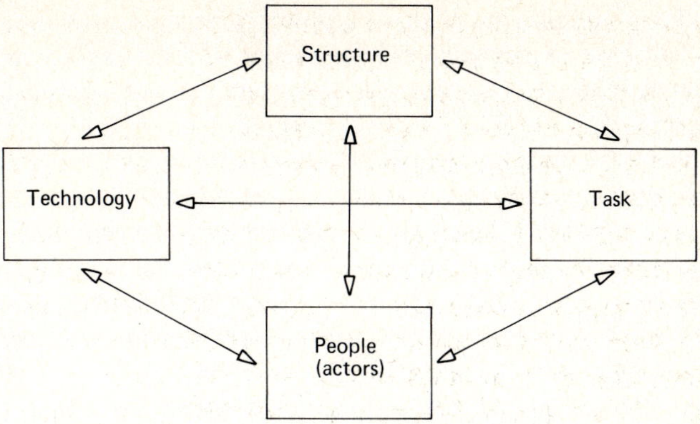

Fig. 2. The multivariate system of organization (Leavitt, 64).

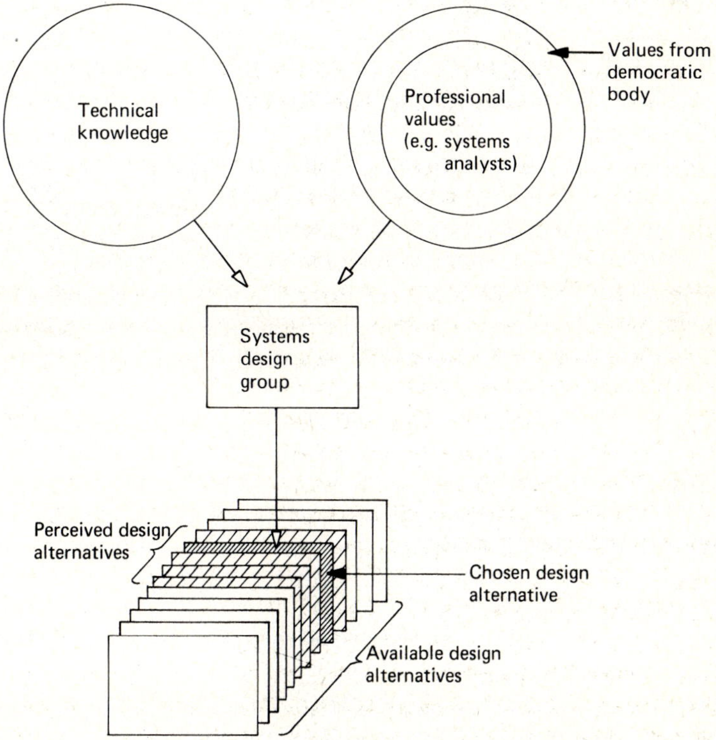

Fig. 3. Facts and values in the system design process.

(2) Facing a complex problem with several alternative solutions, systems designers will have to use subjective judgement to make explicit or implicit choices between alternatives. Facts as well as values will intermingle in the design process.

These basic assumptions identify the systems design process (the core of the metasystem) as an important influence point, which should be considered in industrial democracy models. Interested parties in an organization could influence the distribution of information processing resources (and obtain power) by setting up procedures so that the *value* input to the systems design process becomes representative of a wider group than that of professional systems analysts and programmers (Fig. 3).

There should be little need here to discuss the assumption that computer technology offers design alternatives, and that whether we perceive computers as bad or good is primarily a result of how we have chosen to utilize the technology. If we want to use the new information technology to improve conditions for individual *decision-making* in a decentralized organization, the new computer systems could be designed to provide decision aids as well as improved decision-bases for a number of widespread decision centers. The technology offers a potential for improving the "information irrigation system" of the firm. The quantity as well as the quality and timeliness of the information transports can be improved to support the vision of decentralization and individual self-determination. On the other hand, the same information technology can potentially be used to brush up the "information vacuum cleaner" of the firm. If we envisage an organization with centralized control and increased power at the top of the pyramid, it is clear that computer systems can be designed to be instrumental to that vision. There are alternative computer systems. Values and visions play an important role to determine the direction of technical change.

7. The rules of the metagame

A smoothly functioning metasystem should be able to revise more or less continuously the existing information systems of the firm. The following requirements can be specified:

(1) It should be possible and easy for all interested parties to *trigger* a design or re-design process.

(2) All interested parties should be *able* to influence the outcome, once the process is triggered.

(3) All interested parties should be *motivated* to participate in design or re-design activities.

(4) The system should provide for *feedback* and learning.

The basic requirement for easy triggering is that the organization as a whole regards designed systems not as *ultimate products*, but as intermediary solutions and momentary states of a changing system. Systems development should be seen as an integrated part of ongoing organization development, and the implementation of new systems should be thought of as efforts which can accelerate change processes, rather than bringing them to an end.

Feedback information is a necessity for learning and adaptation. However, performance assessment requires that standards are set against which outcomes can be compared. A very important task of the metasystem is to formulate these standards and to project the desired state of the organizational system, so that the actual state that is the outcome can be evaluated and changed. In fact, to transform values to guidelines and workable visions and to evaluate outcomes in terms of these values should be the major task of the metasystem.

Making values explicit and evaluating results in terms of these values can be thought of as the *strategic function* of systems design. The *administrative function* is to transform these values into technical interpretations, and the *operative function* is to implement and maintain these solutions in the organization. Today there is seldom any clear distinction between these three levels of systems management in the development of information systems. System analysts and computer scientists are often given entire responsibility, and when other parties are included in the process, they are not included in the whole process. *Systems design* has hitherto been treated mainly as a technical problem, and problem-solving has taken place in the specific language of the computer specialists or management scientists. Hence the need for education and training of employee representatives in design groups. However, including employee representatives in actual design activities and training them to become good systems analysts, may be a waste of time and skills. Worse than that, it may take their interest away from their major strategic task, to formulate and re-formulate the *values which should guide the development* of the systems design activities over time.

Designing computer systems is a complex task. Technical, human, structural, and task variables are intertwined in complex systems into which the design group intervenes (cf. Fig. 2). The whole network of constraints and possible outcomes is in most cases far beyond what any human mind can perceive at one time. There will be extremely few cases where only one solution exists to a decision problem. There will be about as few cases where anyone can be certain that the chosen solution is the best solution. Systems design today is partly handicraft, partly guesswork.

There is little reason why laymen should be called in to perform the handicraft part, but good reason why they should participate in the "guesswork". While the administrative and operative functions of systems management should probably be left to the computer scientists and other experts, the strategic function should be performed by a representative body as a part of industrial democracy. The strategic function should initiate change, request design proposals, and monitor the systems development process in interaction with the value system.

The strategic level of the metasystem should not involve itself in the technical details of systems design. It is the "message of the sentence" which it should produce, not the "translation" into different languages or dialects. Since the number of pitfalls in this mission is high, a simple flowchart could be useful as a guideline and to illustrate a possible influence strategy (Fig. 4).

There is no reason to assume that the computer staff or the operations research group would be better suited than other members of the organization to formulate goals and visions for organization development. The strategic discussion in the metasystem should concern general policies which express organization philosophy ("how do we want our organization to be?") and models of man ("what kind of people are we dealing with?", "what do they want", and "what could be done to help people realize themselves?"). There is little reason why expert–client discussions should be carried out in expert language. If the client has to become an expert in order to use an expert, then the original expert is no longer needed. The knowledge of the operational research model makers and computer scientists should help the strategic system clarify action alternatives and possible outcomes. The major task of these experts, however, should be to translate metasystem input into technically operational solutions. They should be the interpreters, not the speech-makers. In too many organizations today systems departments have been given the dual role. Not necessarily because they wanted it, but because too few other parties have been ready to prepare strategic input for the process. The computer staff is seldom to be blamed.

The design of computer-aided systems and other forms of formalized information systems is an increasingly important part of the organizational *power*-game. Democratic bodies as strategic levels of permanent metasystems for systems development and maintenance seem to be a missing link in existing industrial democracy schemes.

Employee representatives in the metasystem who try to stay clear of "bytes and halfwords" and instead concentrate on human, organizational, and societal values and visions could be very powerful actors in the power-distribution process of systems design. Having recognised their ability to exert

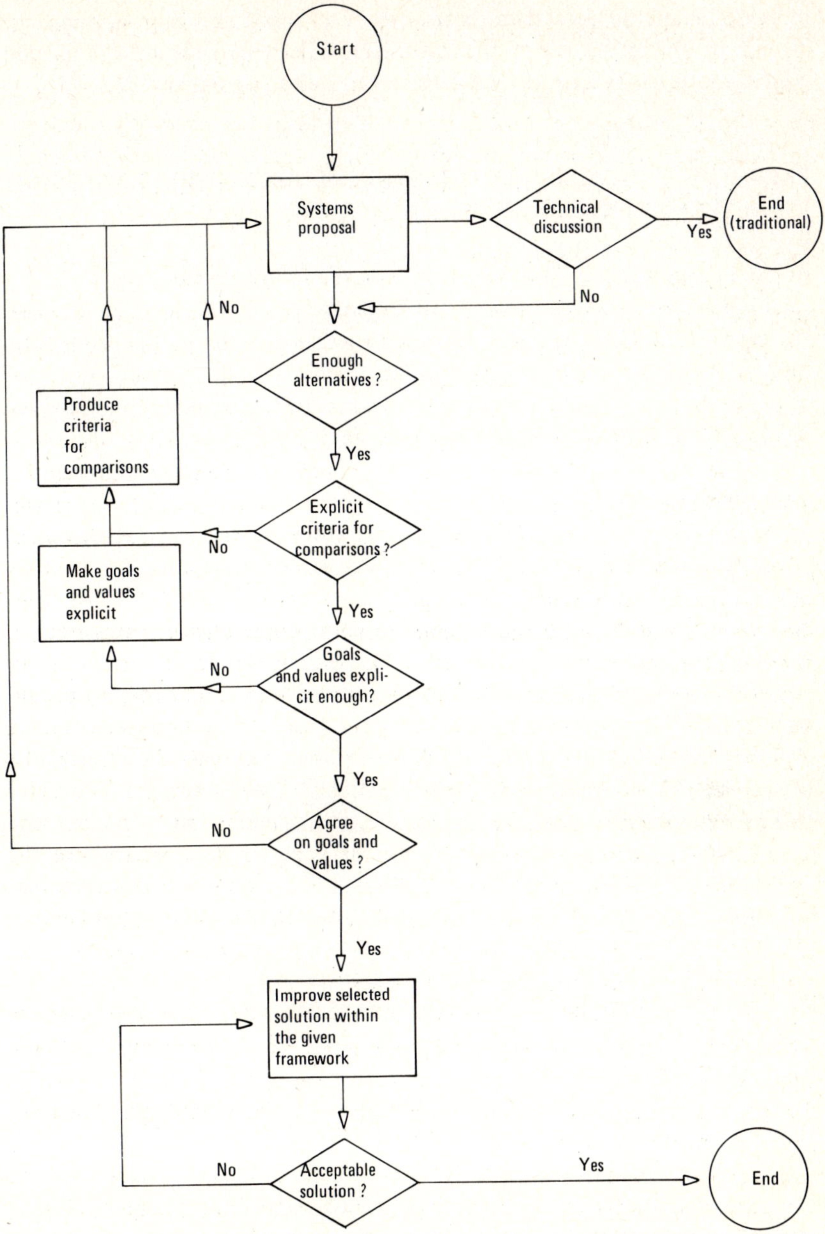

Fig. 4. Flowchart showing laymen influence on expert solutions.

influence, and the fact that things *can* be changed and improved for the benefit of the collective or the individual, it is reasonable to assume that elected metasystem members would be motivated to participate.

PART TWO: "HAVE COMPUTER SYSTEMS BEEN USED TO SUPPORT INDUSTRIAL DEMOCRACY THUS FAR?"

In order to answer this question I have used the following strategy:

(1) Short survey with some 15 participants from West-European countries visiting an Industrial Democracy research workshop at the International Institute of Management in Berlin, May 1973.

(2) Postal questionnaire to 11 trade unions (FFI, blue collar) and 18 trade unions (FIET, white collar) in Western Europe.

(3) Survey of recent articles in scientific journals, computer journals, and trade union journals.

(4) Follow-up of hints and suggestions from colleagues in the areas of computer systems, personnel planning, public administration and management.

The short survey with European researchers in the area of Industrial Democracy asked the following principal question:

"Do you know of any explicit attempts to design computerized systems especially for worker councils (Betriebsrat, etc), or worker representatives participating in the management of firms or other organizations: (Keywords: "participative management information systems", "non-manager-MIS")?"

Two indications were given by the 15 participants. One stated that the Commission of the European Communities is about to start a project on "collective bargaining agreements" in early 1974. The other indicated that the Institute of Worker's Control, Nottingham, is interested in the area. In neither case were any actual computer systems yet designed.

The result of the survey of European trade unions was about as meagre.[1] Two Scandinavian unions (one in Norway–white collars, and one in Sweden –blue collars) and one British (blue collars) replied to the English questionnaire. The main items read:

(1) "Has your organization yet developed a formal policy on computer-related issues?" (please supply documents).

[1] It should be noted that the Austrian white collar union (Gewerkschaft der Privatangestellten) was not included in the sample. This union has been active in arranging this conference. However, in this case also the answer to questions 1 and 2 is "no".

(2) "Is your organization involved in (or do you know of other) efforts to design or promote computerized systems especially for:

(1) employee representatives in participative management groups, or

(2) employees in semi-autonomous groups or departments?"

(3) "Which – in your opinion – are at the moment the most important computer-related issues for your union to tackle?"

The unions who answered the questionnaire replied that (1) they did not have any explicit policy or program concerning computer-related issues, and that (2) they were not involved in, or knew of, any explicit efforts to design computer systems to support industrial democracy. With respect to important issues for future union action the following areas were mentioned:

(1) The integrity problems in connection with data banks containing personnel data.

(2) Computer impact on centralization/decentralization and the amount of discretion left to individual workers in highly computerized environments.

(3) The problem of accumulating appropriate know-how and expertness in information technology, computer science etc., within unions.

(4) How to develop broad and informative EDP courses to raise the general level of knowledge among TU members.

The survey of professional journals together with the follow-up of individual hints resulted in the following observations:

(1) The Norwegian Union of Steel Workers (Jern-og Metallarbeiderforbundet) is making some active efforts together with a research group at the Norsk Regnesentral, Oslo, to develop a strategy for worker influence on the computerization process.

(2) In connection with the construction of a new assembly plant in Kalmar, Sweden, Volvo AB is developing a set of computer systems to support the functioning of auto workers in semi-autonomous assembly groups.

(3) The Swedish Immigration Authorities have completed a small project where a terminal-oriented operative computer system has been developed by the workers to support increased autonomy in a new job organization.

No doubt these examples are not the only ones. However, judging from the surveys and several talks with trade union officials and professional colleagues, the level of non-computer specialist activity in the studied area seems to be surprisingly low compared to the hectic activity which currently goes on in the field of computer systems design.

There seem to be very few activities underway today (if any) concerned with designing computer systems to support employee representatives in democratic bodies. Computer systems have, in other words, not yet been used to support co-determination as one component of industrial democracy. Since numerous management information systems are presently installed, one can guess that *employee representatives in participative bodies are at the moment losing rather than gaining power as a consequence of the ongoing computerization*. Trade unions do not seem to control – or even to have realized – the potential power of possessing information processing capacity and information to process.

With respect to *self-determination*, or semi-autonomy, the situation looks slightly different. Efforts are underway, although seemingly seldom initiated or actively supported by trade unions.

The Norwegian effort to develop strategies and procedures for worker influence on the systems design process is an extremely interesting attempt to design what we earlier referred to as metasystems – systems which are set up to develop and re-design systems. Local units of the Steel Workers' union have initiated study programs in cooperation with a group of researchers from the Norwegian Computing Centre (Norsk Regnesentral) in Oslo. Initial efforts have been devoted to increasing the union's competence to deal with EDP problems and problems of planning and control. A set of basic text books on EDP, planning and control have been written to educate local union members and union officials (Nygaard and Bergo, 73). These educational activities have led to the formation of action groups and task forces at various plants. Groups of workers, together with some researchers, have studied proposed systems designs and produced their own alternative proposals. Others have worked out their own programs, or policies, for union action in areas related to automation and computerization (Bedriftsklubben, 73). These activities have even resulted in one negotiated agreement between employers and employees. The agreement regulates the use of computer technology and numerically controlled machines, and establishes procedures for worker influence in the design process.

The Norwegian Steel Workers' initiative has spread rapidly. The number of participating local unions (and firms) has increased from four in the initial phase to more than ten in the Spring of 1974. Other unions have joined. Groups of salaried workers have started similar task forces. The unions plan to have studies underway at some 100 Norwegian firms in two years time. Compared to traditional union activities, the Norwegian activities are strikingly decentralized. Local union clubs perform their own studies of their own factories. Although the applications and general conditions are very different, the Norwegian experiment seems to have much in common with the Latin American "conscientisation"-strategies, which have been used to initiate social change in connection with teaching programs for illiterates (cf. Freire,

70). The Norwegian unions clearly do try to combine efforts to reduce EDP illiteracy with efforts to initiate social change in organizations. Their further developments deserve wide interest.

8. Computer systems for semi-autonomous groups at Volvo-Kalmarverken, Sweden

The new assembly plant in Kalmar represents an interesting attempt by the Volvo Corporation to design production technology to better fit human needs. The traditional *assembly line* is broken up, and each car body is placed on an electric, partly computer-controlled, transportation vehicle. The vehicle follows a magnetic tape in the floor, and the logistics of the production system can be relatively easily changed. The plant is divided into 28 so called "team areas", semi-autonomous groups of 15–20 employees, each of which is responsible for one complete function of the car (e.g., electrical system, steering and wheels, brakes, doors etc.). Each team area forms a separate workshop of the plant with its own hall with separate entrances, own equipment, own coffee rooms and restrooms, and collective responsibility for the workshop performance.

The participants of each team can influence the layout of the production flow within their area to a certain extent. The transportation vehicles can be directed to follow an assembly line arrangement, or they can be stationary in the workshop, while workers move around. Typically the vehicles are programmed to move from a certain station after a specified interval of time. The workers can press a button on the vehicle to indicate to the computer system that a vehicle will be delayed.

The arrangement allows the group to exert some control over its pace of work. Arriving vehicles can be stored in an arrival queue, while the group, for example, takes a break. However, the buffer areas between various teams are limited. Interdependencies between work stations in the plant reduce each group's autonomy considerably. The vehicles can be programmed to allow for different time intervals at different stations of the flow.

The new assembly layout requires a significant increase of information processing and control. An overall picture of the production systems has to be compiled, at the same time as required information is fed forward to other teams for planning purposes, and fed back for performance evaluation and correction.

The package of computer systems which has been installed includes the following:

(1) *A process control system*, which controls and directs the transporta-

tion vehicles in the production system. Information from the process control system is fed forward to working groups so that they can get a picture of their potential work load via their computer terminal.

(2) *A production control system*, which delivers written specifications for each separate car to the work group (extra equipment, options, etc.).

(3) *A quality control system*, which feeds back quality control results to the working group. Quality control is normally carried out on a specified sample of the production. When errors are detected, the sample size of the quality control is increased by 100%. The responsible group receives a twinkling message on their terminal screen and they are supposed to take corrective actions. (Later on it is envisioned that the system should include an "error memory" and that a mistake should be fed back to the working group together with a diagnosis including a set of suggested action alternatives to improve performance. When the error rate is back to normal, the alerted quality control is set back to standard sample size after a time delay (Fig. 5).)

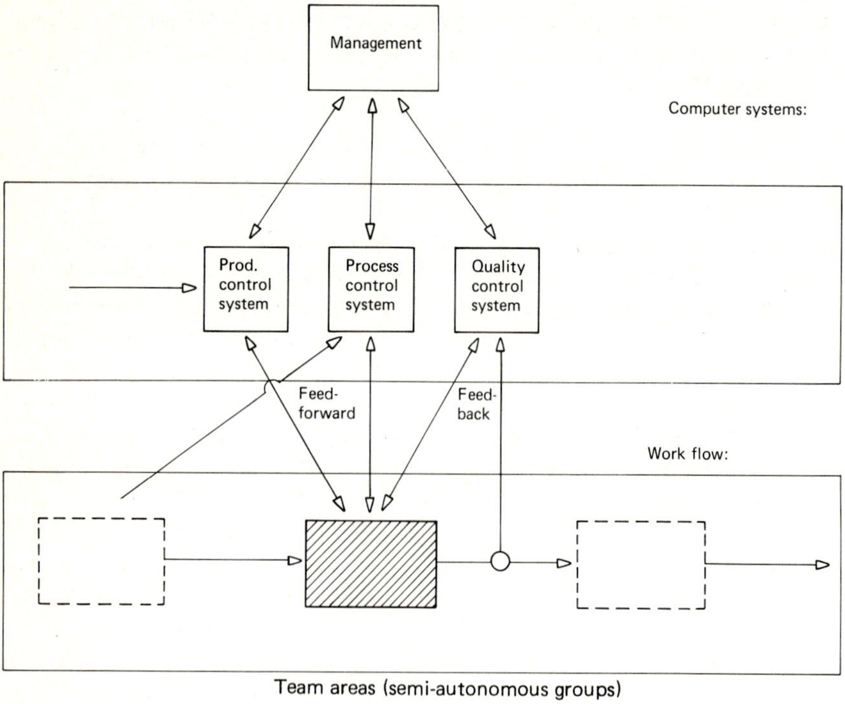

Fig. 5. Feedback-, feed forward- and management-information with respect to one team area.

The quality system monitors some 3000 control points in each car and uses its stored information to build up experience based upon correlation studies and regression analysis. Like all computer technology, the set of new computer systems introduces possiblities for centralization as well as for decentralization. The apparent decentralization of responsibility to the work group will be matched by a corresponding centralization of the ultimate control. The supervisors of the factory can study detailed performance figures in terms of error rates, error types, and rate of work for each separate station along the line. The managers receive summary reports on hard copy. Only workers, supervisors, and quality control units have continuous access to on-line terminals.

The new information technology undoubtedly strengthens management's overall control. At the same time it is clear that the new technology offers a potential for increased autonomy in each group of workers. Each team area can be made into an intimate workshop with its own discretion and responsibility. The computer technology offers a potential for improving worker influence in one of the most criticized areas of modern production. The Volvo experiment is just about to start. It deserves the attention of management as well as unions.

9. Self-determination in work groups at the Swedish Immigration Authorities

Like card punching, simple registration tasks in terminal systems connected to large data banks potentially represent areas where the new information technology could impoverish rather than enrich work, and could increase the monotony and alienation in the work roles substantially. In order to avoid these effects, and to use advanced computer technology in a manner which permits job enrichment and job rotation in operative job tasks, the Swedish Immigration Authorities recently involved the whole group of potential users in a long-run learning process and search for new alternatives for organizing work in a computerized environment.

According to early calculations, a group of about 60 people would be directly involved in registration and retrieval activities at the computer terminals. In a traditional job organization ten of these would be responsible for the preparation of input material for the data bank; twelve employees would be involved in inputting at the terminals; four would punch information on to magnetic tapes, and ten would be responsible for follow-up activities. Four persons would work full time with question-answering tasks via terminals, and eight would be involved in the maintenance and updating of created files.

Finally, four persons would transport punch manuscripts, magnetic tapes, and four would supervise the unit. Most of these work roles would be restricted and boring.

A project group of nine individuals was first set up – including two union officials, two representatives of the future users, one representative from the personnel department, the potential manager of the new unit, the person in charge of the reorganisation, and two computer specialists. Beginning with the assumption that the new technology should be used to make each individual job more interesting, and that, if possible, semi-autonomous work groups should be created, the group came up with a proposal for a new job organization for the registration unit. A small staff was envisaged for monitoring the work of four semi-autonomous registration units. Each unit would decide on the division of work within its area of responsibility. It was thought that most groups would decide to use some system of job rotation between the preparation, registration, maintenance, and question-answering tasks. A new wage system had to be designed in cooperation with the union in order to facilitate the new job organization. The system users collectively agreed to limit the working time at the terminal for each individual to a maximum of four hours per day. In order to enable various forms of job rotation, everybody would be trained to handle all occurring tasks at the unit.

Compared to the old technology, the new information technology allows the organization to provide its employees with somewhat more stimulating jobs. The terminal system, as it is used, facilitates job rotation. The new job organization has opened up possibilities for the delegation of power and responsibility. Each terminal group plans its own work and chooses its own methods to accomplish its tasks. The semi-autonomous groups themselves handle personnel planning and introduce newly employed persons into the technical and social environment of the group.

Although on rather small scale and from the outside not very elaborate the Immigration Authority terminal system is a good example of conscious planning to use the new information technology to improve working conditions and individual self-determination in organizations. So far the results are positive, but more time has to pass before a final assessment of the experiment is possible.

10. Harnessing information technology. The challenge to labor unions and other non-computer specialists

Computer systems as a support for industrial democracy. The message of this paper has been that computers and new means of communication *can be used* to support industrial democracy. However, at present the development seems to be in the opposite direction. Workers and other non-management groups in the organizations do not yet seem to have realized the full potential of the new technology and the need to control its development. To a certain extent the computer specialists themselves – consciously or unconsciously – currently direct the development of the new technology.

There seem today to be few computerized systems which have been designed for participative management. The fit between new and more democratic forms of co-determination and the corresponding information and decision systems seem to be poor. In the area of self-determination a few small experiments are reported. Computer technology has actually been used to try to support the functioning of *semi-autonomous groups*.

In actual use in business and government computer technology is about 15 years old. However, we are still only beginning to realize the full potential of the resource. Computerization is just about to start. If we want it!

When finishing this paper my eyes fell on an article in the Harvard Business Review, written by two traditional authorities in the computer area. The article was called "How to control the computer resource?". The authors state (Dearden and Nolan, 73):

> The computer resource exists solely to help staff offices and operating units to execute their responsibilities better through cheaper processing of data, more efficient organization of information systems, and procurement and development of information that is too expensive to obtain otherwise. The resource has no reason for existing except to provide such services, and these services should result in greater profits. In short, the resource has a purely economic purpose.

For those persons who have understood the full implications of Leavitt's organization model (Fig. 2) and who have taken seriously the task of using the new technology to improve organizational efficiency in a wider sense than in sheer profit terms, it must be alarming if the cited passage represents the message of the recognized business schools. There must be other visions for the future.

The new computer technology is a resource. It is indeed potential power. Systems design implies decisions about how power is to be distributed. Computer systems can support – or prohibit – industrial democracy. To harness – not to stop – the development should be a challenge to the unions. A metasystem strategy is needed.

References

Andersson, G. (1972). Här utbildas man till att påverka den nya organisationen, Stockholm, *Tema*, No. 2.

Annerstedt, J. (1972). Data till hjälp i den fackliga kampen, Stockholm, *Tema*, No. 3.

Bedriftsklubben ved A/S Hydraulik, Bergo, O.T. and Nygaard, K. (1973). *Bedriftspolitisk handlingsprogram*, Oslo: Tiden Norsk Forlag.

Dearden, J. and Nolan, R.L. (1973). How to control the computer resource, *Harvard Business Review*, Nov/Dec.

Edström, O. (1973). Några effekter av införandet av datoriserade styrsystem, Gothenburg University, Working Paper (mimeographed).

Freire, P. (1970). *Pedagogy of the Oppressed* (Pedagogia do Oprimido), New York: Herder and Herder.

Hedberg, B., Sjöberg, S. and Targama, A. (1971). *Styrsystem och företagsdemokrati*, Göteborg, BAS,

Innforing av EDB i bedrifter. (1973), Oslo, *Handel og Kontor*, No. 3.

Leavitt, H.J. (1964). Applied organization change in industry: Structural, technical and human approaches, in: W.W. Cooper, H.J. Leavitt and M.W. Shelly II (eds.), *New Perspectives in Organization Research*, New York: Wiley.

Nygaard, K. and Bergo, O.T. (1973). *Planleggning, styrning og databehandling*, Part I and II, Oslo: Tiden Norsk Forlag.

Pettigrew, A. (1972). Information control as a power resource, *Sociology* 6 (2).

Simon, H.A. (1971). Designing organizations for an information-rich world, in: M. Greenberger (ed.), *Computers, Communications, and the Public Interest*, Baltimore: Johns Hopkins Press.

Starbuck, W.H. (1973). Information systems for organizations in the future, International Institute of Management, Berlin, Preprint Series No. 1/73–53.

VOLVO AB. (1973). Introduktion till KVIK. (Kvalitetsinformations-system Kalmar), Gothenburg, August 1973 (mimeographed).

Whisler, T. (1967). The impact of information technology on organizational control, in C. Meyers (ed.), *The Impact of Computers on Management*, Cambride: MIT Press.

E. Mumford and H. Sackman, eds., Human Choice and Computers
North-Holland Publishing Company (1975)

THE PEOPLE'S COMPUTER, AN AID TO PARTICIPATORY DEMOCRACY*

John M. CARROLL

Computer Science Department, University of Western Ontario, London, Ont., Canada

and

Jean M. TAGUE

Department of Mathematics, Memorial University of Newfoundland,
St. John's, Newfoundland, Canada

1. Introduction

This paper presents the view that the computer is becomming a repressive instrument in the hands of big governments and corporations. It stresses the need to provide the common man with easy access to computer facilities to even up the social, economic and political balance of power. It discusses problems involved in bringing computer power to the people, and describes preliminary steps taken in connection with a non-governmental municipal information service in London, Canada.

Throughout history, various items of technology appear to have served as instruments to divide the human race into classes and enable one class to exert its will over others.

Today the computer is regarded by some as a repressive instrument that serves the cause of governments, corporations and large institutions.

The common man often sees himself as billed by it, taxed, enumerated, administrated, manipulated, and controlled.

The computer makes it easier for big countries to dominate small countries, for senior governments to control local governments, for large corporations to take over small companies.

* The research reported in this paper was performed under contract with the Canadian Department of Communications whose support is gratefully acknowledged.

We may well be experiencing the emergence of cybernetic imperialism. To those in government who are sincerely committed to participatory democracy, hegemony fostered by the computer would be an undesirable synthesis. There seems to be a growing awareness that it is necessary to restore the actual and the apparent balance of power; to make computer power available to the people at large.

2. Background

There is a vast literature on the computer in relation to social services and social programmes. Unfortunately, in most cases it reports failures in application.

Fortunately, one does not have to take time here to review the literature in general as Gotlieb and Borodin (73) have done this very well.

The specific issues relating to a community information utility have been treated at length by Sackman and Nie (70) and by Sackman and Boehm (72).

Much of the prior discussion centers upon cost/benefit analysis and break-even points and appears to point towards eventual control of such a utility by private business or by a senior level of government.

In our specific context, either of these outcomes would be viewed as unfortunate.

Control of an information utility by the central government could negate much of the information utility's potential as a device to correct administrative shortcomings.

Control by private business, judging from past experiences with mass media, usually leads to cynical manipulation of public attitudes and, in the Canadian context, eventual domination by Americans.

Thus far we have been able to work as a coalition of voluntary organizations. The University of Western Ontario (a quasi-public institution) has generously made computing time and equipment available. Our federal government seems quite willing to make grants in aid to persons working full time on the project. Another group in Vancouver is starting on a similar operation.

It is early to foretell what the eventual organizational synthesis will be. The Canadian Broadcasting Company appears to have been able to avoid both political and private domination in its structure as a Crown Corporation and provides one possible model.

3. Computers and the underprivileged

Making raw computer power available to persons not sophisticated in its use, provides little more than distracting entertainment, however. Extrapolating experience gained from several Open House sessions, it is our observation that people play TIC-TAC-TOE, CHEQUERS, or CHESS; they run ELIZA; do simple CAI lessons in High School maths; or use AID to perform arithmetic.

None of this is bad. In fact, each summer we set up a terminal in the Public Library to provide just such "rainy-day" amusement.

However, we have in mind an ultimate move toward more socially significant uses.

It is well to digress at this point to introduce the term HUMAN SERVICES DELIVERY SYSTEM. This is becoming a fashionable catch-all which includes the rendering to citizens of services such as health care, education, welfare, housing, employment counselling, recreation, and legal and protective services. It is easier to use the inclusive term HUMAN SERVICES than to enumerate all of them and this we will do.

The problem, of course, is that no unified human services delivery system currently exists, although it would be desirable if it did.

Canada is a parliamentary monarchy with a federal system of government. As in the European democracies, the government guarantees every citizen a basic standard of living, including education and health care irrespective of his ability to pay.

However, the actualization of human services delivery, or how people really get the benefits to which they are entitled, is delegated to a varied assortment of federal, provincial and municipal agencies; quasi-public institutions; voluntary organizations; associations; private philantrophies and businesses.

We felt that one way the People's Computer could make a socially significant contribution would be by helping potential benefit clients find their way through the bewildering maze of human service organizations.

In the context of human services delivery, assistance to both the helpers, the needy, and the public is urgently required to:

Create awareness of human needs, human problems, and gaps in the existing human service delivery system.

Co-ordinate the activities of existing services to improve the quality of human services rendered, promote joint-case co-ordination, increase the accessibility to human services of those who require them, decentralize the delivery of human services, and foster a multi-disciplinary neighbourhood-centered approach.

Plan and order the priorities with which human service delivery problems are attacked concentrating upon deficiencies, unmet needs, and the need for greater accessibility.

Furnish computational and informational support to research workers, planners and protesters, policy makers and critics.

Central to success of any movement aimed at improving the delivery of human services, is an information system that makes available facts regarding the services, programmes, and activities of helping services. This information is needed by individuals whose problems make them potential clients for human services, and also by workers in various human service delivery roles so they can better co-ordinate their activities, and by the public at large to recruit volunteer workers and promote a more sympathetic climate of opinion regarding human services delivery.

4. Human resources information system

Like everything else, implementation of a Peoples Computing Network in all its possible ramifications is too large an undertaking to be done at one time. It is the old question of ordering priorities. In this context, the Human Resources Information System (HURIS corresponding to the Greek *ευροκω* I discover) appeared to be the most promising implementation in terms of payoff, because it would:

(a) be highly visible;

(b) provide urgently needed assistance in an area which currently accounts for the bulk of government spending;

(c) utilize existing instruments and schemes which have already proved successful in other ways.

The conceptual problem in applying the computer was to identify the unique capabilities of a modern time-sharing computer and match them against the perceived information needs of the underprivileged.

(1) The computer can untiringly and reliably accept and store data about the availability of new or expanded services; the needs of the people as articulated by their requests; and the effectiveness with which these needs are met as disclosed by rebuffs reported. A social worker with a scratch pad can do the same thing, but slips of paper get mislaid and each person has his personal "shorthand". The computer can exert format control and once data is entered, it is there to stay.

(2) A computer can sort, collate, and cross-tabulate large amounts of these data. No social agency has the manpower to do this on a regular basis. As a

result, unmet human needs now left to become festering social wounds could become immediately apparent as would slip-shod administrative work on the part of an agency or a developing pattern of arrogant behaviour by some functionary or other.

(3) A computer can retrieve data from a file by affording many points of entry and thus fulfill requests occurring in unanticipated contexts. A social worker with a good manual card file and several local directories can do this too. However, it takes months for the social worker to attain such a level of competence. We can send young cadres into depressed areas to work from a computer terminal after only a few hours of training.

(4) In making personal referral, it is handy to give the client a page of printout containing the name, address and function of the agency to which he is being sent. It makes him feel like he is a "somebody", and in this cold and impersonal world that in itself is worth something. There also seems to be an ego boost to the client in just seeing the computer (terminal) doing something for him.

HURIS would then have four functions:

(a) Referral,
(b) Production of summary reports,
(c) Conduct of longitudinal studies,
(d) Support of research activity.

4.1. Referral

The referral service will answer questions from benefit clients and other citizens and direct them to social agencies that can handle their requests.

The heart of the referral subsystem will be a computer stored bank of information regarding human resources. It will contain information about human service agencies (e.g. city welfare, provincial social services, federal manpower, the Salvation Army, etc.), and associations, programmes, and activities. It will also identify individuals in those agencies who should be approached: those responsible for case intake (establishing in the first instance the need and eligibility of the client), those responsible for decision-making with regard to appeals and administrative matters, distinguishing those who do the work, and those who wield the power from those who have shown themselves to be ineffectual.

Information would be entered into this data-base on-line and in real-time (that is, as received by the individual entering it). It may be received in publications, memoranda, briefs from various groups, or letters.

An independent voluntary information service has an advantage over a government information bureau in that is can report actual practice, rather than administrative intent. If a particular case worker is unsympathetic or negligent, the client can be advised how to by-pass him, for example.

A real-time computer-based system has the additional advantage of being able to modify its information as conditions within a social agency change from time to time.

Requests for referral may be expected to come from friends, neighbours and family of persons requiring help; professional and volunteer workers; other agencies to whom the individual has applied, and the individual himself.

Eventually, they may come from consoles at neighbourhood centres. The most frequent medium for contact will likely be the telephone.

The whole point of the referral service is that the citizen wishing information will not be referred from one functionary to another; he will get his answer with only one telephone call. If there is a runaround, the referral service will get it and not the person seeking help. Furthermore, contact with inept agency workers and other frustrating experiences will constitute another source of input to the data bank, one that could be used to plan agency budgets and evaluate the efficiency of agency personnel.

Follow-up entries will originate as the result of the referral service contacting agencies to which people have been referred to determine what was done about the case, and contacting the individual to determine his level of satisfaction. In making these contacts, *the referral service will act not in the role of an advocate, but as a fact gatherer* and the facts of unmet needs, clients perceiving themselves to be unfairly treated, and inter-agency buckpassing (the practice of one agency foisting its responsibilities onto another) will speak for themselves when statistically analyzed.

4.2. Summary reports

The reporting function would consist of compiling information gathered by the referral service in the course of its referral and fact-gathering activities. Those reports would:

(a) provide a measure of agency activity in terms of referrals, intake, and appeals;

(b) measure agency effectiveness by feedback from recipients and additional information-seeking activity on the part of clients;

(c) determine relative accessibility of various human services;

(d) disclose deficiencies in existing human services;

(e) reveal unmet human needs;

(f) assist in ordering priorities in human services delivery planning according to (i) special groups (aged, youth, newcomers, etc.), (ii) areas within the region served, (iii) relative urgency of various problems handled, and (iv) relative magnitudes of the various types of problems;

(g) summary reports will, of course, provide HURIS with a basis for self-evaluation.

4.3. Longitudinal studies

Existance of the HURIS referral data bank will permit long-term follow-up of cases. It is expected that these studies will:

(a) promote joint-case co-ordination by the various human service agencies;

(b) determine the actualization of human services;

(c) determine the quality of help and its long-term effects;

(d) permit greater insight into the origin and development of human problems, their inter-relationship, and the effects of human service intervention at various phases of problem development.

4.4. Research activity

In addition to the referral data bank HURIS will also operate a Social Planning Information Bank. Inputs will consist of:

(a) the periodic summary reports produced by the Referral Service;

(b) applicable statistical data of a local nature;

(c) applicable statistical data extracted from the national census;

(d) information produced by municipal or regional planning groups (City Planning Maps);

(e) information produced by educational administrators (Board of Education Planning Maps);

(f) results of ad hoc surveys;

(g) contents of local land-use data banks not already covered in (d) and (e).

(A land-use data bank is a computer-stored inventory of land parcels and the uses to which each is put. They are used for regional planning. One exists in the Lake Erie region of the Province of Ontario.)

5. Implementation

Our immediate objective was to implement a subset of HURIS in a defined local area to determine requirements for hardware, software, systems planning, and training of human intermediaries. Two principal vehicles were created:

An interactive computer-based community information system.

A method for capturing and analyzing data regarding information sought by clients.

6. Community information network

Our computer-based community information network is now operating in London, Canada (population: 233 000).

Its data base is disk resident within the PDP-10/50 computer at the University of Western Ontario. This computer had previously been configured to optimize its time-sharing capabilities.

Three remote terminals are connected by direct telephone lines to the computer.

(1) A cathode-ray-tube display terminal is installed at Information London.

Information London is an agency that furnishes information and assistance to persons requiring human services of all kinds.

Requests from clients are received principally by telephone although clients sometimes write or call in person.

The staff consists of three to five workers some of whom are volunteers.

The telephones are answered continually during the five-day business week.

The agency is financed on a year-to-year bases by grants from United Community Services, the municipal government, and the federal government. The provincial government assists with some logistic support.

Information is acquired by the agency from a variety of sources. These include newspaper clippings, pamphlets, handbills, agency memoranda, letters, directories, and, perhaps most importantly, personal contacts by the staff.

The agency's data bank has existed historically as manual card files, a large bulletin board, notes, and, to a considerable extent, the memory of the staff.

(2) A cathode-ray-tube terminal is installed in the Humanities Reference Section of the London Public Library and Art Museum. The Library is considering making a parallel installation of a terminal that will provide hard copy.

(3) A cathode-ray-tube terminal is installed in the main office of the Visitors' and Convention Bureau of Greater London. This will be replaced by a terminal which produces hard copy.

The Visitors' and Convention Bureau is a municipal agency that provides information to tourists. It serves principally a walk-in clientele at its main office in downtown London and three sub-offices at each of the major highway approaches to the city.

Occasional or dial-up users of the system include:

Bell Telephone of Canada,
School of Library and Information Science, UWO,
Computer Science Department, UWO.

It is our intention to invite the leading users, gatherers, and creators of community information to become part of the network.

We have begun discussions with

London Free Press (the local newspaper which has TV and radio outlets),
Information Canada – Canada's federal information agency.

To demonstrate the potential of our computer information network, we installed a display terminal at the UWO booth at the Canadian Computer Show in Toronto last fall and showed that we could answer visitors' questions about London by querying our data base by long-distance telephone.

The Data Base consists of three main parts:

Master Resource File,
Ephemeral Files,
Annotation File.

The *Master Resource File* contains approximately 5 000 records. Each record consists of four fields.

Amplified name of the resource agency,
Street address,
Telephone number,
Descriptive code.

The *amplified name* of the resource agency consists of its full legal name, common name, acronym (e.g., ARF for Alcoholism and Drug Addiction Research Foundation), and a descriptor (e.g., J.J. Smith – LAWYER).

The *descriptive code* consists of four digits:

1st digit – affiliation (e.g., municipal),
2nd digit – primary service category (e.g., health care),
3rd digit – secondary service category (e.g., clinic),
4th digit – tertiary service category (e.g., venereal disease).

The Master Resource File was compiled from the following sources of information:

Allocated Members, London and District Dental Society,
Clubs, Organizations, Groups, etc. in London, Ontario (C of C),
Community Directory (Information London/London Public Library),
Community Groups by Planning District,
Community Leaners' Catalogue,
Directory of Ethnic Organizations in London, Ontario (S of S),
Directory of Program Resources (London Public Library),
Extracts from Files (Information London),
London Chamber of Commerce Industrial Directory,
London Drama Council Newsletter,
London Inter-Church Council Church Directory,
London Legal Directory,
London on the banks of the Thames (V & CB),
London Telephone Directory,
Province of Ontario Community Services Directory,
Senior Citizens' Groups of London,
United Community Services Funded Agencies.

Ephemeral Files are created by the users of the computer network by use of the CREATE operation in our retrieval programme and the text editing facilities of the PDP computer system.

The Visitors' Bureau has created several files which collectively answer the questions most frequently asked by tourists among which are:

- Directions to and details about points of historical and cultural interest;
- Hours of operation and admission prices of places of amusement or recreation;
- Availability of facilities for conventions and meetings.

Information London has created files containing information about:

- Eligibility criteria at child day-care centres;
- Camps and day camps for children;
- Location of polling places, names of candidates and deputy returning officers for elections.

The Public Library has created files containing information about:

- Cultural activities at branch libraries;
- New acquisitions of books and periodicals;
- Newly formed clubs and citizens' groups.

We think of our ephemeral files as a community-wide *electronic bulletin board.*

Annotation File. The annotation file is made up of one-line comments expanding upon information in the master file. For example: the master resource file entry: "Joe's Restaurant" might be linked to the annotation: "Italian food, prices start at $3.00."

It would be technically feasible to link complaints about pollution violations and consumer dissatisfaction to the master file entries of the offending companies and organizations.

Data Base Management. These operations have to do with creating and updating the Data Base.

The programmes were written in COBOL and run on a CYBER 73-14 computer, which is much faster than the PDP-10/50.

There are three distinct procedures:

Create the Master Resource File from a manually prepared punched card file.

Print hard-copy directories of which there are three kinds:

(a) Directory of human resources indexed by affiliation of the agency:
0 = unspecified,
1 = municipal,
2 = provincial,
3 = federal,
4 = quasi-public,
5 = service and voluntary organizations,
6 = associations,
7 = private business,
8 = resource centres;

(b) Directory of human resources indexed by primary service category:
0 = unspecified,
1 = basic income maintenance,
2 = other human services,
3 = legal and protective services,
4 = health care,
5 = education,
6 = recreation and travel,
7 = employment,
8 = public affairs,
9 = community affairs;

(c) Directory of human resources indexed by keywords in the amplified title (KWIC index):

Print mailing labels to send out periodic questionnaires revalidating the master file entries.

Update the master file by:
(a) correcting inaccurate information,
(b) deleting duplicate or irrelevant entries,
(c) adding new entries.

Information Retrieval. These programmes were written in FORTRAN for the PDP-10/50. They have to do with retrieving information from the master file, managing ephemeral files, and managing the annotation file. They run in real-time from the remote terminals.

Search. This operation is based upon a combination of digits from the descriptive code or combinations of strings from the amplified title joined with the Boolean operators: AND, OR, NOT, NAND, or NOR.

Display. This operation permits the user to read the ephemeral file corresponding to a specified record in the master file. Each master file record is uniquely identified by a number made up of its descriptive code and a computer-assigned four digit sequence number.

Create. This operation encompasses a set of commands which enable a user to manage ephemeral files over which he has been granted authority. The integrity of the ephemeral files is ensured by hedging these operations with a system of special passwords.

The set of commands comprising the CREATE operation are:

(a) LOCATE:	enables the user to obtain his allocated file,
(b) STORE:	enables the user to create a file by typing in a natural way at his remote terminal,
(c) CLEAR:	permits the user to erase existing material in the file,
(d) SUPERCEDE:	enables the user to create new information to replace that erased from his file,
(e) RELEASE:	permits a user to relinquish an ephemeral file when he no longer has a need for it.

Creating an ephemeral file is no more difficult than putting out an internal memo announcing an upcoming event or a new or expanded service.

7. Capture and analysis of questions

When a client requests help from Information London, certain data are recorded on mark-sense cards which we process monthly to produce several statistical cross tabulations of the types of service rendered and inquiries received.

This information can be stored and added to each month.

Data regarding cases handled was formerly collected on forms and in format developed by Ontario Provincial Cummunity and Social Services during a research project which studied the operations of this and similar centres. The forms were sent to Queen's Park, keypunched by the Provincial Government and processed by computer to create a 25-page summary monthly report.

This service was discontinued in December 1972 after the Province finished its study.

We wrote a computer programme to process the case records produced by Information London. We had their handwritten case slips keypunched and produced the same cross-tabulation of case data that had formerly been produced by the Government of Ontario. We did this for five months – January to May 1973.

Working with the Director of Information London, we revised the data collection format to overcome some deficiencies in the scheme devised by the Government of Ontario that became evident in actual use. We devised a mark-sense card format for collecting the data to replace the handwritten case slips. The new format was put into use in June 1973.

The data collection format permits characterizing a case by: age of client, area of city; problem dimensions including urgency, complexity, whether the problem involves physical handicap, language difficulty or criminal involvement, whether the client belongs to a minority group or is a welfare recipient; whether or not the social service the client requires is available and whether the client has any complaint regarding the level of service; and the steps taken to solve the problem including identification of the agency or class of agency to which it was referred.

8. Future plans

The rest of our implementation plan will take advantage of the fact that by this time there now exist two computer-based data banks: a community-wide structured inventory of human service resources having some 5 000 entries (Master Resource File) and a structured data bank of human problems growing at the rate of some 1 500 cases a month.

Some future tasks will involve:

The monthly reduction of individual case data to pertinent summary statistics for long-term storage.

Providing Information London with the facility to make retrospective coordinate searches of its case data bank to answer its needs for summary statistical information of an operational nature between delivery of periodic cross-tabulations, and to obtain data encompassing several reporting periods.

Implementing a computer based question-answering system utilizing a matrix of problems versus solutions.

Developing special terminal display units to be installed at one or more Neighbourhood Resource Centres where clients can be served on a walk-in and self-help basis.

It is noteworthy that the problem of whether clients can communicate more freely with a machine or a human intermediary is a subject for research. One can hypothesize situations in which the machine would be preferred as well as situations in which human communication is essential. The question is doubtless situation-dependent, but is not sufficiently well understood.

Also in the research area is the problem of designing access facilities of a visual, tactile, or oral nature to enable unsophisticated or aliterative individuals to communicate effectively with a computer resource.

One can project the networking concept upward from the local level. A single system such as we have described would scarcely tax a dedicated time-shared computer, so possibly a single computer could serve several cities and facilitate interchange of information among them.

On the national level, a handful of regional computers would suffice to fulfill the total need for community information service and, of course, these could be linked for interchange of information on a national level.

9. Summary

Our Community Information Network, while aiding in the work of local human service agencies, initiates the systematic study and incremental build-up of a project having long-range national significance. We visualize HURIS as:

(a) a nationwide social early-warning system,

(b) a means for co-ordinating the delivery of human services that will tend to reduce regional disparity, and

(c) a control that will prevent overlapping and redundant expense in an area that for some citizens' likes is already too costly.

References

Gotlieb, C.C. and Borodin, A. (1973). *Social Issues in Computing*, New York: Academic Press.

Sackman, H. (1973). *Some Exploratory Experience with Easy Computer Systems*, AFIPS Conf. Proc. 42.

Sackman, H. and Boehm, B. (1972). *Planning Community Information Utilities*, Montvale: AFIPS Press.

Sackman, H. and Nie, N. (1970). *The Information Utility and Social Choice*, Montvale: AFIPS Press.

E. Mumford and H. Sackman, eds., Human Choice and Computers
North-Holland Publishing Company (1975)

THE CONTRIBUTION OF COMPUTERS TO PARTICIPATORY DEMOCRACY

Yochanan MANOR

Hebrew University, Jerusalem, Israel

0. Introduction

In recent years "democracy" and democratic government has come under strong attack, the target of many insidious criticisms. Distrust and scepticism of national democracies and the democratic "way of life" are voiced not only by sophisticated observers but also by the very groups that are supposed to benefit most from government "of . . ., by . . ., and for the people." This sceptical attitude applies to all levels of government, national, state and local. It is the author's belief that this present trend against democracy can be curbed if citizen participation is enhanced and enlarged, and that the use of electronic data processing (EDP) and computers can play a central role in this enhancement. Thus it is the aim of this article to show that EDP and computers can be a powerful tool in the strengthening and promotion of democracy, particularly on the level of local government.

Strangely enough, even as democracy has become much derided, it remains a "hurrah!" word – a term with "good" emotional connotations that arouses prompt and passionate support, a concept praised by everyone, favored by everyone, and applied by everyone to his own way of doing things. While this split view is most apparent at the national level, a similar development has occurred on the level of local government, traditionally viewed as the genuine birth place of democracy and the best school for learning it. The decline, even the decay, of democracy on this level was increased by the loss of autonomy by local authorities. Even in countries known for well-rooted and developed self-government, a shift from self-government to decentralization has been noticed (Drago, 68).

Surveys carried out in several countries – including the United States,

United Kingdom, West Germany, Italy, Mexico – show that "the sense of subjective competence [of the citizen] occurs more frequently vis-a-vis the local government than the national government . . . and the proportion [of the citizenry] that says it can influence the local government is higher than the proportion expressing national competence" (Almond and Verba, 65). These results confirmed widely held views about the closer relatedness of citizens to local government, because on this level it seems far easier for them to grasp, understand, and explain the issues at stake and the trade-off between individual satisfaction and collective needs (Club Jean Moulin, 68).

Since it seems reasonable to assume that the challenge to democracy on one level is linked with a similar challenge on the other level, and that on both levels the problem is of a similar nature, this study is centered on the local government level. First I shall endeavour to expose briefly the main sources of distrust and scepticism about democracy and then, to investigate the possible contributions of computers in restoring faith in democracy and in strengthening its operation.

1. Sources of distrust and scepticism in "democracy"

Generally, when one refers to "democracy" one has in mind a regime of representative democracy, a system of government which must fulfill at least two basic requirements: "First, to be able to elicit as accurately as possible the opinions of as many people as possible on who shall be their representatives, and how the country ought to be governed ... . Second, it must provide a way of ensuring that those chosen by the public do in fact do what the electorate wants them to do, or that they can be replaced if they do not." (Pickles, 70.)

In fact, representative democracy is built on the fundamental hierarchical model of leaders that has led to a system of decision making to which "leaders are more or less responsive to the preferences of non-leaders" (Dahl, 56). Revealingly, Dahl noted that this system seems to operate with a relatively low level of citizen participation.

The concept of decentralization, which very often is associated with democracy, is but a transposition of representative democracy to the level of local government. Of course, decentralization is more democratic than administrative deconcentration (Meyer, 57), but we must remember that it is no more than a new avatar of representative democracy. This is not to down grade the importance of decentralization with regard to democracy, but one should not forget that this type of democracy is related to what Pranger terms "the politics of power" in contrast with the "politics of participation" (Pranger, 70).

However, democracy can also be viewed as participatory democracy, that is, a regime in which citizens actually have adequate opportunity to influence and decide on public policy, in which the people not only act as watchful citizens, but "meet face to face, interact freely as equals" (Mumford, 67), and are active participants in public affairs.

Participatory democracy often evokes the concept of direct democracy as illustrated in ancient Greece in the Agora, or at present in some cantons of Switzerland (Siegfried and Heguin, 48). In such a regime the citizens have the possibility of discussing public issues, of being critical, of making suggestions, and of initiating laws. However, direct democracy seems to be an exceptional phenomenon confined to marginal situations and specific societies. Even in the places where it still exists as in the Swiss cantons of Glaris, Unterwald, Appenzell or the Israeli kibbutzim it is very hard for direct democracy to be a regime of total participation.

As an example of modern democracy we should rather point to the French clubs (Mossuz, 70), which create for numerous citizens the possibility of being informed about public policies, of learning about them, and of taking part in the drawing up of various propositions which will be thrown into public debate. Obviously, this type of participatory democracy is somewhat spoiled by confining it to the category of new middle classes, and the very limited nature of the effective influence on the process of public policy making. In any case, democracy – representative as well as participatory – is a rule and system of government that is quite difficult to run satisfactorily.

As a matter of fact, participatory democracy is rejected as being an impracticable utopia. Sometimes this assertion is worded as a categorical statement: "If every one will deal with public issues, who will remain for work?"

Moreover is it not an "established" fact that today, perhaps even more than yesterday, the citizen has not the qualifications to be an active agent in solving problems at the level of the community he is living in. He has not the information, the knowledge, or the expertise: he has not the time to deal with these problems, and he lacks rationality. Under these circumstances what can one expect from collective cacophonic processes of decision making?

Participatory democracy is but a utopia, and most of a citizen's life is cluttered with problems where he has no responsibility for initiating or for solving. Citizens at large do not seem to be really interested in participation, and although it sounds very satisfying and soothing to state that people are equal, in fact they are not, especially in their ability to discuss public matters.

Thus the only workable compromise between democracy and rationality, and in consequence between democracy and efficiency, is the regime of representative democracy. Unfortunately even the latter does not display a genuine propensity to democracy as well as to efficiency.

The low state of democracy stems from the fact that its "natural tendency is to degenerate into despotism or aristocracy", as Montesquieu observed long ago. The process of representative democracy enables a small group of representatives to rule without having to take into account the views of the citizens, not only between elections but even during election periods – because the citizens have no effective alternatives. The process by which representatives are chosen and alternatives worked out is a pseudo-democratic one, because there is no democracy in the political parties which very often are governed and run by their apparatus, the party "machine".

In other words, citizens have the impression that they are short-circuited, and they do not feel that they are able to reverse this situation; they believe that they do not have the power to participate actively in the public policy process and to influence it. They feel frustrated, alienated, or, more simply, apathetic to the regime. These very feelings jeopardize the basis of a democratic regime. One day this growing indifference may lead to the collapse of the democratic regime itself, because imperceptibly the citizens are removing their support from it and are ceasing to give it further credibility. This is especially true when, in addition, the practical benefits of being governed under such a regime are not evident, and even quite dubious.

Indeed, reality contradicts the usual assumption or claim according to which representative democracy is the best compromise between democracy and efficiency. Many authors have emphasized the contradiction between efficiency and democratic regimes. As a system of decision making democracy is less efficient in large part because it must pay tribute to political pressures and this leads to the taking of non-rational decisions. On the level of local government this contradiction is perhaps still more acute because local government displays a very limited ability in the field of decision making (Leemans, 70).

Yet, on this level citizens are more able than anywhere else to evaluate the actual achievements of such a regime. In most cases they would have to conclude, perhaps bitterly, that representative democracy is not really efficient. On the contrary, carelessness and an inability to provide vital services seems to be the rule. It is worth noting that on the level of local government, citizens have been inclined to take for granted the excuses and justifications voiced by their representatives to explain their failures and lack of efficiency – that is to say, the loss, the shrinkage, of the local jurisdiction's autonomy.

Obviously this is first of all a matter of constitutional distribution of functions between these two levels. For example, in France the present rule of distribution has been described by E. Pisani as leaving "to local authorities what others are not able to carry out". In place of this Pisani has proposed leaving to local authorities everything they *can* carry out, and to transfer to central authorities matters that the center can best deal with (Pisani, 69). The main problem is to discover which is which. In other words, is it possible to draw up an objective criterion of distribution which will give a satisfactory answer to one of the central issues of every management and government system, that is, the degree of desirable complementarity/self-containment and of required coordination (Morris, 68). There is little doubt that generally – not only in France – the criteria of distribution were a product of guesses and intuition or of moral principle, and much less a matter of systematic learning and testing.

But even when local authorities do have some constitutional autonomy, they do not really take advantage of it. The excuse called forth is the lack of sufficient means, especially financial resources. The validity of this excuse can be assessed by investigating the magnitude of grants by central authorities to the budgets of local authorities; the substantial totals involved tend to suggest that the problem is not precisely the level of means available for use, but the conditions binding their disposition. That is to say, the main problem is one of management, and unfortunately local authorities do not display "natural" gifts in this field.

In contrast, the traditional leadership has displayed impressive talents in the "politics of power" in its attempt to overcome its very limited competence in the field of management. The traditional local elite has woven very special links with the central administrative authorities. It has obtained the backing of the public administration to support its political dominance, in exchange for its acceptance of the public administration monopoly to set up the "rational general interest", based among other things upon the public administration monopolistic hold on information and on its tendency to throw "a veil of secrecy on public affairs" (Catherine and Thuiller, 69). Sooner or later, this mystification will be disclosed and will aim a fatal blow at representative democracy.

In short, there are three main sources of distrust and scepticism concerning democracy: (1) the complete loss of control over the leaders by those led, (2) the inability of democracy to provide public services efficiently, and (3) the impracticability of participatory democracy because of the "deficiencies and inabilities" of the citizens. We shall try to establish that computers and EDP can help change this state of affairs and especially can promote participatory democracy.

2. Potential contributions of computers

Actually, the three main sources of distrust and scepticism in democracy can in some way be considered problems of information. Therefore, since computers are machines which "deal with the very core of human society, with information, its communication and use" (Diebold, 69) and since "the aim of cybernetics is to develop a language and techniques which will enable us effectively to deal with the problem of the regulation of communication" (Wiener, 71), one can expect vital help from cybernetics in overcoming these problems. Computers can, in fact, be used to improve representative democracy; they can even be utilized to establish participatory democracy.

2.1. The improvement of representative democracy

First of all, computers and EDP can contribute to strengthening the autonomy of local government, so that it is more capable of assuming its responsibilities; its ability to provide public services to its citizens. EDP is recognized universally as an effective means for increasing the efficiency of management in public as well as private administration. EDP has already been used with success on both the levels of central and of local government (OCDE, 73). In order to evaluate the developments on this latter level we shall use a classification of computer uses borrowed from the main level of utilization identified by John Diebold (Diebold, 69b), because in contrast with other types of classification (Flanagan et al., 66; Elizur, 70; Sackman, 67) Diebold's classification concentrates on decision making.

In the first stage, the computer is used as a clerk, performing menial work characterized by a large proportion of routine: calculation of salaries of local government employees; bookkeeping of local authorities' accounts; preparation and implementation of local budgets; taxes for water and sewage; management of local taxes; and many other such necessary but routine chores (Hadas-Lebel, 73).

No doubt under particular conditions the use of EDP can increase efficiency by saving time and money and by providing better and quicker public services with less bureaucratic annoyance. However, this is not a one-sided and irresistible tendency, because what is sought is not efficiency from the point of view of the citizens securing services, but efficiency from the internal point of view of the administrative machinery.

The use of EDP to supervise and control processes constitutes the second stage of penetration. There are only a few beginnings in this field and a wide range of plans. For instance, in Israel a program is being worked out which will enable local authorities to supervise the implementation of technical and security norms in the construction of houses and buildings. This project will help local authorities fulfill a basic task which is not practicable today because they lack capability for following up the finishing of buildings and for checking if the construction answers technical and security specifications. The possibilities of this stage are very wide, and there is no doubt that they would help local authorities to regain some of their raison d'etre. Among possible utilizations is the field of local land uses and supervision of land prices, which is not only a matter of political will and determination, but also a matter of knowledge and follow-up.

The third stage is perhaps the most promising, although little experience has yet been gained in this area. In this stage computers are used as tools for planning and forecasting; for testing alternatives; and for gaining experience by simulation, making it possible to have an overview of problems and to look for better solutions.

An example of this potential contribution is displayed by the Urban Performance Model (UPM) developed in Israel. The UPM is a "predictive and distributive urban growth model and a tool for organizing and processing large amounts of metropolitan area data in a manner which predicts the effects of change in the distribution of land uses, facilities and services . . . one of the main purposes of the UPM is to assist urban decision makers in the allocation of urban resources by providing quantitative estimates of the consequences of policies and projects on overall urban performance" (UPM, 72). This model was used to test the policies under consideration by the municipal council of Tel Aviv to halt and reverse the trend to depopulation of the city's center.

Thus EDP can bolster the autonomy of local authorities by helping to improve their management and by assisting them to take advantage of the formal authority they do have. An entertaining example of this can be found in the recent initiative of an Israeli mayor who decided to break the quasi-monopoly of "Kadishah societies" over Jewish funerals. The mayor introduced a new tax – which he was entitled to do – although the new levy seemed impracticable both politically (The Interior Ministry supervising local government was in the hands of the National Religious Party) and technically (because the cost of introducing and managing this new tax was prohibitive). The mayor succeeded because he was affiliated to the Local Government Automation Corporation and was able to introduce this change at a bearable cost.

There are real opportunities for local authorities to find out new margins of effective autonomy, arming them with valuable information for their negotiations and confrontations with other authorities, especially with central authorities and public administration. Moreover the local government's ability to provide valuable public services can be raised by using EDP and computers in order to organize continuous citizen pressure and constant public checking of the operations of public bodies and the actions of authorities. The structure of EDP makes it much easier for citizens to check the decision making of public authorities, because EDP works on the basis of organized files and well-structured programs, explicit objectives and policies. If citizens and groups have access to this information – which must exist in an organized form somewhere – they will be able to follow up and check policies. In this way they will become accustomed to the practice of experimental methods and adopt a scientific attitude, a development seen by various authors as a vital condition for the survival and blossoming of democracy (Bennis, 66; Sackman, 67).

It is also possible to look toward improving the democratic process of representative democracy, especially by making arrangements to obtain more frequently the views of the citizenry on public issues and to learn the range of citizen preferences about solutions (perhaps by means of on-line voting systems). Creating new habits of democracy will perhaps lessen current fears and tensions arising from political confrontation once every four or five years.

Nevertheless, it is our conviction that despite the valuable technical improvements which may be introduced, thanks to computers, in the functioning of representative democracy, this is not enough. It will not be possible to deeply root democracy, to secure active popular support for it, and to liberate its full potential unless democracy develops into full participatory democracy. And in this respect also, EDP and computers can prove very useful.

2.2. Furthering participatory democracy

EDP can also contribute to the promotion of participatory democracy by helping to set up the conditions for an increasing and successful participation of citizens in public affairs. EDP can reveal itself as an extraordinary means to reinstate the citizens as a central factor in democratic government. In order to assess this view we shall use the four political variables identified and related by Pranger to participation in democracy: distance, space, communication, and choice (Pranger, 68).

(i) *Distance*. Generally the concept of distance is taken to mean geographical segregation between leaders and led, a problem dealt with by techniques such as deconcentration and decentralization, with very limited results – especially because the criteria of distribution between central and decentralized authorities are a matter of guess and intuition. Although in this respect computers can help us to uncover more objective rational and tested criteria, it is important to remember that the subjective distance perceived by both the governors and the governed is not less important than physical distances. If one accepts the idea that social distance is "immaterial and stems from ignorance, incomprehensibility, apathy or aversion" (Jessua, 68), it is reasonable to expect some help from computers in order to reduce ignorance and incomprehensibility at the very least, since EDP offers a means of providing, processing, and pooling data. But computers may as well contribute to reducing apathy and aversion, because the introduction of computers seems to modify the structure of organizations, enabling more cooperation and new administrative arrangements to be introduced. The tensions and strains so often associated with automation are in part caused by administrative arrangements that became inadequate as interdependence increases in an organization (Mayer, 72). Furthermore one can anticipate that computers will provide the kind of flexible technology which will enable the establishment of new organizational non-bureaucratic models, mainly to get rid of the constraints of the hierarchical Weberian model, and replace it with new trans-bureaucratic structures, such as the matrix organization formula (Shull et al., 70; Bennis, 69).

(ii) Space refers to the amount of room given, in relative terms, to participation and to power. To over-simplify it, one may assert that because politics generally is viewed quite exclusively in terms of power, similar effects are to be expected in the decision making process. The interference of groups of citizens is often perceived as an irritating phenomenon although an unavoidable one. The general tendency in public administration has been to limit and reduce the impact and the magnitude of such interferences in the name of the general interest, because they are too difficult to manage. The prospect of more extensive interferences down to the level of individuals and private citizens seem shocking and even more unmanageable. In this field the possibilities opened by EDP and various associated techniques are tremendous because it is no longer a utopia to associate a large number of citizens in the several stages of public policy making, for instance by means of the on-line voting systems already mentioned, or more generally through what Nie names the Interactive Communications Systems, which "may directly increase the flow of information and messages to government" (Nie, 70). A very crucial stage emphasized by the introduction of computers is the determination of criteria according to which decisions are taken, a stage which has to be clearly discriminated from the decision itself (Hadas-Lebel, 73). At this stage it is of decisive importance to present and clarify the expected consequences of the criteria of decisions, or of the decisions themselves. Computers can help to build representations of expected consequences, similar to what occurs when wood scaffolding is erected before construction begins, in order to sketch concretely for the neighbors what the new building will look like.

(iii) *Communication.* There are two kinds of political communication: socialization and education. Information processed by socialization is directed mainly toward the inducement of social attitudes and responses. Education puts more emphasis on learning and independent judgment. Thus, in the latter there is a more genuine tendency to secure real access to information and to dispel the veil of secrecy which covers many fields of public affairs. In this respect EDP may very soon appear as a useful tool for securing real access to information. For instance, in Israel in the last two years a municipal automatic data processing system terminal network has been developed that enables every citizen to know instantaneously the current status of his tax accounts. Tomorrow, similar techniques will enable the citizen to ask many other questions and to obtain a wide variety of information which is denied today – information about laws, rules, projects, plans and data of various kinds. The development of integrated systems of information and data banks will increase tremendously these possibilities (OCDE, 73), although this raises other problems. In any case EDP can contribute substantially to overcoming the lack of access to information, a well-known limiting factor to popular participation and democracy.

(iv) *Choice.* The concept of choice is related to decision making and public policy making, to which we referred earlier; it is included here because the formal provisions for citizen participation in the different stages of decision making is not enough to secure effective and significant interference on their part. As hinted above, citizens may be deprived of vital and basic information; moreover, they generally lack the basic knowledge and expertise to deal with the information. EDP can help the citizen not only in getting valuable information and expert advice, but also in learning about problems and the ways to solve them: in learning how to decide, how to choose with responsibility, how to make meaningful choices. In other words computers can assist the citizens in acquiring what it is alleged they are deprived of – a rational approach to dealing with public issues. In this respect, one must mention different "games" set up and tested in several places ("Perou 2000" by R. Schneider and J.A. Villegas; "Squatter City 2000", "Ghetto 1984" by J.A. Villegas and others). The prospect of millions of people being involved in the creation of their own future is truly fantastic, as sketched with gusto by Alvin Toffler in his *Future Shock*. Finally the principal contribution of computers and EDP will perhaps be to create realistic conditions for citizens to confront themselves and "interact freely as equals." EDP seems to have an equalizing power; it seems able to reduce the differences between people in their ability to be active participating citizens.

3. Conclusions

In the light of these remarks, it seems fair to expect a positive contribution from EDP to the promotion of democracy, especially at the level of local authorities. However, this prospect may be constrained by strong limiting factors. EDP's possible contribution may be limited by technical factors associated with the structure of computers and their use – such as the emergence of a new category of intermediaries who will try to impose their ideas, the high cost of EDP equipment, the risk of non-use of the equipment, and the rigidity of programming techniques.

But the main obstacles are of a social and political nature. In fact, there is a strong tendency, especially among specialists and systems designers, to view the human being as the main factor limiting the success of these techniques (Boguslaw, 65). In this, they show that they are prisoners of the techniques they are supposed to use and to control. This tendency is not confined specifically to this particular group. In our "modern" societies, technics imposes more and more its own logic. This process is not completely blind and unconscious. Some groups try to use the universal acceptance of technics, science, and rationality in order to promote structures on which their dominance in society is built. For them EDP, cybernetics, automation are useful and profitable tools.

But for the people at large, the perspective is somewhat different, and actual developments do not corroborate the enthusiastic vision of potentialities already referred to. On the contrary, today the dominant impression is that the introduction of computers is increasing centralization, turning these tools and techniques into a powerful instrument of domination in the hands of new oligarchies, which display no eagerness to relinquish it. Moreover the actual ability of EDP to increase rationality, to liberate the mind, and to promote human thinking and creativity is not established. Is it not amazing that in the most computerized society, the United States, a recent study shows an increasing proportion of Americans are certain of the existence of the devil? (Nunn, 74). And is not the extreme splitting of skills entailed and generated by the introduction of computers – in the way computers are used (Cooley, 73) jeopardizing the essence of man, his creativity and turning man into "a machine with a human envelope, a kind of cybernanthrope"? (Faure, 70).

In other words there is no "natural" trend or irresistible tendency in the contribution of computers to the promotion of democracy. On the contrary, some definite dispositions have to be taken in order to harness computers to the promotion of democracy, especially of participatory democracy. The first step to be taken is a determined stand in favor of participatory democracy and a readiness to fight for its institution. More concretely, one has to find out and look for ways to favor systematically the participation of citizens in the processes of policy making and in public affairs. This implies structural and constitutional changes which it will be wise to base upon formal social experiments in local communities. The second step is to work out data legislation, or information laws, which, taking into account the legitimate concern for secrecy, the protection of private liberties, and the prevention of thievish misuses, which will above all, enable effective access to information and data by groups, organizations, and private citizens (Lenk, 74). The third step is to give very special attention to the growing divorce between these techniques, their mythification, and the people's common sense and ability to make judgments about how their lives should be run. EDP and computer techniques should be widely diffused. Knowledge about EDP and computer techniques should be spread in a way that will strengthen the people's confidence in their thinking potential and common sense. Finally, the additional efficiency expected from the use of computers and the associated techniques should be applied first to improving the supply of public services to citizens. Efficiency has first to be considered from this point of view and decisions about acquiring computer facilities first must answer and fit into this point of view.

References

Almond, G.A. and Verba, S. (1965). *Civic Culture*. New York: Little Brown.

Bennis, G.W.(1966). *Changing Organizations*. New York: McGraw-Hill.

Bennis, G.W. (1969). The coming death of bureaucracy. In: D.I. Cleland and W.R. King (eds.), *Systems, Organizations, Analysis, Management: A Book of Readings*. New York: McGraw-Hill, pp. 11–18.

Boguslaw, R. (1965). *The New Utopians*. Englewood Cliffs: Prentice-Hall.

Catherine, R. and Thuillier, G. (1969). *Introduction a une philosophie de l'administration*. Paris: Colin.

Club Jean Moulin (1968). *Les citoyens au pouvoir*. Paris: Seuil.

Cooley, M. (1973). Rentabilisation capitaliste et chomage scientifique. In: A. Jaubert and J.H. Levy-Leblond, *(Auto) critique de la science*, Paris: Seuil.

Dahl, R. (1956). Hierarchy: democracy and bargaining in politics and economics. In: *Political Behaviour, a reader in theory and research*, Free Press of Glencoe.

Diebold, J. (1969a). *Man and the Computer*. New York: Praeger.

Diebold, J. (1969b). Bad decisions on computer use. *Harvard Business Review*.

Drago, R. (1968). *Cours de Science Administrative*, 1967–1968. Paris: Les Cours de Droit.

Elizur, D. (1970). *Adapting to Innovation, a facet analysis of the case of the computer*. Jerusalem: Jerusalem Academic Press.

Faure, E. (1970). *L'Ame du combat, pour un nouveau contrat social.* Paris: Fayard.

Flanagan, D. et al. (eds.) (1966). *Information*. Scientific American.

Hadas-Lebel, R. (1973). *L'Informatique dans l'Administration Francaise*. Paris: Editions Cujas.

Jessua, C. (1968). *Couts sociaux et couts privés*. Paris: P.U.F.

Leemans, A.F. (1970). *Changing patterns of local government.* The Hague: International Union of Local Authorities.

Lenk, K. (1974). Information protection problems facing broadband communications. In: *OECD Seminar on Data Protection*. Paris, 25–28 June, 1974.

Mayer, M.W. (1972). *Bureaucratic structure and authority*. New York: Harper and Row.

Meyer, P. (1957). *Administrative Organization – A comparative study of the organization of the public administration.* Copenhagen: Busck.

Morris, W.T. (1968). *Decentralization in management systems*. Ohio State University Press.

Mossuz, J. (1970). *Les clubs et la politique en France*. Paris: Armand Colin.

Mumford, L. (1967). *The Myth of the Machine, Technics, and Human Development*. New York: Harcourt, Brace and World.

Nie, N. (1970). Future developments in mass communications and citizen participation. In: Sackman and Nie (eds.), *The Information Utility and Social Choice*, AFIPS Press.

Nunn, C. (1974). Devil-belief rising with mood stress. *International Herald Tribune*, April 5, 1974.

O.C.D.E. (1973). *Gestion automatisée de l'informatiques dans l'administration publiques*. Paris: O.C.D.E.

Pickles, D. (1970). *Democracy*. London: Methuen.

Pisani (1969). L'importance de la décentralisation somme remède contre la technocratie. In: *Movement Communal.*

Pranger, R.J. (1968). *The eclipse of citizenship*. New York: Holt Rinehart.

Sackman, H. (1967). *Computers, System Science, and Evolving Society, The Challenge of Man-Machine digital systems.* New York: Wiley.

Shull, Delbecq and Cummings (1970). *Organizational Decisionmaking*. New York: McGraw-Hill.

Siegfried, A. and Beguin, P. (1948). *La Suisse, Démocratie témoin.* Neuchatel: LaBaconniere.

Toffler, A. (1970). *Future Shock*. New York: Random House.

U.P.M. The Urban Performance Model; General Description. (1972). R.S.A. (Research and System Analysis), Jaffa.

Wiener, N. (1971). *Cybernétique et Société.* Paris: Union générale d'éditions.

E. Mumford and H. Sackman, eds., Human Choice and Computers
North-Holland Publishing Company (1975)

THE COMPUTER AND DEMOCRACY

Françoise GALLOUEDEC-GENUYS

Centre National de la Recherche Scientifique, Paris, France

1. Introduction

The history of the world is bound up with technical discovery. Technical discoveries have had an influence on politics and have at times helped to revolutionise societies by their economic and social effects. Computer science, being the technique used for the dissemination of information, hardly contradicts this rule of thumb; indeed, since its objective is both a criterion and a condition of the democratic state, it confirms the rule. But in what ways will the changes operate? Will the principles and the methods of distributing information be completely transformed, thus creating both ease of access and ability to keep secret – both equally dangerous?

Strangely enough, our worries have been confined to the new ease of access to information and to its effect on our private lives; and this has been without any sense of proportion or reason. This conception of computer science is widely accepted, and provides that mythical aura which surrounds the electronic scientist; however, without enumerating examples of these ideas, it will be useful to investigate their causes, especially the reasons why our private lives have appeared the most threatened, while the much more serious and deep-seated problem in a *democracy* of withholding news and interfering with information received has been pushed into the background.

2. Protection of our private lives

2.1. Private lives and computers

2.1.1. It is accepted that we have such a thing as a *private life* though this conception has varied according to era, to regime, to individual. However, directly after the Second World War, an ever increasing and persistent desire to protect the individual from the multiple interferences in his private life has made itself felt in the international community – both as regards private people and private associations who may wish to pry, and as regards public authorities. If we look into our recent past, the reasons for this desire are obvious; they are no less so when we consider our present-day politics and technical abilities, although one may be permitted to have doubts, as far as the latter is concerned, as to their full relevance.

Thus, the General Assembly of the *United Nations Organization* (UNO) adopted, in 1948, the *Universal Declaration of the Rights of Man*, of which Article 12 stipulates: "No one will be the object of arbitrary interference into his or her private life, family, home, or correspondence nor of attacks upon his or her honour and reputation. Every man has the right to protection of the law from such interference and such attacks."

A very similar text was included in the International Treaty relating to Rights, both civil and political, which was passed by the vote of the General Assembly of UNO in 1966.

The European Convention for Safeguarding the Rights of Man and his fundamental liberties called by the *Council of Europe* in 1950 takes its inspiration chiefly from the Declaration of the Rights of Man in demanding in Article 8:

(1) "Everyone has the right to respect for his or her *private life*."
(2) "No public authority may infringe the exercising of this right except when this infringement is allowed by law and when it constitutes some measure which, in a democratic society, is necessary to National security, to public safety, to the economic well-being of the country, to the defence of the Law and Order and to the prevention of violations of the Penal code, to the protection of health and morals or to the protection of the rights and liberties of another."

In France, to mention only one of the European countries, a law dated 17th July 1970 has, for the first time, been put into the *Code of Civil Law* Article 9 which states thus: "Each person has the right of privacy."

If these repeated declarations simply make statutory a right which formerly was merely recognized as traditional in many countries – and still is, in a great number –there has not yet been a clear definition of what is meant by "privacy". Moreover, neither theoretical study nor jurisprudence have yet helped to enlighten us on this matter or to give us clues as to its exact meaning.

2.1.2. This lack of precision regarding the concept of privacy has not prevented an increasing sensitivity of opinion in the face of attacks on our private lives which have occurred or may occur in the future. Data banks have rapidly become the prime area for condemnation amongst the various eventual sources of danger; they are represented as monsters of an insatiable appetite, sinister holders of our most intimate secrets, and providential supporters of dictatorial and police-ridden regimes (an idea which is hardly substantiated by history or by present-day events).

Are there any technical reasons for this quite subjective fear? They appear to be weak ones, except that computer science has been used to underline and reveal a state of things which existed before. One cannot accuse the computer of being the origin of the art of compiling personal files nor of the dangers these files might expose individuals to. Ought we to lay at the computer's door the responsibility for the vast increase of such files and for the ensuing exacerbation of the dangers? For example, one can quote just the most recently proclaimed perils: the celebrated centralised filing system on all the populace and the international links of such systems; the immediate compilation of complete dossiers on every individual and the uncontrolled distribution of these dossiers; or, lastly the unreliability of the facts in the dossiers and their perennial ability to harm the individual.

Certainly, computer science does increase temptation; but at the same time, it offers us unrivalled means for protecting ourselves. It is too easily forgotten that computer's freedom of action is only that of the men who use it. Indeed, the computer is often only the alibi for desires which fear to reveal themselves openly.

2.2. Private lives and politics

2.2.1. The feeling of fear which becomes concentrated around data banks containing dossiers on the individual has arisen through factors other than technological progress. It is the expression of the major crises of our time: the crisis of tolerance, in a world where conformity imposes itself increasingly in every domain – social, economic, political; the crisis of popular confidence which especially concerns those who hold power; and the crisis of democracy whose leaders have become distant and all-powerful while the citizens are harassed, or reduced to passive acquiescence.

It is interesting to note that assaults on our private lives have been generally blamed more on the State than on private enterprises in so far as data banks are concerned; as though the contract which ties the individual to such private enterprises constituted a sufficient guarantee to his or her privacy, while any interfering State organisation has been considered incapable of respecting its undertakings.

2.2.2. In fact, the deep causes of anxiety aroused by the collection of information in these personal files – and I do not here wish to judge whether or not they are well founded – do most certainly not justify the almost unanimous restriction to the area of our private lives.

Now it is a fact that certain states which are deeply concerned with this problem are only campaigning actively as regards this particular area. And the international organisations such as the UNO, the OECD and the Council of Europe have all stressed this same point while leading their crusades for the *Rights of Man* and while multiplying their words of warning about the misuse of technological advances.

This similarity of approach is revealing – it shows that all of these organisations have the same motivation. There is nothing more natural, nothing easier than to mobilise public opinion in defence of privacy against the computer. Peoples' sensitivity is delicate in this matter: our private lives are our concern day by day, indeed, they remain for many of us the last bastion of individual freedom, the last right in our democracies to uphold against outside interference, either by individuals or by the state. Besides, this concept fits in perfectly with the predominant liberal ideology; it satisfies an endemic distrust of everything modern. This well-advertised campaign has allowed all our attention to be directed to this one aspect and to conceal the other eventual dangers of computer science such as an increasing imprecision of information, along with a major development in the means of information which ought to provide more knowledge of our society and a greater ability to participate in its government.

We can see already that this campaign contains within itself the seeds of its own inadequacy; especially as its results have, at times, overstepped the wishes of some of us. On the one hand, studies undertaken to ensure protective legislation for our private lives have brought out into the open certain difficult or embarrassing problems: for example, who should choose which files to be inspected – should they be the information files in which case there would be a risk of creating inequalities, stagnation and fraud; or should they be just those files which reveal dangerous traits in an individual – but how could one identify them? Or perhaps just the public files – and then, should it be all of them, with no exceptions, not even those needed by the police?

Then again, how should one inspect the files? Should it be an impartial inspection of all the facts given? Should it be after the event (or the judgement) or before? Will it involve public statements, prohibitions, sanctions, and, if so, of what nature? Finally, who will be entrusted with such a job? A specialized institution? Drawn from the legal profession or from state administration?

On the other hand, these same studies have emphasized the instability of a problem which is in any case far from being defined, and the need, in order to achieve a satisfactory solution, for a generalized set of rules about secret information: this would be the charter for all information media in democratic states, under regimes which remain the supreme guarantee of individual liberties and of privacy.

3. Future action with regard to information

Democracy consists of a balance between authority and liberty, between the demands of society and the needs of men, which they themselves determine and control. In a world of continual and rapid evolution, this balance varies according to necessity; it is this democratic *power* which guarantees its continuity and limits its prerogatives, which decides what is and what is not to be regarded as "secret" when considering information.

3.1. Information and law

Secrecy is not, in fact, an absolute; secret material – and indeed public material – does not exist as such because of its nature, but rather because of convention. For example, the secrecy accorded to the individual or to the doctor's patient, or to the subjects of any administration, is a result of a privileged contract between two or more persons: it confines certain pieces of information to particular persons who take it upon themselves to refuse to reveal them outside the authorised circle or beyond the predetermined aims. If one looks at it this way, there is no such thing as a private life on its own. Democracy insists on a frank and clear display of state affairs in order that its citizens may be able to judge the political programmes carried out and their elected and responsible governments. The need for secrecy itself postulates a law which will determine in what fields it holds sway and to what extent; the content and sanctions for its application, and finally, at the same time what rights there will be to any information.

3.1.1. Immediately, we can understand why there have been demands both for greater secrecy and better means of information – demands which are interconnected and by no means contradictory – and their links with computer science. This science has not altered the right to secrecy, but rather its application. It has permitted the forming of infinitely more accurate systems of information than those systems termed "manual". If it is easy to read a dossier, to act on one's own, without leaving any trace of one's action – and thus to break confidences without risk, it is certainly a very different matter when the facts are stocked in a computer's memory. Then, any fraudulent consultation presumes a special knowledge of the machine and operations which are simply detected, often implying the activating of powerful levers or the help of compromising underlings: all serious obstacles to the theft of personal files. Moreover, there are all sorts of technical methods of prevention and control which protect the access to the computer and to its memory banks; and these methods are continually being improved.

Thus the right to secrecy may well be more respected; but at the same time, there is a greater risk of our seeing established a "secret of fact". Without mentioning the mystique which surrounds the computer and extends to everything concerning it, computer science creates constraints which are favourable for the withholding of information. Thus, the change in the form in which data are expressed makes necessary new and relatively expensive technical knowledge and means before they can be interpreted; it means that, in order to understand them, they have to be presented together with their sources and their methods of treatment, and the models and programmes used when they were collected initially; it tends to dispense with the usual procedures of editing and sale of information and leads to a concentration of information in new centres, which, for various reasons, will be able to impose conditions upon access such that they will limit or prohibit the diffusion of formerly public documents.

This new restriction in access to information, the risk of an unreasonable proliferation of secret material, more than ever before calls for an exact recognition of the rules and of the practice of secrecy, so that we can be better assured of their implementation and so that those modifications considered necessary can be introduced.

3.1.2. It is in this domain that imprecision and incoherence arise. For both technical and political reasons which are obvious, this state of affairs can not be continued for long. For it constitutes not only a danger for secrecy as such, but also a hindrance to the adequate dissemination of data which it is vital to improve. We all know how much various administrative bodies in all countries are separated from each other and how jealous they become of their information, often to the detriment of good management, to the disrespect of the law, to the inequality of our citizens; we all know how both the administrators and the administrated aspire to a greater explicitness in public affairs. Revelations of lack of trust, and of scandalous deceptions are only the extreme manifestations of a legitimate desire for the truth on all our parts. So recourse to computer science involves the risk of perpetuating pernicious attitudes while, at the same time, suggesting ways to improve them. It would be wrong not to profit by technical innovations and not to seize the opportunity they offer us to revise the right to secrecy and to develop the right to information. Sweden has shown us the way; the Swedish government has carefully thought out the measures necessary to respect the principle – accepted since 1766 in that country – of public knowledge of official documents when these are banked in a computer's memory, and the new problems of protecting our private lives when data banks are used to assemble certain individual data. A law to this effect was promulgated on the 1st May 1973.

3.2. Information and truth

However, would it not be right to go further and ask ourselves about information itself in this new computer era?

3.2.1. If the constitution of data banks and their reliability presuppose a very active control of the quality of data provided – a control which the computer itself allows us to improve upon – full use of such banks and their economic value encourage us both to rationalize them, to harmonise the data themselves and to centralize the collection of data. The cost of these data banks, the vast needs of power which they represent, tend to the monopolisation of information by a few powerful groups, and principally by the State. The state's intervention, under cover either of giving aid, or of a need for rationalization, will give it the authority, besides, to control all information, if indeed it does not withhold it entirely. It is significant in this regard to consider the dissemination of economic information.

3.2.2. It is not difficult to imagine the eventual consequences of such practices and of such an overlording: inevitably, information will be both partial and patchy, and we will not even be able to contest its truth. What would a decentralisation of the powers of decision mean in such conditions, even if there were widely dispersed terminals giving access to the central computer? What would remain of democracy?

The safeguard of the freedom of information which is not just an empty formality is one of the grave questions of our time and it is in need of urgent attention if we are not to see the right to information, but lately recognized, go by the board. The creation in every country of "a central bureau whose duty would be to draw up a blueprint for the dissemination of information, a coordinating service which must enjoy the trust of the executive power but . . . must be completely independent of all political parties or leaders" has been proposed by the OECD. No doubt, we can conceive of other such means, but it is essential that we find the right one soon.

4. Conclusion

The exercise of any democracy depends on the techniques that democracy employs, but democracy itself is in the hands of the men who choose it as a way of life. If we are to preserve it and strengthen it in a world of new and ever-changing techniques, we shall have to discover appropriate solutions to the problems raised by them. Does the computer threaten to undermine our private lives, our individual liberties, is it going to deny our access to information, in short – to corrupt democracy? The answer will not come from computer science which only advises us, allows us to do things hitherto impossible, but never decides. Computer science is a tool in the hands of the human beings who use it and subject to their will and thus to the will of all of us. Do we wish to continue to live democratically? Let us then seize the opportunity that computer science has offered us.

Bibliography

Braibant, G. (1971). La protection des droits individuels au regard du développement de l'informatique. *Journées juridiques franco-nordiques,* 24–27 Octobre.

Braibant, G. (1970). L'informatique dans l'administration (introduction). *Cahiers de l'Institut francais des sciences administratives,* Paris, Cahier No. 4, 5–15.

Caldwell, L.K. (1968). *Science, Technology and Public Policy.* A selected and annotated Bibliograph (vol. 1), Indiana, pp. 207–210.

Conférence sur l'ordinateur, la vie privée et la liberté d'information, Kingston (Canada), 21–24 Mai, 1970 (notamment les exposés de C.C. Gotlieb, H. Lawford, D.F. Parkhill).

Dunn, E.S. (1967). The idea of a national data center and the issue of personal privacy. Am. Statis. 21: 21–27.

Gallouédec-Genuys, F. (1971a). "L'informatique et les libertés", La Documentation Française, Problèmes politiques et sociaux, no. 55, Janvier 1971, 48 p.

Gallouédec-Genuys, F. (1971b). Participation à la table ronde sur "le droit aux secrets". *l'Informatique*, Avril 1971, pp. 58–68.

Gallouédec-Genuys, F. (1971c). Problèmes juridiques posés par l'utilisation des banques de données. *Bulletin de L'I.R.I.A.*, no. 9, Novembre 1971, pp. 45–52.

Gallouédec-Genuys, F. (1972a). L'administration et les administrés devant le secret. *Informatique et gestion*, no. 40, Août–Septembre 1972, pp. 45–50.

Gallouédec-Genuys, F. (1972b). Informatique et secret dans l'administration. *Revue internationale des sciences administratives*, no. 2, pp. 141–148.

Gallouédec-Genuys, F. (1973a). Le secret et l'information. *Le Monde*, 20 Septembre 1973, p. 36.

Gallouédec-Genuys, F. (1973b). Le droit des fichiers: cas français et propositions générales. In: *I.B.I. - I.C.C. World conference on Informatics in government*, Amsterdam.

Gallouédec-Genuys, F. (1973c). *Le maintien de la protection des documents confidentiels*. A paraître dans la collection "Etudes d'informatique", O.E.C.D.

Gallouédec-Genuys, F. (1973d). L'informatique et la décision administrative. Institut international des sciences administratives, Septembre 1972, 14 p.; Avril 1973, 28 p. Juillet 1973, 38 p.; Octobre 1973, 10 p.

Gallouédec-Genuys, F. (1974). De l'influence de l'informatique sur la centralisation/-decentralisation de l'Administration. Institut international des sciences administratives (Congrès de Mexico), Juillet 1974, 22 p.

Gotlieb, C.C. and Borodin, A. (1971). *Social Issues in Computing*. New York.

Hoffmann, L.J. (1969). Computers and Privacy: a survey, *Computing Surveys*.

Laroque, P. (1969). L'ordinateur et les libertés publiques, *Congrès international "Gestion automatisée et humanisme"*, A.F.C.E.T., Paris.

Maisonrouge, J.G. (1973). *L'ordinateur menace-t-il la liberté individuelle?* Conférence à l'Académie des Sciences morales et politiques, Paris.

Mehl, L. (1970). L'informatique juridique et les droits de l'homme. *Revue de Droit contemporain*, Paris, no. 1.

O.E.C.D., Etudes d'informatique, Paris, no. 1, 1971 (Thomas, U.) no. 4, 1973 (Lenk, K.); no. 4, 1973 (Pipe, R.).

Rapport présenté par le Ministère des Communications et le Ministère de la Justice, *L'ordinateur et la vie privée*, Ottawa, 1972, 239 p.

Report of the Committee on Privacy (Ch. Kenneth Younger), London, 1972.

Report of the Secretary's Advisory Committee on Automated Personal Data Systems, U.S. Department of Health, Education and Welfare, *Records Computers and the Rights of Citizens*, Washington, 1973, 346 p.

Sackman, H. and Norman, N. (1970). *The Information Utility and Social Choice.* AFIPS Press, Montvale, N.J.

Ware, W.H. (1967). Security and privacy in computer systems. *Proc. AFIPS Joint Computer Conf.* 30: 279–282.

Westin, A.F. (1967). *Privacy and Freedom*. New York:

Westin, A.F. and Baker, M.A. (1972). *Data Banks in a free society*. New York.

E. Mumford and H. Sackman, eds., Human Choice and Computers
North-Holland Publishing Company (1975)

COINOCRACY – A GROUP-STRUCTURED DEMOCRACY

Poul SVEISTRUP

University of Copenhagen, Copenhagen, Denmark

1. Introduction

The theme of the conference is Human Choice and Computers.

The problem is to make human choice more humane.

The question is whether this old problem has been made more difficult or easier to solve by the computer.

The problem is old and well-known and not caused by the computer.

It is due to a growing complexity of modern communities, which has made the existing steering systems – democracies as well as autocracies – inefficient. Several ways have been tried to solve the problem by giving more influence and more power to technocracies and bureaucracies, but it seems more and more evident that this is not a real and durable solution. First of all because it does not make human choice more humane.

It is essential that common people and people in common make the choices, i.e. take part in the decision processes of the steering systems. But it must be realized that the fulfilment of this requirement will add to the already growing complexity of modern communities. Thus the crucial point is that the problem can only be solved if we are able to overcome the growing complexities of our communities. Not in the way taken by most technocrats or bureaucrats, namely by reducing complexity through making systems inflexible and oversimplifying solutions. But in a new way, by a new type of . . .-cracy – I call it coinocracy – which makes systems not only more complex but at the same time more flexible and more steerable.

In systems design we have to recognise that complexity is due to a need for flexibility and not just to technical inefficiency. We must find new structures which make our communities more flexible and more steerable, and in this search the computer may be the tool. Instead of considering the computer as a threat to humanity, we shall see it as the tool which is indispensable for a solution of the main problem of modern societies, namely the problem of growing complexity.

If we do not succeed in finding new flexible and steerable structures we run a great risk of getting a systems-paralysis. Lack of flexibility will produce a type of stability which is unstable because it will cause dangerous tensions and challenges which sooner or later will lead to an explosion. A centralized manipulative technocratic control system may postpone the crisis, but the final chaotic state is unavoidable.

The problem of making human choice more humane is not easy to solve. But it has to be solved, and to be able to discuss the phrase "to make human choice more humane" in a meaningful way, we have to find out what human beings consider as humane, i.e., we have to study human feelings and ideas to find out what people really need and want. Of course we cannot expect to find a simple set of goals and objectives which express human needs, wants and ideas, because a most essential need is not to be told by others what one should want or think.

What we have to do is to formulate a very general and common ideology, which can cover all essential ideas necessary for human choice. The ideology must be so common and general that it can cover even conflicting ideas and wants. It should never be required of an ideology, that only one rational choice is possible. That is simply not humane. Human choice cannot be a simple rational choice, but has to be a result of a decision process in which all human beings interested in that specific choice may take part, and in which all relevant arguments have to be used in the reasoning and disputation.

2. Human choice – a decision process

Choice is a decision process. More or less conscious. More or less organized. More or less formalized. But if we want to use the computer, it has to be formalized, and therefore organized and conscious too. That is in my opinion the most essential impact of computers on man and society.

The problems of choice are:

(a) how to find and formulate the alternative possibilities to choose among,

(b) how to find the right possibility, i.e. the best or most relevant possibility, and

(c) who shall do it, i.e. who shall formulate the alternatives and who shall make the choice.

The variety of realistic and relevant possibilities has grown due to the computer. But the new possibilities are not well-known, not well-described, and in many cases not even seen as relevant. The main reason for this is, that the computer makes it possible to operate and to steer more complex systems, but that the steering models for such systems have not yet been designed and discussed seriously. This is because it has not been worth while up to now to try to design systems which require a computer to be implemented. A possibility must be regarded as realistic to be treated seriously. If not it is only utopian. And most ideas about computerized societies are still regarded as utopian.

The difficulty in most industrialized countries is a growing complexity, which causes problems because the traditional steering systems in both the private and the governmental sectors have lost control. Some traditional thinking people believe that control may be reestablished by making systems – the structure of society – less complex. Some of them will do it by centralizing in a more autocratic and bureaucratic system. Others by reducing governmental control drastically in a super-liberal system. Only very few people have realized that the computer makes it realistic to operate very complex systems with very decentralized structures.

To make human choice possible most systems have to be changed – and the change itself should be possible inside the system if evolution is preferred to revolution. That is, the flexibility of social systems has to be increased to allow for the possibility of changes in social structure. However, not all possible structures of such systems can be catered for because this is neither realistic nor relevant.

The computer makes such flexibility a realistic possibility. The real challenge of the computer is therefore to design and implement systems which are able to create new variety – in life and in the community. But to do that we must know more about what kind of variety may be needed, or – in other words – what variety is most relevant. However, we can never know enough to design the ideal amount of variety. Hence, systems mutations may be allowable.

To understand how this may be possible we must see the structure of a community primarily as a structure of communication. If the right to communicate is free and unrestricted the structure of the community cannot be fixed and stable. Using the computer as a tool of communication the flexibility of the computer may increase the degree of freedom in the structure of the community.

The question is, however, freedom for whom? Will it be freedom for all or only for the specialists – the technocrats? To be able to talk about human choice and not only about "technocratic" choice it is necessary that all people should be able to communicate with the computer and via the computer. As the industrial revolution was based on "homo oeconomicus" the information revolution must be based on "homo communicans". To change "homo sapiens" from "homo oeconomicus" to "homo communicans" is the real challenge of the computer. Do we really want that change, or is it – again – an unpleasant impact of a pure technological development?

I believe we want that change because we cannot make decisions in common without communicating, and common decisions should be basic to all democratic communities. How can it be satisfactory only to communicate once in a while – and not even every year – in the most primitive way, i.e. by voting in a democratic election or referendum? And how can it be satisfactory only to be able to communicate by saying "yes" or "no" to a given question by putting a cross on a voting paper?

One suggestion has been to utilize the computer in decision processing by making automatic voting systems. In my opinion that would be a misuse of the computer, because it increases the risk of manipulation and increases the power of the technocrats.

To utilize the computer in decision processing, participation should be made easier by generating more information and more alternatives through the computer. More information does not mean a greater volume of data but, on the contrary, more relevant information and less data. Today information tends to drown in a huge mass of data in the mass communication media. In computerized communication systems the process of selecting relevant information may be made easier. But it is only possible if we know the criteria of relevancy.

The problem of relevancy is a problem of argument. To be able to argue we need general and acceptable arguments, i.e. arguments which are based on generally acceptable ideas, values, aims and purposes. Such basic norms and beliefs can be called a common ideology. The function of a common ideology is to be a common frame of reference for all argument and discussion in a community. It has to contain all specific ideologies of special interest groups to facilitate communication about conflicting ideas, and all ideas have to be formalized in an operational way to make it possible to communicate in a computerized system.

If we succeed in generating a common ideology formalized in a general reference system for communication, we will be able to communicate both facts and feelings. The old claim prevailing in most existing communication systems that only facts can be communicated – and not the opinions of writers and editors – will then be recognized as a fundamental mistake, one which can facilitate manipulation.

To be able to understand a message the receiver needs argument because the content of the message depends upon the relevance of the information.

Hence, pure facts should generally be regarded as polluted information. And to avoid pollution a common ideology is needed.

Thus the crucial questions appear to be:

(a) how to formalize the concept of relevancy in a common ideology, and

(b) how to implement such ideas in new structures of a computerized community.

3. Quality of life and of community

To find and formulate a common ideology which can form the basis of human choice and of the design of the necessary computer systems – so that we can be sure they will be relevant for all of us and not only for the designers – we need to know what we want from life.

To be common the ideology has to be complex. It must contain all the different individual wants, attitudes and values if it is to be adequate as a general and acceptable reference system for communication. And ideas will be contradictory. Otherwise people cannot communicate about conflicts and in that way change a conflict from a possibly destructive state into a constructive state which leads to resolution.

A quality of life is an attribute of life. Hence, what we want of life may be expressed in terms of qualities of life. And we have to express and discuss different qualities – that is a whole pattern of attributes – among which the ability to choose, the freedom to choose and the practical possibility of making a relevant choice are very essential.

It is often claimed that the problem of human choice could be solved by setting clear goals and objectives, but that is – as all who have tried to know – impossible. We cannot formulate and formalize our wants as goals and objectives simply because beforehand we do not know what our wants are – with the exception of the most elementary ones which are self-evident. It is meaningless to ask:

what qualities of life do human beings need?

the formulation of the question must be changed to:

what qualities of live do you expect from live?, or even

what qualities of life do you want to create in life?

Life is a process and we cannot know and do not wish to know the future flow of the process. But we know that not all of the possible flows will be satisfactory. Therefore we want to be able to choose among the possible flows, and the best formulation of the question must be:

what qualities of life will form a satisfactory profile of life? To formulate a common ideology we have to discuss and evaluate the different profiles of life as patterns of changeable qualities. And in my opinion change itself is an inevitable and preferable quality of life. A satisfactory profile of life cannot be a flow of stability. It sounds contradictory. And it is. A life in which nothing happens, without challenge, without anything other than the constant repetition of the already well-known, is not a life worth living. Thus, we want change, but not forced change. We want free choice of change. We want what we feel is a relevant change.

The possibility of change is a challenge which we both want and need. But to make relevant changes we must be able to steer the process of change. So we need also systems which allow steerable changeability. That is the real challenge to systems design. However, we still have to remember that steerability is not claimed by only one human being. Systems have to be steerable by all human beings in a community. Therefore systems have to be designed on the basis of a common ideology covering all individual ideas. But even that is not enough.

The qualities of life of one human being are relative to the pattern of qualities of all other people in the community. Hence, human choice depends not only on the quality of life but on the quality of community as well. And such qualities have to be included in the ideas of a common ideology. Therefore: qualities of communities should be patterns of qualities of flows and not only a structure of stability.

It is often claimed that technical development has created the pattern of flow of today, i.e. the pattern of growth, and it is often asked: how will the human being be able to keep up with the technical development?

But growth stopped several years ago in the most developed countries. Thus the question should be: how can technology in the future move in phase with human development?

Economic statistics have not yet registered the changed pattern of development because of deficiences in statistical methods. These are partly due to the way concepts are defined in national income statistics, and partly due to the measuring and estimating techniques used with those statistics.

The factors that have stopped growth are not those usually mentioned in the literature on limits to growth, i.e. natural resources, population, capital investment and pollution. The main limiting factor is the human being himself. As trees cannot grow into the sky, so man does not want to push himself beyond any limit. In fact so many people in the most developed countries have already reached a point of stress that the patterns of flow have changed. There are two reasons for this, the accelerating speed and restlessness of modern life and the lowering of the stress boundary due to a higher level of education and more personal freedom compared to life in the old autocratic and Victorian days. So growth should not be regarded as a highly valued community quality in the most developed countries.

On the contrary growth should be replaced by flexibility, in the sense of steerable changeability as the preferred quality of community.

To increase flexibility in social systems means to increase the variety of such systems, but an increased variety implies an increased need for steering and control. To make a very flexible system steerable the steering processes must be well-structured, and the arguments in the decision processes must fit these structures. It follows from the discussion of qualities of life and communities that the design of such structures should be based on an ideology of change:

(a) Change has to be made possible because the possibility itself is desirable – not because it has to be made. It is the variety itself which is needed, not a maximum amount of change.

(b) Change should only be the consequence of a free choice, i.e. it should never be enforced on people when they do not want it.

To design and implement such systems requires more research into possible patterns of change, i.e. in planning. A plan is a pattern, and a process plan is a pattern of flow – and of change. Remember: plans are not made because they have to be followed. Plans are made because it is then easier to change plans, i.e. to change flows.

We need planning because structure creates freedom, if – but only if – the structure is flexible and steerable. Hence, planning should be based on an ideology of change. Not on an ideology of stability. The ideology of stability is based on the law of great numbers:

The law of great numbers says that the distribution of the means of different samples taken from the same population is the so-called normal distribution.

This law is well-known in stable technical systems, and it is, for example, found in the distribution of errors in measurements. From this law some people have got the idea, that it is the mean which represents the normal state and that all deviations from the mean should be regarded as errors, cf. the term mean error for the standard deviation.

An ideology of change may be based on a law of small numbers, which I suggest to be the following:

The law of small numbers says that in social systems a more uncommon state – i.e. a state with a small probability of occurrence – is a more probable basis for change than a more common state of the system.

In such systems the terms normal and error are completely misleading as the most abnormal states are in fact the most attractive when seen from the point of view of desired change, and a big error is consistent with a high variety and therefore desirable from the same point of view.

It follows that we have to find a new steering principle for the steering systems in a community based on an ideology of change. The old principle of directive steering was appropriate in an autocratic or bureaucratic system with a high degree of centralization. Now we wish to utilize the computer to design decentralized systems and the basic steering principle should be one of coordinative steering.

Directive steering requires only power. The aim of the design of the steering system is integration.

Coordinative steering requires communication and cooperation between relatively autonomous subsystems of the community. The aim of the design of the steering system is to create a coordinated whole.

The structure of a community with directive steering is a hierarchy. What is the structure of a community with coordinative steering? – Anarchy?

The answer is no, if anarchy only means chaos, but the answer may be yes, if it is possible to talk about a coordinated anarchy. As the basic ideas and principles introduced in the discussion above are the reverse or inverse of traditional ideas and principles, the structure of a community with coordinative steering may be the inverse structure of a hierarchy. Hence the question is, how to design an inverse hierarchy or coordinated anarchy.

4. The coinocracy – an inverse hierarchy or coordinated anarchy

The terms inverse hierarchy or coordinated anarchy are not easy to use in introducing a new concept of the structure of a community. The risk of misunderstanding is too great because of eventually misleading associations. I therefore suggest a new term, the coinocracy. The term is made from the Greek word for common, namely koinos, and the Greek word for power, namely kratos, cf. the ending -cracy in words like democracy or autocracy. In Greek the word koinos is used in the same way as the word common (from Latin) to create the words koinonia, which means community, and koinonikos, which means communication.

The term coinocracy is chosen to emphasize that the structure we seek has to be based on a simple principle which facilitates communication to form a community. The question is whether the communication structure will be strong enough to form the structure of a community, or – in other words –

whether the coinocracy will be able to create the power necessary to a steering system.

To facilitate communication we should recognize the fact that people communicate best in small groups. The size of such small groups can be debated, but experience tends to show that the ideal group should consist of 7 ± 2 persons. Groups with more members tend to have difficulties in communicating unless there is a formal leader using a directive steering principle, and groups with less members tend to produce strong tensions between different members because of lack of sufficient variety and flexibility in the communication.

Further the size of the ideal group seems to have some useful characteristics. If a new member is added to a group of maximum size, i.e. 9 members, one group may split into two ideal groups of minimum size, i.e. 5 members. And if a group of minimum size loses one member it may be combined with another ideal group of minimum size to form a new ideal group of maximum size. Hence the size of the ideal group gives the greatest flexibility between groups as it will always be possible for one person to change groups so that the size of a group always remains 7 ± 2. The only condition is that the population is big enough.

If we regard ideal groups as elementary systems we can design a bigger system according to the following coordination principle. Each group on the elementary level chooses one member as a representative of the group. All representatives form a population on the next level which may be structured in ideal groups (if the population is big enough). These groups may again choose representatives who form a population on the next level, and so forth until we reach a level with only one group. Of course we cannot be sure that the group on the highest level will be of the ideal size, but if that is wanted it is not difficult to introduce further restrictions to meet such a requirement.

By using this principle a tree structure is built up from below, i.e. we have created an inverse hierarchy. Will it be a coordinated anarchy too?

I can imagine it will depend – among other things – on the total size of the population. Let us look at a simple example:

If all groups consist of exactly 7 members, there will be one group on the top level, 7 groups on the second level, 49 groups on the third level and 343 groups consisting of, in total, 2401 participants on the fourth level. And so forth. If we consider a total population of – say – 2000–3000 people it may be structured in a coinocracy of 4 levels. That means that all people may belong to at least one ideal group, about 300–400 will belong to two groups (namely on the two lowest levels), about 40–60 will belong to three groups and the 7 ± 2 in the top group will belong to four groups – one on each level.

I am sure that it will be nearly impossible for 2000–3000 people to communicate effectively if the population is not structured at all. On the other hand I can imagine it will be possible to communicate effectively inside the group-structure of a coinocracy, as an individual is only required to communicate with at the most – say – 20–30 people, namely if the person belongs to the top group. If all groups consist of exactly 7 members, he has to communicate with 4 times 6 other persons, i.e. 24. I imagine it will be possible to communicate effectively even in a coinocratic structure with more levels. I do not know the upper limit of the ideal number of levels, but if we – for the sake of discussion – say that it is 7 levels, the maximum population to be structured in a coinocracy is only a few million people as $7^7 = 823\,543$ and $9^7 = 4\,782\,969$. In any case we have to take account of what usually are called smaller countries.

Now, let us return to the question of coordinated anarchy. The problem is whether people can trust their representatives – and they can do it in a higher degree than in a traditional democracy. The answer depends first of all on the effectiveness of communication in the system and the flexibility of the system.

The effectiveness of communication will depend upon the possible contact between people who need or want to communicate, and on the existence of a generally known and understandable reference system containing the necessary concepts and an adequate terminology for a common ideology and for what should be regarded as common basic knowledge. Besides these more formal requirements it must of course be assumed that people in a coinocracy are able to communicate, i.e. are able to express themselves and to understand other people by listening or reading. This seems evident but may not be taken as a generally fulfilled assumption.

The crucial point in the structure is that people are able to communicate directly or indirectly through a very few people with the members of the top group, but of course it depends upon whether the top-members are sufficiently motivated to take part in that communication. However, I am sure that the flexibility of the coinocratic structure will force them to be motivated, as people will renew their representatives or change groups if the communication does not function.

As representatives may be renewed and group change may take place whenever it is wanted general elections will not be necessary in a coinocracy. In this way the usual tactical considerations and operations before an election are avoided, and "Gallup's" will be meaningless as the attitudes of a population will be known and represented in any point of time in the actual structure of the coinocracy.

To implement a coinocracy requires:

(a) a perfect registration system which can update the structure daily, or weekly, with regard to group relations and representations, and

(b) a generally accessible information center which can facilitate the informal communication inside the system, i.e. a kind of mass communication of basic knowledge about facts and attitudes steered by the receivers and not by the senders in the communication process.

The first requirement can only be met by a manual system in a rather small population of, say, a few hundred or at most a few thousand people. In bigger populations a computerized registration system built on a data-base will be necessary. The main reason for that is the demand for flexibility and actuality in the registration of the structures which in practice can only be met by the computer. On the other hand we will get rid of general elections and assemblies. The second requirement is very difficult to meet in a manual system due to the information explosion. Only if the variety of interest in a specific coinocratic system is narrow, as it may be if we only look at small subsystems with little autonomy like, for example, education systems, it may be possible to establish an information center based on the manual media as we know them in our libraries. If the variety is greater the accessability can only be obtained through a computerized information system with a very flexible and high standard information retrieval system. Such a computerized "library" may be called a logothec.

Of course the logothecs should contain all the necessary basic knowledge for communication, and it must be emphasized that this should include data on the general attitudes of the members of the coinocracy. All members of such a community need to present themselves to all other members in order to facilitate contact between people who need or want to make contact. This basic idea of a coinocracy is however in strong contrast to the ideas of privacy in a traditional society which are based on ideas of competition and survival of the fittest and not on ideas of cooperation and coordination of different and even contradictory ideas. Thus, to implement the idea of a coinocracy demands a major change in the attitudes of most traditionally thinking people who may be afraid of living in an open and open-minded community.

To implement the idea of a coinocracy, experiments in small communities seem necessary and are perhaps the only way of selling the idea. Sceptical people always want to see the successful results of experiments, and much practical experience in the establishing and functioning of the necessary logothecs are needed. To manage such experiments the variety of interests has to be small. The crucial point is that it should not be so small that the experiment itself is without interest.

As most people are not used to taking part in democratic decision processes the implementation of a coinocracy demands a considerable and long term learning process. For that reason the first experiments with coinocracies should take place within the education system. Human choice with the computer should be introduced into schools. And not only as simple answers to silly questions.

5. Conclusions

Human Choice means for me:

(a) a conscious choice between a large and well-known variety of relevant possibilities, which include the possibility of changing the variety itself,

(b) a well-argued choice as a result of an appraisal which considers all relevant purposes and values in a common reference system,

(c) a common choice in a community as a result of a common decision process in which all people may have some influence if they wish this, and

(d) a free choice to all common people who are interested in making specific choices but who are not forced to take an active part in decisions which for them are less relevant or even irrelevant.

Thus human choice should include all decisions which imply change in qualities of life and communities relevant to a human being.

Computers mean for me:

(a) a tool of flexibility which makes more complex structures steerable in social as well as automatic systems, – but is at the same time

(b) a tool of stability which by reducing or excluding steerability increases the risk of systems-paralysis, and

(c) a tool of data-processing which facilitates the communication processes in a community through the requirement to structure both facts and attitudes in models and ideologies so as to form a common reference system for communication, – but is at the same time

(d) a tool of data-processing which makes it easier to manipulate data if we do not succeed in creating the common reference system.

Thus computers should be used in all systems where a high degree of complexity and flexibility is needed to secure a steerable changeability in the system.

Human Choice and Computers means, consequently, for me a combination of a common need for influence and of tools for communication and control, which make it feasible to introduce a more democratic structure into a society – the structure I have called the coinocracy.

The computer is used to communicate structures of facts, i.e. models, and structures of attitudes, i.e. ideologies, and to administer structures of people in groups of 7 ± 2 persons in an inverse hierarchy, where it is permitted to change group and/or attitude whenever it is desired but only if this is communicated through updating the database-system in which the coinocratic structures are registered.

The problem of this conference on Human Choice and Computers is to make HUMAN choice more HUMANE. The question is, whether this old problem has been made more difficult or easier to solve by the computer. My answer is that the problem can only be solved in a very flexible and very complex system if the system is well-structured and steerable. Thus the computer is a necessary – but not sufficient – condition for human choice.

Challenge is a necessary condition of satisfaction, but the challenge of unsolvable problems provides only stress and frustration. In a coinocracy based on an ideology of change and with computer systems of high but relevant flexibility, the problem of making human choice more humane is, in my opinion, solvable. Not easy to solve, but solvable.

In a traditional democracy or autocracy, technocracy and bureaucracy will prevail, and the problem is then not only more difficult to solve by computer, but probably unsolvable.

Thus to reduce stress and frustration people have to take a chance, accept a challenge, and make the human choice of a coinocracy.

May the future impact of the computer be the relaxed community.

SOCIAL CHOICE AND COMPUTERS

E. Mumford and H. Sackman, eds., Human Choice and Computers
North-Holland Publishing Company (1975)

COMPUTERS, PERSONAL PRIVACY AND HUMAN CHOICE

Willis H. WARE

The Rand Corporation, Santa Monica, Calif., U.S.A.

1. Introduction

While computer technology influences society in very broad ways, its effects have been largely invisible to society at large until recent years. For example, the application of computers to scientific and engineering chores in the 1950's could be perceived only through the impact on research and engineering design. More recently, notably in the 1960's, data systems have been widely introduced into organizations for the conduct of business, but even here the effects of such usage are often apparent only to people within the business itself. In each case, it is important to note that the individual who used the computer for scientific or engineering purposes or interfaced it in the course of his job, became accustomed to the intricacy, complication and awkwardness that any given system might have.

In the late 1960's and the 1970's, information systems have been introduced that interact directly with a large segment of the public, e.g., billing systems, magazine subscriptions, financial accounting systems. For the first time, a large cross-section of the public saw personally the behavior and effect of a computer-based system. There have been expressed extensive concern about the dehumanizing effect, the impersonal interface and, when the application is to factory or office automation, there has also been concern about the lack of job satisfaction or unacceptable working conditions. Moreover, as personal information in such systems is used more and more widely, there is the ever-increasing risk that people will be harmed by the operation of the system.

Thus, society at this point in time needs to achieve a balance among (a) the needs for information of management and an organization for the conduct of business; (b) the needs of people who in the course of their daily job will interact directly with some computer system; (c) the needs of people that will be affected by the system whether they interact with it or not; and these collectively are subject to the pragmatic constraint that the technical feasibility and economic acceptability must be satisfied.

This is not the first time that society has grappled with the consequences of a new technology. It has, for example, over a very long period of time learned how to live with fire as a natural phenomenon and the broad technology based on it. We have learned how to exploit the advantages of fire, while protecting society from harm by such means as fire insurance and fire departments. For such protection, society has implicitly agreed to pay, either as an individual through insurance premiums or collectively through taxes. Analogous protective mechanisms must now be found with respect to personal harm that can ensue from the operation of computer-based information systems, but there is a significant difference from previous occasions. The introduction of information systems has been moving very fast and will continue to do so because there is ample reason for society, industry, commerce and government to need them to process their voluminous information demands.

While computer technology per se is in its third decade, the application of that technology to information systems that broadly influence and affect people is a development of the last 10 years at most. Thus, the present performance of such systems and the concerns that are raised about them reflect the collective state of understanding – or level of ignorance – of organizations that need and commission the design of such systems, the technologists who implement such systems and the people who run them. Nearly all personal information computer systems are first generation ones in the sense that there has not yet elapsed sufficient calendar time for successive cycles of improvement. Furthermore, the historical pattern has been that an organization that wished to use a computer would abdicate the responsibility for the detailed design to computer experts that were retained to implement it. Thus, the resulting system reflected the technologists' own perception of system requirements as well as the level of understanding that existed at the time of design. When the final product did not culminate as the management or organization expected, there was, of course, disillusionment, recrimination and costly revisions.

Some of what has often been called poor performance on the part of computer technologists is rather the inability of organizations and management to communicate concisely and clearly what is wanted. The situation, of course, is changing rapidly and improving. System designers have accumulated substantial insight and experience with the design and behavior of their product. Organizations and managers have learned to better formulate and communicate their wishes. However, what has not yet developed is a mechanism for people affected by the operation of a system to express their needs, their views and their concerns over the very existence of the system and the way it functions. A very important aspect of the interface between information systems that deal with personal information and the people that they affect is the so-called invasion of personal privacy.

2. The problem

In many Western countries but certainly in the United States, the individual citizen is surrounded by record-keeping and data systems that contain extensive personal information about him. Many such systems are computer based; but others are still manual or just being converted to a computer basis. Relative to the balance of power between himself and the totality of data systems that surround him, the citizen finds that he is increasingly in a position of significant disadvantage.

The proliferation of record systems has come to pass (a) partly because of the increasing size of population and the sheer necessity to keep track of people; (b) partly because of the demand for services that society now makes on government; (c) partly because of the need for improved efficiency in the conduct of government; and (d) in business, because of size and complexity, and for economic reasons. Contemporary computer technology provides society with the tool that it needs to accommodate growing information requirements, not only for the conduct of government but also for industry and commerce.

The use of computer-based data systems is not limited to the things that used to be done manually. Increasingly, data per se is becoming an item of commerce and a growing industry is discovering that substantial profit can be made from sale of its product. Increasingly, personal information is finding its way into diverse uses that were not anticipated when it was collected originally; consequently, such other exploitation does not imply the explicit or implicit consent of the data subject for such use. This paper addresses the relation between data banks and personal privacy, especially as the issue is now developing in the United States.

3. Privacy in record-keeping

Personal privacy often connotes the right to be left alone; the right to withdraw from the influence of one's environment; or the right to be secluded, secret or private. In any of these senses, invasion of privacy implies the intrusion of some aspect of one's environment into his solitude. Relative to record-keeping systems, however, privacy has a somewhat more precise meaning. An individual has given personal information to a record-keeping system for some purpose. Usually this is because he expects in exchange some right, privilege, benefit, or opportunity. Conversely, the organization that holds personal data does so for some purpose; for example, it must administer a public assistance program, or operate a teaching institution, or maintain an inventory of some set of people such as property holders, military reserves, or wanted persons.

The individual, in his action to provide personal information, does so with the expectation that it will be used for the purpose for which he gave it. It is his implicit expectation that such information will be used in his best interest and certainly not in any way to his detriment. He does not expect to be annoyed, pressured, harassed, or harmed by its use. Thus, the holder of personal information and the individual have a *mutual* interest in the proper use of such information. Neither should have unilateral control over its use.

The sense, therefore, in which this paper addresses personal privacy relates to the interface between an individual and any record-keeping system that holds personal information on him. Personal privacy implies the expectation by the data subject that information about himself will be used in his best interest and in no way contrary to his expectations. Thus, invasion of privacy implies that the holder of personal information has misused it to the detriment of one or more individuals, or has exploited it in some fashion other than for the purpose for which collected.

The nub of the issue today in the United States is that the "data owner" has one-sided control over the use of personal information. Except in isolated categories of data, the individual has nothing to say about the use of information that he has given about himself or that has been collected in other ways. In particular, an organization can acquire data for one purpose and use it for another; e.g., perhaps for its own bureaucratic end, perhaps for financial return, perhaps for harassment and perhaps for combining with other data to create more extensive records on individuals. What is worse, the data owner can do such things without consulting or informing the data subject.

4. Computer security

Shoulder to shoulder with the privacy issue stands the related one of computer security. The two need to be carefully distinguished. The goal of protecting personal privacy is to assure that personal information is used properly. Therefore, it follows that information must be protected within the information system that stores and manipulates it, be it computer-based or manual; furthermore, it must be released only to authorized users. Protection of information within a computer-based system is commonly called "computer security" and for the purposes of this discussion, it will be defined as: (a) the protection of a computer system per se and the information within it against accidental or deliberate damage, (b) providing such information only to authorized users, and (c) doing so on a timely basis.

In the sense as defined, computer security is a necessary aspect for assuring privacy, but, of itself, is not sufficient. In particular, the users served by a computer-based record system are not considered part of the security problem.

By now, it is reasonably well understood how to provide computer security (Anderson, 72; Turn and Peterson, 67; Ware, 67). In particular, it is understood that:

(a) Physical safeguards such as locks, fire protection, water protection, etc., are needed to prevent damage to the equipment and its associated information.

(b) Computer hardware safeguards such as memory-protect, a non-user mode, etc., must be provided to implement an access control mechanism between user and computer file, and to isolate users from one another.

(c) Software safeguards such as a file access control scheme must be provided to create, in conjunction with hardware, a protective barrier between a user and data files to which he is not authorized while permitting him access to those for which he is.

(d) Communication safeguards must be provided when necessary to assure secrecy of information when in transit over communication channels.

(e) Personnel safeguards such as background checks, bonding, training, and disciplinary actions are required to minimize potential leakage of information due to an individual's actions.

(f) An administrative and management overlay must be created that oversees all aspects of the security safeguard system; inspects, tests and audits them; and controls movement of people, magnetic discs, magnetic tapes, paper, etc.

Thus, within a fence that conceptually surrounds the security problem, one finds the computer itself, its software and application programs, its communication circuits, its terminals, its files such as discs and tapes, maintenance people associated with the system for both hardware and programs and the operational people.

5. Privacy related to security

A record system is created to serve some set of users; moreover, a record system that contains personal information is created to influence some right, benefit, privilege or opportunity for an individual. So long as such information is used properly, all is well; but, if it is not, then an individual may find himself without a job, publicly ridiculed, with a damaged reputation, harassed, pressured, in an extreme case blackmailed, or having lost some right, privilege, benefit, or opportunity. Thus, as contrasted with the computer security problem described above, the privacy problem relates to the individual's perception of how information is used to influence him; in a larger sense, to the extent and comprehensiveness of the information collected about him; and in the fullest sense, to these matters measured against his social environment.

6. Users of records

Between the individual and the record system are the users that the system is designed to serve. One such class contains the legitimate users who include people authorized to have information from the system; this implies that such information is required to perform some job. A second class contains the malicious users who are perhaps unknown or hidden, and deliberately attempt to penetrate the record-keeping system to pirate information for some purpose. It is against them, of course, that computer security safeguards are erected and intended to be effective. However, the legitimate user does not have to act properly; he clearly can acquire information on a presumably authorized basis but pass it to a third party for some private purpose, e.g., financial gain, spite, ideological conviction, or a favor. By doing so, he can cause one or more individuals to suffer loss of job, public ridicule, embarrassment, or some other damage. Against the misbehaving legitimate user of a record-keeping system, there is not now in the United States an adequate set of restraints nor legal mechanisms to deter undesired action. Furthermore, to the extent that computer security controls do not completely stop the malicious user, there is likewise no adequate mechanism to provide redress to the harmed individual. Thus, the system user is an important interface between a record system and the individuals intended to be influenced by it. On one hand, he confronts the computer security safeguards of the system and with the other, potentially threatens the privacy of the individual.

7. Dimensions of the issue

The computer security matter is largely a technical and management one, whereas the privacy matter is largely a legal one, certainly in the sense with which the term "privacy" is used here. Thus, there is a need to construct a set of legal safeguards so that the individual citizen has some leverage over owners and operators of data banks and such that the individual citizen has legal recourse should he be harmed by the operation of a data bank. The question is: "What is an appropriate legal structure and how should it be implemented?"

Is this a real problem? Unfortunately, there is not now a documented comprehensive record of the extent to which individuals are harmed by data systems. In the United States, the Fair Credit Reporting Act (U.S. Code, 70) does provide the individual citizen with certain rights relative to the so-called consumer reporting data banks, but there is little published data concerning the economic impact of this act on the credit reporting industry. For example, the consumer is given the privilege to inspect his record, to contest its accuracy and to cause it to be corrected. Moreover, he is given the privilege to be informed when certain negative actions against him are taken on the basis of information in such a data bank. However, even for this industry that already functions under constraints, there has not been assembled a documented record of how many individuals challenge records in such data banks, or of how many individuals are wrongfully denied some privilege because of information in it. While there are many anecdotes and word-of-mouth stories describing specific instances in which an individual is harmed, it is generally felt that the problem is real and, in some countries at least, popular sentiment has been substantial.

Lacking documented evidence of the extent of the problem, there are still several important points to be noted.

(a) In the United States, there is no way for an individual to discover what data banks hold information on him and what information each contains. Every citizen knows of obvious ones that he expects to exist, e.g., military records, social security records, census records, health records, financial transaction records; but there are also hidden and unknown ones that he does not know about. Some that have come to light are a master insurance industry data bank, criminal history records, police intelligence records, and various data files of government.

(b) Even if the citizen should find out that he is in some data bank, in most instances, there is no way for him to cause it to be affected. Furthermore, should he discover a system holding information on himself, there is no way for him to control the use of such information. Once it has been acquired, the data owner uses it as he sees fit.

(c) In the United States, the bulk of such personal information is subject to court-ordered seizure, e.g., by subpoena or court-writ. Only in the case of census information, certain public health data and a few other categories is there any legal protection of personal information. Even in special categories, the protection is often not absolute and only partial.

Thus, as of now, the citizen of the United States is at a disadvantage relative to the totality of data banks that surrounds him and influences his life. Decisions to implement new data banks or to extend old ones, to exploit personal information, or to use personal information already held in a new way, are made by government agencies or private organizations for their convenience, efficiency or professional preference, not necessarily with the interests or concern of the data subject or society in mind. How can a comprehensive umbrella of legal protection be erected to assure personal privacy in this situation?

8. Approaches

There are several options for a framework of legal controls, some of which are already in use within the United States.

(A) Special legislation could be created for each category of problem that is identified. The Fair Credit Reporting Act is such an example (U.S. Code, 70). It reflects the concern of Congress with the behavior of the consumer reporting industry and with potential risks to individuals from the operation of this industry. This approach has the disadvantage that it deals with the problem after the fact; it waits for the difficulty to develop before acting. It implies retrofits and modifications to the data systems themselves and represents a piece-meal remedy to the larger problem.

(B) There are already in the United States a number of industries that are government-regulated, e.g., banking, communications, transportation. A variation of the first approach would be to amend all such regulatory acts to include appropriate safeguards for personal privacy; there already is some protection in communication legislation. This approach has all of the disadvantages of (A) above, and in addition has the shortcoming that it does not, of itself, encompass situations where regulation is presently absent.

(C) A federal-level regulatory body could be created that controls, licenses, and oversees data bank operations and the use of personal information. Sweden has already adopted this approach (Sweden, 73; Computer Decisions,

73). The Swedish Data Act provides for a Data Inspection Board that licenses, regulates, controls and disciplines all "personal registers" which are defined to be any automatic data processing system that deals with identifiable personal information. This Board has complete control over non-government data banks but only an advisory relation with government data banks. Its object is to make certain that [personal registers do not] "cause undue encroachment on privacy".

The regulatory approach can certainly provide the necessary protection if regulation per se is acceptable. There is a residual concern that regulation will impede progress or will stand in the way of exploiting data banks and data processing for societal good. It is also to be noted that at least in the United States, regulation tends to be used only where there is a monopoly or oligopoly situation, where there is a scarce or public resource that must be allocated (e.g., electromagnetic spectrum), where public resources are required for operation (e.g., transportation), or where substantial damage to the public at large or at least a large segment of it potentially exists (e.g., banking). Regulation is not normally used as a mechanism to deter crimes against the individual, but it should not be ruled out summarily as a means to contain privacy regulation.

9. A code of fair information practice

A different approach to the subject was conceived by a Special Advisory Committee that presented its findings to the Secretary of the Department of Health, Education and Welfare in the Summer of 1973 (Department of Health, Education and Welfare, 73). The recommendation of this body is to create, by legislation, a Code of Fair Information Practice that would define the desired behavior of a data bank, the desired relation between the data subject and the data bank and establish certain rights for the citizen. It rests on these basic principles.

(a) There must be no personal data record-keeping systems whose very existence is secret.

(b) There must be a way for an individual to prevent information about him that was obtained for one purpose from being used or made available for other purposes without his consent.

(c) There must be a way for an individual to see, correct or amend a record of identifiable information about him, and to find out how it is used.

(d) Any organization creating, maintaining, using, or disseminating records of identifiable personal data must assure the reliability of the data for their intended use and must take precautions to prevent misuse of the data.

The Code would deter the misuse of personal information by stipulating that any deviation from the Code would be an abuse of personal information subject to criminal and civil sanctions, recovery of punitive and actual damages, and injunctive relief. The Code, as recommended, would be implemented by a series of safeguards, the collective effect of which is to specify the preferred behavior and method of operation of data banks and to describe the rights and privileges of the individual citizen relative to them.

The safeguards suggested by the Committee are similar in the broad sense to those incorporated in the Swedish Data Act and to those identified by various other studies of the privacy issue. For example, one safeguard would require an annual public notice that is intended to inform the public at large as to the name of a record system, its nature and purpose, its data sources, the categories of data maintained, the organizational policies and practices regarding data storage, etc.

A second set of safeguards would stipulate the behavior of the organization maintaining a personal data record system. It would be required to identify a focal point to whom complainants could come; it would be required to take affirmative action to inform its employees of the safeguards and to specify penalties for any infraction of them; it would have to take precautions against transferring identifiable personal information to data systems that may not include adequate safeguards; it would be required to maintain records with sufficient accuracy, completeness, timeliness and pertinence as is relevant to their intended use.

A third set of safeguards gives the individual data subject certain rights. When asked to supply personal data, he would be informed whether he is legally required to or may refuse to supply it; he would be informed, upon his request, whether he is a subject in a given data system; he would have the opportunity to inspect the record, to challenge it, and to cause corrections to be made; he would be assured that data about himself is used only for the stated purposes of the system.

There are significant arguments in favor of this approach.

(a) It uses the existing legal and judicial institutions of the country to implement privacy protection.

(b) It is consistent with the United States' approach to deterring societally or personally undesirable actions against the individual, e.g., a criminal act, unfair labor practice.

(c) It implies the creation of minimum new bureaucratic function.

(d) It applies equally to government or private data banks.

(e) Relative to private industry, it focuses the problem in the office of the General Counsel, an entity which industry already needs for other purposes.

(f) It encourages preferred behavior of data systems by levying financial penalties for misbehavior.

(g) Through the medium of court decision and interpretations, it provides an adaptive solution to the issue of personal privacy as the attitudes of society and the needs for personal information change.

(h) It puts the control where it seems proper, namely, in the hands of the individual who has been harmed rather than in the hands of a government function that paternally watches out for him.

(i) It deals with the issue across the board rather than piecemeal.

(j) It represents a minimum of government intrusion into the affairs of the individual and of industry.

The dominant argument against a Fair Code approach concerns the slow response time of the judicial system and the expense of prosecuting an action.

10. Conclusion

As of the end of 1973, many countries or states have considered the personal privacy issue or have taken explicit action to provide some measure of protection for citizens. A number of states of West Germany, for example, have passed data protection acts that establish certain measures of control over government files (DHEW-1, 73). Sweden has passed its Data Act that established a federal Data Inspection Board. France (DHEW-4, 73) has studied the problem but taken no definitive action. The Younger Committee (DHEW-2, 73) in Great Britain and the Department of Communications and Justice in Canada (DHEW-3, 73) have produced substantial studies and recommendations on the issue. In the United States, proposed legislative action at the federal level seeks to implement a Code of Fair Information Practice (Goldwater, 73; Koch and Goldwater, 74); the State of California is considering similar legislation (Bagley, 73). The State of Massachusetts has created a Commission on Privacy and Data Banks to review the operation of all state data banks and the relevant law and administrative procedures (Computer World, 73).

Thus, there is substantial concern in many countries of the Western world about the relation between the individual citizen and government or private data banks that use information about him for various purposes. It would appear that many legislative and administrative actions will occur in 1974–75 that will significantly redress the balance of power between citizen and data bank; the relationship between them will become more equitable and bilateral. In this matter of personal privacy, society now faces a truly central question of human choice as people collectively decide how they wish information about themselves to be controlled and used.

References

Anderson, J.P. (1972). *Information Security in a Multi-User Computer Environment; Advances in Computers*, Vol. 12. New York: Academic Press.

Bagley, W.T. (1973). State of California Assembly (U.S.A.), draft legislation A.B. 2656 (August 31, 1973).

Computer Decisions. (November 19, 1973), pp. 50–51, U.S.A.

Computer World. (December 19, 1973), pp. 1 and 7.

Department of Health, Education and Welfare. (1973). *Records, Computers and the Rights of Citizens*. Stock No. 1700-00166. Washington: United States Government Printing Office.

DHEW-1, (1973). *ibid*, pp. 168–170.

DHEW-2, (1973). *ibid*, pp. 173–174.

DHEW-3, (1973). *ibid*, pp. 174–175.

DHEW-4, (1973). *ibid*, pp. 171–172.

Goldwater, Jr., B. (September 12, 1973). United States Congress, House of Representatives, draft legislation, H.R. 10042.

Koch, E.I. and Goldwater, Jr., B. (March 6, 1974). United States Congress, House of Representatives, draft legislation, H.R. 13303.

Sweden, Data Act, Ministry of Justice (May 11, 1973).

Turn, R. and Peterson, H.E. (1967). System implications of information privacy. *AFIPS Conference Proceedings*, Vol. 30, Montvale, N.J.: AFIPS Press, pp. 291–299.

15 U.S. Code 1681-1681t. (1970).

Ware, W.H. (1967). Security and privacy in computer systems. *AFIPS Conference Proceedings*, Vol. 30, Montvale, N.J.: AFIPS Press, pp. 279–282.

Ware, W.H. (1967). *ibid*, pp. 287–290.

E. Mumford and H. Sackman, eds., Human Choice and Computers
North-Holland Publishing Company (1975)

THE INDIVIDUAL, PRIVACY AND THE COMPUTER

Laurence E. MALLETT

British Computer Society, Thames Ditton, Surrey, United Kingdom

The potential of the computer to collect, record, sort, analyse, collate, compare, reproduce and retain data makes it a powerful tool in the hands of those whose work objectives (whether incidentally or otherwise) are the invasion of the individual's privacy.

What is privacy? Tot homines, quot sententiae. One definition is that it is the condition of seclusion, withdrawal, or freedom from the knowledge by others of one's personal concerns. A blanket definition such as this is inevitably defective, and experts have variously characterised privacy as made up of zones or of different elements. Thus, for example, there is the innermost zone containing the ultimate secrets of an individual, which will not be shared with anyone; then come the intimate secrets which can be shared, but only with a restricted class of persons; then a series of wider circles concluding in the least sensitive facts. Professor Westin (67) analyses privacy into the four elements of solitude, where the individual is left with the "familiar dialogue with the mind or conscience"; intimacy, in groups such as family or work mates; anonymity, where the individual is one of a crowd and not identified; and reserve, where the individual keeps his distance from others.

Different cultures have different views on privacy. For example in the United States, there is a tradition of hospitality, and strangers are readily invited into the home; but in certain European countries only a person's very closest friends will ever see the inside of his house or apartment. Within a culture classes have different attitudes to privacy, so that in education the difference in England is most pronounced between the experiences on the one hand of the under-privileged and the boarding school belt, and on the other of the middle-class day school category. The former are accustomed to living intimately together in cramped and over-crowded surroundings, thus knowing a good deal more about the habits and personalities of their associates than the latter, many of whom from an early age have a room of their own. A further complication is that an individual may at different times require a different level of privacy for the same facts: thus it may be that as a man comes more into the public eye he wishes a fact in his past life to be shrouded by the passing of time. Two legal definitions of privacy perhaps exemplify the difference between a straightforward approach and a qualified definition. Justice Cooley called privacy "the right to be left alone", while Justice, the British section of the International Commission of Jurists talks about "that area of a man's life which, in any given circumstances, a reasonable man with an understanding of the legitimate needs of the community would think it wrong to invade".

Whatever the definition chosen, more and more people are realising the importance society must attach to the basic principle that, however true it is that in a modern welfare state the authorities must know certain facts about people's circumstances simply in order to plan the provision of such necessities as housing subsidies, social security benefits, clinics, local authority services, etc., there must be a point at which society recognises that it does not need, or is not entitled, to enquire further into an individual's life; beyond that point, enquiry and interference is properly called an invasion of privacy, and as such is a threat to what we understand to be freedom in a democratic state. Responsible people in the world of computing want to ensure that the massive potential of computers is harnessed for the benefit of society rather than being used indiscriminately to create what one commentator has described as "the gold-fish bowl society" in which information about individuals is readily available, and the invasion of privacy is quicker, more effective, and more comprehensive than was possible before the widespread use of computers. It is the responsibility of society to draw the line between legitimate enquiries and invasions of privacy.

There are existing legal protections of privacy, of a greater or lesser effectiveness, in many jurisdictions. In England there is no common law remedy available for invasion of privacy as such, though there is nothing to stop the Courts from developing such a right. After all, much of English law is common law, made by the Judges, rather than Statute law. In the absence, however, of a clear right, the aggrieved individual has to try to fit his claim into one of several other remedies available – for example, defamation, breach of confidence or breach of contract. But none of these remedies is tailored to provide protection of privacy, and it must therefore be said that privacy is inadequately protected in England.

In France, there is also no legislation, although case law has created the concept of the "right of the personality", which is supplemented by some specific safeguards – for example, truth cannot be used as a defence in a defamation action where the statement complained of concerns the person's private life. Nevertheless French law gives better protection than English law to the individual, in that it does, in theory, embody this idea of a basic right to a private life which could be developed to cover databank abuses. In Germany also, case law has established a right of the personality on which privacy decisions have been based. The cases reveal that in the absence of consent or of reasonable public interest, it is illegal for a person to publish facts concerning the private or family life of another, and this line of interpretation of the basic privacy right may be extended to cover the databank situation. One of the German states, Hessen, has also a Data Protection Act of 1970 which ensures data secrecy, gives a right to demand rectification of incorrect information, and appoints a Data Protection Commissioner.

The new Swedish Data Act of 1973 is the most comprehensive European legislation so far produced. It gives a Data Inspection Board power to regulate the operation of private databanks, and in certain limited cases, that of public databanks. Under the Act, a personal register or databank can only be kept by permission of the Board. No information can be kept of highly personal matters, such as data on a person's alcoholism, arrest record, or psychiatric treatment, except with special permission from the Board. No registration can be made of an individual's religious or political views, though churches or parties may keep membership lists. The Board issues regulations on how each databank may be set up and used, and each individual has the right to a free print-out of what a databank contains on him; he can sue a databank if it spreads false information about him; and can demand that corrections be made to erroneous information in the databank.

In the United States, the Courts have over the years built up a considerable case-law on privacy to the extent that there is a fair protection of rights not to have one's seclusion intruded upon; not to be placed in a false light by publicity; and not to have one's name used in publicity without consent. But this common law right fell short of giving protection in the computer databank situation, so specific situations have had to be dealt with by statute. The Federal Fair Credit Reporting Act 1971 provides the individual with new protections and rights in the consumer credit field, considered by many to be the greatest danger area in the computer/privacy context. The Act gives the subject, a potential consumer, the right to be told the name and address of the consumer reporting agency when he is rejected for credit, insurance, or employment. He thus knows of the existence of a record about him and can use his right to correct wrong information on the file. On a rejection the subject has the right to free access to examine all information on file except medical data and the sources of investigative information. He has the right to know who has received information about him, in the last six months for credit or insurance purposes, and the last two years for employment purposes. He has the right of confidentiality for the data, which may only be reported for credit, insurance, employment, government licence or benefit, or other legitimate purposes. Where he disputes the accuracy of stored information the agency must re-investigate, and correct items found to be inaccurate. Any unresolved dispute must be noted on file together with a brief statement of the subject's version of the dispute. Agencies have duties to ensure that information is accurate and not obsolete. The Act provides the individual with legal remedies for enforcement, and in general provides protection in an area of considerable potential abuse. On the other hand, it has to be said that the very narrowness of its scope means that it does not succeed in resolving all the difficulties created by databanks.

Recent proposals to increase the protection of individuals in the face of increased use of computer databanks have in England included the following:

(a) A legislated general right of privacy by which would be established the right of any person to be protected by whatever means from intrusion upon himself, his home, family, relationships, communications with others, his property and his business affairs.

(b) A system for the registration of databanks along similar lines to those of the Swedish Data Act referred to above.

(c) The regulation of activities of consumer credit agencies along lines similar to those in the United States Fair Credit Reporting Act.

(d) Specific rights for individuals who are the subject of computer databank files to receive print-out, to challenge, to correct, and to have a reply inserted on the record.

(e) The establishment of a personal right of property in information about oneself so as to create the right to restrict or control the dissemination by others of that information.

(f) The developement of high professional standards in data processing so that at the very least every installation would be controlled by a Manager with defined professional standards and duties. He would have imposed upon him the responsibility for ensuring compliance with any legal provisions of the databank he controlled.

(g) The Home Office Committee on Privacy has made recommendations at the invitation of the British Government for the adoption of principles which would regulate the handling of personal information in computer databanks. That Committee also recommended that a standing commission be established to investigate the desirability of legislation or other controls for safeguarding the handling of personal information.

These proposals, though made in England, are of general application to the computer/privacy problem in Europe and elsewhere. As, however, the English proposals are geared specifically to the English legal system, no attempt has been made to state them otherwise than as outline proposals. It will be noted that other jurisdictions have established a lead in the field especially of databank registration and of consumer credit reporting. It is submitted that every jurisdiction must give thought to the desirability of imposing legislative or other controls on the operation of computer databanks to ensure that international conventions to which they adhere are observed in the spirit and the letter in the computer databank context.

References

Editors (1972). *Computers and the Year 2000*. Manchester: National Computing Centre.

Home Office (1972). Report of Younger Committee. London: Her Majesty's Stationery Office.

Justice (1970). *Privacy and the Law*. London: Stevens.

Niblett, G.B.F. (1971). *Digital Information and the Privacy Problem*. Paris: O.E.C.D.

Westin, A.F. (1967). *Privacy and Freedom*. New York: Atheneum.

E. Mumford and H. Sackman, eds., Human Choice and Computers
North-Holland Publishing Company (1975)

MAN–COMPUTER SYMBIOSIS: FEARS AND HOPES

Lew KOWARSKI

CERN, Geneva, Switzerland

1. Early misgivings

Since the Renaissance, Western society vastly increased the use of machines for performing useful tasks in ways more and more remote from the traditional reliance on human muscle directly controlled by human will and thought. Motive power, at first, still came from the muscle, sometimes stored up, as in a clock or a catapult. Windpower, waterpower and finally steam-power came next, and the existence of these extra-human providers of goods and services was almost immediately recognized as a competitor to human workers. Their products were never quite suited to human demands; rather the demand had to be adjusted to what the machines were able to supply. This encroaching inhumanity began to be resented at first on purely philosophical and esthetic grounds. Already in the early 18th Century Jonathan Swift attacked the inventive scientists of his time. In *Gulliver's Travels*, Fellows of Royal Society are described as one of the four inhuman races, along with midgets, giants and horses. Towards the end of the same century, William Blake spoke of the first steam-driven factories as "black satanic mills". A generation later, automatic weaving became a reality and a target for the destructive hostility of displaced Luddite weavers: the man–machine antagonism had reached the level of economic survival.

On the same Jacquard loom principle, Charles Babbage began to develop a mechanical extension and substitute for the hitherto exclusively human capabilities of sustained computation and logic. With remarkable foresight, Samuel Butler denounced – in *Erewhon*, a century ago – the danger of the machines acquiring the powers of reproduction (first machine tools?), then of logical manipulation and finally bending human desires and values to an imperative of keeping the master machines in existence and absorbing their output. In our own century, the increasingly self-controlling production machines first reduced many categories of workers to submissive slavery (as in Charlie Chaplin's "Modern Times"), and then made them altogether redundant. The collapse of employment patterns in 1930's produced a new awareness of the man/machine clash; the ideas of Swift and the Luddites then became a matter for serious consideration by ideologists and governments.

By an unlucky coincidence, electronics, much more efficient than mechanics as the means of processing information, was made available exactly at the same time. It took World War II to provide a strong enough incentive for taking this new and decisive step into the machine age. The postwar needs of reconstruction and economic growth continued to make all increases in productivity seem attractive, by whatever means and whatever the side effects.

2. Arrival of the thinking machines

In this postwar climate, all recent technological breakthroughs were greeted by public opinion with expectation and glee. In particular, the "giant brains" would "relieve mental drudgery" of all kinds connected with arithmetic and figures. It took some time for the public, and even for the specialists to grasp the whole width of this new prospect. If decimal arithmetic is a pretty narrowly specialized chain of elementary logical operations, binary arithmetic stands in a more immediate connection to these elements, and makes the transition from a "computing machine" to a "thinking machine" much more obvious. Non-numerical tasks of the kind described today as "artificial intelligence" began to be envisaged before even the first IBM 700's became available; translation and indexing were hastily relegated to a menial level from which all detailed intervention of the human brain would, hopefully, very soon be eliminated.

The rapid progress of the commercially produced computers all through the 1950's spurred the first preliminary attempts to achieve such "intelligent" devices. The transition towards actually serviceable systems of hardware and software proved, however, much more arduous than expected. When launched into a real environment of texts, sets of individual objects or optimizing selections, the faultlessly logical devices proved to be singularly helpless, thus showing – as if such a demonstration were really ever needed! – that there is much more to human thinking, than mere logic. From then on, the inventive effort no longer sought to remove human intervention altogether; rather to understand the exact nature of the task, and see which of its features can or cannot be easily reduced to formal logic. Man and machine should be put to work symbiotically rather than competitively; only in this way the twin dangers, denounced by anti-machine prophets, of displacement and dehumanization can be averted.

They can, but will they? To say that symbiosis represents the final equilibrium is to beg the question. To clarify this issue it is, perhaps, appropriate to focus our attention on one concrete illustration.

Before we do so, in the next section of this paper, a point of terminology is worth mentioning: the word "symbiosis", as applied to the performance of a task jointly by man and machine is not new (c.f. Licklider around 1960), but even now it still appears to be controversial. "Life together" – *are* computers a form of life? Even if scientifically doubtful, the term "symbiosis" has enough intuitive meaning to serve at least as a clearly understandable metaphor.

3. A case history

Computerized processing of visual data in physical research may be invoked here as a suitable example. It has been, for many years, my privilege to be connected with the development of this technique since its inception around 1955 – a long enough period to witness, at first hand, the typical succession of its various stages: the first appearance of the computers as an aid to an essentially human performance; the drive towards full automation and its first failures; the new look at the task in terms of man–machine symbiosis. The symbiotic idea is prevailing today, in terms of man–machine symbiosis. The symbiotic idea is prevailing today, yet attempts are already in sight to compress the human sector, to achieve a more complete automation; how complete ultimately? The case history ends on this question mark.

We do not propose to describe here the nature of an experiment in elementary particle physics (often called high-energy physics), or how the paths of particles to be observed become visible in a specially prepared sensitive material medium in the form of linear strings of drops, bubbles or sparks. The strings can be photographed; their lengths, angles, intersections and curvatures form the meaningful physical information. The full processing of such visual records comprises three stages: "scanning" (first examination of an image and decision as to whether its content is worth more detailed attention); "measuring" (translation of a track into a numerical sequence of point coordinates); "computing" (treatment of this series of numbers so as to extract physical information on the nature, speed and other properties of the particles whose passage has been made visible).

In the mid-1950's, new methods of particle production and detection have rather suddenly produced a situation (first recognized by L.W. Alvarez in California, and soon afterwards at CERN in Geneva), where the processing of filmed records became the bottleneck of the whole process of physical experimentation. The situation was new, free from established traditions and of their vested interests; computers, as a prospective means of dealing with the problem, were just becoming practicable, and particle-physics laboratories, for various historical and political reasons, were outstandingly rich in talent and money. The scene was set for an energetic and tumultuous development.

The use of "computers as computers", that is for the third of the three stages described above, came quite naturally and developed together with all other numerical and mathematical uses of computers in scientific research. The measuring stage required high accuracy (which can be achieved by an unaided human only slowly and with great effort); the first stage, which comes so easy to a human observer, could conceivably be tackled by a computer equipped with proper sensors and discriminating programs, but such sophistication in 1955 was hardly more than an ambitious dream.

Accordingly, the first generation of computerized equipment for the processing of track-bearing pictures embodied a clear distinction between the tasks entrusted to the human and the machine. Scanning remained entirely human; numerical work was entirely taken over by the computer. In the intermediate stage, a human operator would guide an electro-optical sensor along the track image and, at chosen intervals, would cause it to activate a card- or tape-puncher recording its exact position at that moment. This guiding and punching operation would in fact determine the production speed of the processing chain as a whole.

In the late 1950's this first-generation system became fully operative in America and in Europe. Familiarity with computers and confidence in their reliability became fully established in high-energy physics laboratories, and ideas of further extension of the role allocated to the machine began to be put forward. Once put onto a track, it appeared fairly easy to instruct the machine to follow the track, and to record the position of its properly spaced points, all by itself. Systems in which the human observer had to select only an interesting-looking track intersection (the Spiral Reader, developed in California) or a wide band containing a single promising track (the Flying-Spot Digitizer, developed by P. Hough and B. Powell at CERN and usually known as HPD) came into use in the early 1960's. The sweeping motion of the HPD could be made to transfer into the computer memory a great enough number of point coordinates to cover every region of picture. Plans began to be made for devising programs capable of recognizing line-like sequences of individual points. If successful, this procedure would remove the need for human scanning prior to the machine-performed measurement.

In another device (PEPR, proposed by I. Pless and L. Rosensen at M.I.T.) the sensor was from the start developed towards a capability of recognizing linear tracks. Its exploring element is a linear segment instead of a point-like lightspot. A systematic exploratory motion, at various angles, sooner or later brings it in coincidence with one of the line-like tracks visible in the picture. As soon as such a "hit" is registered, the segment can easily find its way further along the line. This ideal proved to be hard to achieve: a human operator would still have to supervise the sensor's motion and to correct it if it showed a tendency to go astray. But, on the whole, this second generation was conceived with total automation as its ultimate goal.

This dream proved to be unattainable but, at the time, it looked worth dreaming. Physicists began to envisage the production of pictures by the million; a substantial human contribution to their processing would require unmanageable and far too costly armies of processors and, even more important, an irreducible delay in reaching the final result. By mid-sixties the obstacles to full automation were well understood and a third generation of devices made their appearance. This new version of deliberately accepted man–machine collaboration was no longer defined as human work helped by a machine; it was seen as a flow of information through a machine, in which the human, with his superior abilities of discrimination and judgment would intervene only if the machine "yelled for help" (an expression actually used by D. Hodges, one of the main developers of the pioneering Polly system, at Argonne near Chicago). This residual reliance on human faculties enabled the creators of Polly and their followers (notably at CERN) to adapt their requirements more closely to the maximum possibilities offered by today's hardware and software and therefore to make the best use of these possibilities.

This looks like a reassuring re-affirmation of man's superior role, yet with the machine ready to relieve him from all tiresome burdens. But in fact, the story is not ended: this kind of situation never stands still. Acts of human discrimination gradually become codified and expressible in terms of software. Already in some simple classes of sparkchamber pictures the necessity for human intervention is so rare, that the processing can go at an average speed of a picture per second. Bubble chambers, with their visual information picked-up by vidicons rather than by photography, will no doubt follow suit, and with the possibility of assembling final information so easily and so quickly, who will wish to spend laboriously his time on those kinds of experiments where the visual configurations are too novel and too unexpected to be amenable to this kind of dehumanized processing? If this fourth epoch of data handling in high-energy physics does come about, it will mean that we have adapted our demands to what can be supplied by a machine, and not the other way round. The moral of this particular case history is that a tool and a servant, even when blindly obeying its master's orders, has a subtle way of improving its own nature and limitations on the choice of orders to be issued. To pursue our poetic metaphor, this "symbiosis", like any other form of living together – may ultimately lead to a battle of wills.

4. Other fields of symbiosis

I am less familiar with the historical stages of computerization in other domains of human activity, of which my knowledge is either based on less sustained contacts, or is entirely second-hand. In the already mentioned tasks of language translation and document indexing, the gradual emergence of a (possibly not final) symbiotic ideal seems to have occurred on much the same lines as in high-energy physics. In medicine the computerization is more recent and yet its scope seems obvious: diagnosis is based on several categories of necessary information (case records, laboratory analyses, current measurements of bodily functions, etc.); once the diagnosis is clear, intervention is decided by simple logical deduction; many kinds of intervention (e.g. radiotherapy, pacemakers, aerosols) can be entirely mechanized. Is this the end of the human practitioner in all of these medical activities? Or should he always remain in charge, helped but not displaced by the machines?

In any category of tasks requiring scientific intuition and judgement, the increasing reliance on computers threatens to introduce the following undesirable influences:

(a) The questions to be asked, and the problems to be solved, may be chosen on the criterion on being easily amenable to computerized treatment. In a paper given at this Symposium, Dr. Burt Nanus specifically mentions the possibility of a similar trend arising in the use of multinational computer systems in developing countries.

(b) Computers may turn scientific investigation towards a too exclusive preoccupation with what Dr. Zemanek, in his theme paper, calls the "second" or "scientific" world as opposed to the "real" or humanly valid one. The scientific manipulation of concepts may *have* to be performed on this second level, but its fruits are valuable only if transferred to the first level. Computerized manipulation may yet become ultimately incompatible with such a transfer – all logic and no judgement.

(c) Computerized collection and processing of data may lead to the piling-up of factual information of a foreseeable kind – and to the closing of the door on fresh discoveries. In our case history of particle physics there is a growing suspicion that such a trend is already becoming noticeable.

The problem seems to be the same, wherever we turn. Computer-controlled subways and highways; computer-managed business; computerized teaching. All these features of a brave new world are already with us to some extent; all of them carry the threats of displacement and dehumanization. Public opinion, by now fully alive to these threats, reacts to the ubiquitous "IBM cards" with truly Swiftian loathing and apprehension. Then why push the computerization at all?

The usually given answer is cost. Caught between the growing demand for goods and services and the growing price of human labour, the producer resorts to automation, even if the machine's response to individual needs and unusual situations is regrettably imperfect. In many practical situations today the only available choice is between this kind of response and none at all. Yet the cost is not everything: when fully aware of how much we lose by eliminating human intervention, we might be prepared to pay for it. Far more decisive are the requirements of complexity and speed. Contemporary technology tends to create situations, such as air traffic or missile-borne warfare in which the decisions have to be instantly made and put in action on the basis of instantly gathered and digested information: too many factors of the situation have to be appraised and weighed against each other in too short a time for human powers of perception and deduction to be of any use. We may refuse to put ourselves in situations where our lives have to be entrusted to computers, but others may choose otherwise and their chances of survival may then prove to be superior to ours.

5. A. coming conflict?

The ultimate grim prospect is that of a human population kept alive – for how long? – in an idle utopia, where computer-produced consumer goods and computer-created entertainment would be doled out in accordance with schedules based on computer-gathered and computer-digested sociological information.

This threat becomes real only on two consecutive pre-conditions. One is that such a self-maintaining system is materially and objectively achievable. The other, that enough human will and effort goes into achieving it, since it cannot conceivably be brought about in any other way. By "human" we do not mean here resulting from a concerted action by mankind as a whole; much more limited steps in this direction, dictated by narrow-visioned or ill-willed human groups would be quite decisively effective if persistent enough. But first, the bare feasibility. Not with today's hardware and software, certainly; but how far are they capable of developing? Is there anything relevant in human thinking which forever will remain out of machines' reach?

In a classical work of futurology (*The Year 2000*, by H. Kahn and A. Wiener, published in 1967), this question is left open, with some slight bias towards the negative since, in the authors' opinion, "if it turns out that computers cannot duplicate or exceed certain characteristically human capabilities, that will be one of the most important discoveries of the twentieth century." A prominent computer scientist thinks, on the contrary, that no society can be run without a recourse to "imprecise concepts, ambiguous ideas and even contradictory philosophies; the ability to do this is a remarkable attribute of human mind, a capability which is not at all understood at the present time . . . we need people to run systems both directly and by monitoring the output of computers" (R. Bellman, at the symposium on "Man and the Computer", Bordeaux, 1970).

There seems to be therefore, still some room left for hoping that the ultimate fear is not justified at all. But if it is, the second-line hope is that the doom may be averted by conscious human will, and in spite of the no less human trends to the contrary. The vision of a human fifth column, actively promoting the take-over by the computers, has been vividly depicted by one of today's most outstanding astronomers (*A for Andromeda*, by Fred Hoyle). Another science-fiction vision presents an already subjugated humanity, which however succeeds in recovering its freedom through the efforts of an indomitable resistance movement (*This Perfect Day* by Ira Levin). Uneasy feelings which at present seem to be growing in the public mind may yet prove to be only the first unreasoning forerunner of a much more rational and down-to-earth conflict to come.

E. Mumford and H. Sackman, eds., Human Choice and Computers
North-Holland Publishing Company (1975)

THE MULTINATIONAL COMPUTER AND SOCIAL CHOICE

Burt NANUS

University of Southern California, Los Angeles, Calif., U.S.A.

1. Introduction

There can no longer be any doubt that the marriage of computers and communications on a global scale will have – indeed already *is* having – a profound impact upon individuals, nations and the world social order. We have only begun to contemplate the dimensions of these changes, but already it is clear that there are enormous challenges and opportunities to be faced, and that the necessity for social choice in dealing with these developments cannot be avoided. The purpose of this paper is to review very briefly some of the current applications of the use of computers across national boundaries, and to explore two of the more critical issues of human choice involved.

2. What is a multinational computer?

A multinational computer system may be defined as any arrangement whereby computers in one country are linked directly to other computers, data bases or computer users in one or more other countries. Thus the essence of the multinational computer is the direct transfer of data across national boundaries in great quantity and at very high speed. This makes possible the collection and sharing of data bases across national boundaries, as well as the sharing of problem solving algorithms and other software.

The use of computers in this manner today is restricted to very large organizations because of the relatively high costs involved. However, as the costs of computer/communications systems continue to decline, as they have at a very rapid rate in the past decade, such systems will become economical and desirable for many medium-sized multinational organizations as well as nearly all the large ones. To understand the potential range of applications of such systems, a few examples from the public and private sectors should suffice.

In the public sector, by far the greatest amount of experience in the use of computers across national boundaries has been in the domains of military and space research. The U.S. Department of Defense (DOD), for example, has several integrated networks of computer systems tying together facilities around the world for purposes of centralized command and control, logistics and intelligence operations. Similarly, the U.S. National Aeronautics and Space Administration (NASA) uses a worldwide computer/telecommunications system to monitor and control space flights. Indeed, the on-board computers and terminals used during moon landings and other space flights are the world's most remote online terminals. In addition, both NASA and DOD have in operation worldwide information retrieval systems for on-line reference to scientific and technical literature.

There are several other examples of public uses of computers across national boundaries. The World Meteorological Organization employs a global network in its World Weather Watch program for monitoring and forecasting weather conditions. The United Nations is developing a World Science Information System (known as UNISIST) to standardize procedures in the handling of scientific information with the end goal of centralized processing, probably on a regional basis, so that users will have information available to them across national boundaries on an on-line time sharing basis with displays of information virtually anywhere by remote terminals. Similarly, the United Nations is establishing its International Computer Center in Geneva, Switzerland, so that it can provide centralized computing facilities for all UN locations, wherever they are located. Early users of this system include the United Nations Development Program and the World Health Organization. A final example is the world wide movement toward tying together banking operations, particularly in the realm of currency exchange and intergovernmental transfers.

The private commercial use of computers across national boundaries is expanding even more rapidly as illustrated by a few examples below:

(1) Reservation systems – Several international airlines such as SAS, Air Canada, KLM and Yugoslav Airlines have multinational computer services providing a variety of passenger reservation facilities and corporate data processing information. Other services by American Express and International Reservations Ltd., for example, are designed to provide multinational real-time reservations for hotel, car rental and other travel services.

(2) Computer service networks – A number of international time sharing

service networks are available from such organizations as General Electric, Honeywell, ITT and University Computing Company.

(3) News collection and publication – Several systems for international transmission and storage of publishable material have been developed by Triangle Publications Inc., United Press International and several firms specializing in multinational stock quotation services such as Reuters and Ultronic.

(4) Multinational management information systems (MIS) – IBM, British American Insurance Company, Metropolitan Life, Monsanto and Xerox are examples of corporate MIS systems that operate across national boundaries. One of the more dramatic of these may be the Mitsui system which links 115 offices in 69 countries to provide daily information at a central location on a wide variety of environmental information regarding worldwide market conditions.

(5) Corporate control systems – There are a number of systems in existence for controlling transportation and logistics operations (e.g. Gulf Oil Corporation) and for controlling inventories or production on a multinational basis (e.g. Sperry RAND Corporation, Canadian Pacific Railroad and Daimler-Benz).

The evidence is clear. There are many applications today for which the use of computers across national boundaries is already economic, and there will certainly be many more such applications in the future. Thus, we must begin to ask what the long term social implications of such a pervasive multinational phenomenon may be.

3. The AFIPS Delphi study

To explore these issues, the American Federation of Information Processing Societies (AFIPS) sponsored a year long study at the Center for Futures Research of the University of Southern California. The study began with a brief literature search in which more than 40 already existing applications in both the public and the private sectors were identified. The study employed the so-called "Delphi" technique in which a series of three questionnaires was sent to a group of carefully selected participants with feedback to the participants between interactions. The Delphi technique is most useful in cases like this where it is desired to obtain the views of leading experts regarding emerging future issues, but it would be far too costly, even if logistically possible, to assemble them in one location for a group discussion. The technique permits the participants to express their views without the danger of being unduly influenced by a particularly vocal or prestigious person (i.e., bandwagon effect), and with guaranteed anonymity. (On the other hand, the technique has been criticized for not being statistically verifiable or reliable and for other considerations which in this case seemed less important, since the purpose of the study was simply to identify issues and explicate positions.) With the assistance of AFIPS officers, an outstanding panel was assembled consisting of 58 corporate officers, government officials and computer experts, many from countries outside the United States. A carefully prepared list of questions was developed from an examination of the existing literature and extensive discussions with computer experts. The full results of the study are described in a report published by AFIPS Press (Nanus et al., 73), but some of the more interesting findings are summarized below.

The clearest lesson from the study was that there will indeed be some major social impacts of the multinational computer and many of them will occur in the next ten years, but that the nature of these impacts are still only vaguely perceived. There seems to be little doubt that the use of computers across national boundaries in both the public and private sectors will expand very greatly in the next two decades as the costs of computation decline, new applications are proven economic, and the scope and influence of multinational organizations increase. On the technical side, there appear to be few barriers to the development of these systems that are not now already close to solution. The problems that do exist are more in the nature of political or socio–cultural obstacles and while there is no guarantee that these problems can be solved in the next two decades, there are a few promising starts already.

In the public sector, the use of computers across national boundaries is likely to strengthen multinational public enterprises in such areas as public health, criminal justice, pollution control, weather forecasting and disaster control, with major impacts before 1985. For example, in the health field, the Delphi participants expected that medical data banks would be established to service, with on-line capabilities, at least 25% of all multinational organizations throughout the world sometime during the decade of the 1980's. Similarly, in the area of education, they believed that educational data banks will be in significant use during the 1980's across national boundaries and that multinational educational programs at the university level would be operational before 1985.

In the private sector, progress may be even faster because much can be done within individual companies. Thus, the participants strongly felt that at least 25% of all multinational organizations would be using multinational information systems in dealing with manufacturing, logistics, marketing and credit functions by 1985, and that industrial data banks will be in widespread use for these purposes. This is likely to accelerate the trend toward professionalization of business management throughout the world, and also to increase the uniformity in the way in which business problems are handled throughout the world.

These developments are likely to have their most profound and least understood impacts on the socio–cultural level. Within the highly industrialized societies, many people will likely find themselves in some form of man–machine relationship, often involving multinational communications, within the next decade. Delphi participants seemed fairly confident that by 1990, at least 25% of the people living in the highly industrialized societies would be actively involved (say, a half-hour per week) in some form of man-machine relationship and that ultimately, "the inability to effectively interact with computers will be viewed as a particularly disabling form of illiteracy." These interactions may be for educational, health, library, business or other reasons but the net effect is likely to be the enhancement of shared beliefs and values and a growing sense of interdependence on matters of the most fundamental nature. This growing interdependence may be one of the most important results of the use of global data banks since people in different cultures may gradually come to share not only the information they use to solve problems, but the way they understand, analyze and interpret problems.

It is impossible in this brief paper to explore all the ramifications of this new development. Therefore, let us concentrate on two particularly crucial issues of human choice that emerge from a consideration of the possible impacts of the use of computers across national boundaries.

4. Multinational organizations and the nation-state

We live in a world of sovereign nation-states, each jealous of its powers and prerogatives, and many experiencing a growing sense of nationalism as they seek to determine their own destiny in the face of frightful forces under the control of others. Into this milieu comes the multinational corporation whose reach extends across national boundaries and whose interests require the optimization of the use of resources and talents on a global level. Given these realities, it is not surprising that there is an inherent potential for conflict between the multinational corporation and the nation-state.

Now, onto this scene we must project the possibility of widespread use of multinational computer systems. Consider the situation from the point of view of one of the countries in which a multinational corporation is operating. It will be clear to the government of that country that control of the enterprise is being exercised from outside the country in a much more direct manner than has been the custom to date. Further, the intent of the multinational information system is to effect economies of scale by means of policies that may conflict with the host government's objectives. For example, economies can often be realized by transferring production, employment or capital from one country to another, but this may very well be considered undesirable by the host government. Moreover, there is a very real concern as to where the computerized corporate records are being kept and how much access the host nation can have to the records to ensure compliance with local laws, payment of taxes, etc.

Thus, the use of computers across national boundaries may introduce a new dimension into the conflicts that already exist between the interests of multinational corporations and the nation-states in which they operate. At the present time, most conflicts between multinational corporations and nation-states are resolved by a process of negotiation between the two parties involved or between governments. This process does not always lead to mutual satisfaction, equity or convenience, and occasionally leads to very real exploitation of one party by the other. The alternative would be to establish some sort of regulative or judicial machinery at the global level to handle conflicts between multinational corporations and nation-states. Such an entity might be formed within the framework of some existing organization or as part of a new organization established by international treaties.

So far, we have been discussing the multinational corporation and its special concerns, but the problem is really much broader than this. The very essence of the multinational computer is the use of data banks held in one country but accessed in other countries. Currently, there are no legal or political mechanisms to resolve the conflict over who controls these data bases. In fact, there seems to be a lack of international coordination in many areas concerned with the computer sciences, even in the relatively easier realm of hardware and software interfacing standards. However, when one adds the dimension of multinational data bases that may include information on individuals or organizations, one finds that there is a serious lack of multinational agreements on the protection of individual privacy and the limits of government control on data transfers across national boundaries. The issue of social choice here is whether the flows of information across national boundaries should be regulated in order to protect innocent parties and to resolve conflicts that may arise from such transfers.

In the case of the AFIPS Delphi study, many panel members were concerned about the political barriers involved in attempting to regulate data transmission, but they felt some degree of control was necessary and likely to occur in the next fifteen years. Unfortunately, countries have differing legal concepts about the nature of civil liberties, the extent of permissible collusion between organizations, the meaning of fraud and the importance of maintaining individual privacy, and so the resolution of these issues will be a very difficult problem. In the long run, new international institutions may very well be needed for this purpose.

5. Implications for developing countries

It is quite possible that the greatest impact of the use of computers across national boundaries will be upon the developing countries as the globalization of information processing influences world economic development. However, the impacts will be both favorable and unfavorable. On the favorable side, the use of multinational computer systems could help the less developed countries by tying them into advanced technologies. In fact, multinational computer systems could become very potent vehicles for the acceleration of technology transfer to those societies that are attempting to increase their level of industrialization and economic achievement. Furthermore, the use of multinational computer systems could be a strong force in bringing about beneficial changes in education, management, medicine and other public sector areas. It should provide great assistance in improving public administration in the developing countries by permitting the development of more comprehensive plans, the collection of better statistics and the exercise of more control over the allocation of scarce resources.

On the other hand, there are several ways that this development may not assist the developing countries, as follows:

(1) Multinational computer systems may help to enhance the power and influence of multinational organizations whose interests transcend national interests. They would do this by helping to institutionalize a method of socio-economic change whose origins are multinational, thus competing with national strategies for change and establishing a potential for serious conflicts. Since these multinational organizations tend to be financed and dominated by the highly industrialized countries, their increased power and influence may tend to widen the gap between the rich and the poor nations, at least at first.

(2) The use of multinational computer systems in the developing countries may suffer from the paucity of trained native personnel with the needed computer skills to benefit from this technology.

(3) The use of multinational computer systems in developing countries may tend to cause a preoccupation with problems that can be solved with computers at the expense of other important human and social problems for which computers may not be able to make substantial contributions.

The true issue of social choice here is the extent to which the industrialized countries are willing to contribute to the enhancement of the ability of the developing countries to use multinational computer systems. Many people feel that the use of multinational computer systems will have little impact on the developing nations unless the developed countries subsidize their development of computer technology. This implies a need for education and training programs in the application of multinational computer systems to accelerate the processes of economic and social development. If the information-poor countries are not to suffer at the hands of the wealthier, information-rich nations, it will be necessary for the latter to create international organizations and agreements that strengthen the position of the developing countries in regard to all flows of science and technology, particularly the use of multinational computer systems.

6. Summary and conclusions

This paper has focused on two critical issues of social choice emerging from the widespread use of multinational computers. It could have focused on others. For example, will the multinational computer strengthen the hand of management vis-a-vis the worker by making it possible to rapidly (and invisibly) move production requirements across borders to exploit local weaknesses? If so, must unions also develop multinational computer systems and new forms of international cooperation to maintain their relative power? Or again, what impacts might the multinational computer have on unemployment rates in both the developed and the developing countries, or upon conflicts of loyalties between workers in multinational corporations and their countries? These and many other issues could have been addressed, but the conclusion would have been essentially the same.

The use of computers across national boundaries may very well be one of the three or four most important factors tending to bring the world closer together through the creation of new multinational institutions and interdependencies. However, as with all forces for social change, the global marriage of computers and communications technology presents both challenges and opportunities. The greatest challenge is how the world community can exercise social control over the implementation of this technology so as to assure that it will benefit all the world's people and not just those already favored with wealth and power. The greatest opportunity is that if we can exercise social choice wisely in this case, the multinational computer system may enable great progress toward the unification of the world through the sharing of common information, technologies, problem definitions and problem solutions. We may still be ten or fifteen years away from being able to measure the major impacts of this development, but we should view this time as one of research, analysis and careful evaluation of alternative plans for making the multinational computer an instrument for world betterment.

Reference

Nanus, B., Wooton, M.L. and Borko, H. (1973). *The Social Implications of the Use of Computers Across National Boundaries*, Montvale: AFIPS Press.

CONCLUSIONS

E. Mumford and H. Sackman, eds., Human Choice and Computers
North-Holland Publishing Company (1975)

INTERNATIONAL HUMAN CHOICE AND COMPUTERS: CONFERENCE RETROSPECT AND PROSPECT

Enid MUMFORD

Manchester Business School, Manchester, United Kingdom

and

Harold SACKMAN

The Rand Corporation, Santa Monica, Calif., U.S.A.

1. Introduction

The papers in this meeting reflect the remarkable diversity of the subjects covered at the first major international conference on the human aspects of computer systems to enable trade unionists, computer technologists and social scientists to enter into meaningful discussion with each other. This was a conference that all participants agreed was constructive and thought provoking; it demonstrated considerable consensus amongst all three groups on problems of human choice associated with increasing use of computers, and also a stimulating divergence of opinion on how these problems should be solved and the role each group should play in their solution.

One recurring aspect of the discussions was the surprised recognition by the different specialists that others did not have the same view of their role as they had themselves. The social scientists, as might be expected, took relatively academic and analytical views of problems of human choice. They tended to speak from research rather than practice in relation to the problems of computers, and attempted to argue on the basis of what they believed to be a logical and objective assessment of the computer environment and its impact on human beings. Those social scientists, such as the Swedes and the British, who have assumed an action research role and attempted to get human goals – such as an improved quality of working life – incorporated into the design of computer systems – were surprised and somewhat shocked at being accused by the trade unions of acting as the tools of management, although the unions were prepared to concede that they too were, perhaps, unwitting tools. This led to a great deal of useful discussion in which the social scientists attempted to convince the unions of their neutrality and good intentions.

Similarly the social scientists frequently challenged the unions on their seeming passivity when their members were being affected by computer systems, and began to gain an understanding of their ideological and practical difficulties. As the talks continued it became apparent that unions did not all have similar approaches to the problems of computers. Some unions fixed their sights on a change in the structure of society and appeared uninterested in short term ameliorative action such as trying to make the jobs associated with computers more interesting and challenging. Other trade union officials admitted that they were still in a defensive position in their industries and had difficulty in taking any positive action outside the wage bargaining area. Between these two positions were a group of unions who believed that they were now able to incorporate computer systems and job design factors into their negotiating procedures and to insist on computer systems being designed so as to give employees an opportunity for exercising control over their own working environments and for having important and challenging jobs. The unions which had assumed this kind of interventionist role most strongly were the Norwegians and the Swedes, closely followed by the Germans and the Austrians.

The computer scientists, in turn, were surprised that the "neutrality" of their actions was not recognized by the social scientists and the trade unions, and disturbed that their behavior was seen as a product of a technical and managerial value system that took insufficient account of the psychological and security needs of users of computer systems. They were put on the defensive by suggestions from the other two groups that they were designing and implementing computer systems in an anti-humanistic way.

As the week progressed these different perspectives were talked through; the difficulties inherent in the role of a trade unionist, social scientist and computer technologist were analyzed, and a consensus of opinion emerged on what were the most serious problems of human choice, and on some immediate steps that could be taken to ameliorate these problems. It was agreed that the design of computer systems ought to include more formal and explicit values and ideas from both workers and management, while broader community and national interests must no longer be neglected. Dallinger, Chairman of the Austrian Union of salaried, clerical, commercial and technical employees stated, in his opening theme paper, what later emerged as the view of the majority of conference participants. He said that the problem of establishing socio-technical systems "cannot be solved *for* the working man, but only *with* him; and his needs as a human being must take precedence over technological and economic considerations."

The means by which discussion was facilitated at the conference was through a number of seminar groups. Eight working groups were organized each composed of roughly equal proportions of trade unionists, social scientists, and computer technologists. These small, highly interactive seminar groups contained up to sixteen conference participants and met six times during the conference for periods of two hours. The aim of these meetings was to encourage each participant to express his views and opinions on plenary session papers, and on any other relevant issues he wished to discuss, within a small group setting. Each group was given the task of producing a short report setting out its agreements, disagreements and recommendations on key conference related issues. The aim of the conference organizers was to use these reports as a means for providing audience feedback to conference speakers, for evaluating what was achieved at the conference, and for making recommendations on future action and activities. The reports of each seminar group were presented by the group chairmen to the conference as a whole at the final plenary session on the Friday afternoon before the conference broke up.

In the following sections of this chapter the authors have summarized and integrated the reports of the eight seminar groups. Although the discussions of these groups ranged very widely we have attempted to keep within the framework of the objectives of this conference and have set them out in terms of issues related to management, trade unions, democracy and social choice, although there is, inevitably, considerable overlap between these categories. A number of the groups followed a suggestion of Sackman made at the start of the conference, that some consideration should be given to the principles that might be incorporated into a Computer Bill of Rights which would help guide organizational and government behavior in relation to computers. Suggestions on what such a Bill of Rights might include are set out at the end of this paper, together with group recommendations on what future action IFIP could usefully take in focussing attention on problems of human choice and computers.

2. Theme papers

The four theme papers which opened the conference had as their objective the stimulation of group discussion through directing everyone's attention to a number of crucial human choice problems. Zemanek took a wide-ranging historical and philosophical look at the problems associated with man–machine communication. In particular, he presented the epistemological case for the inherent distinctions and differences between human and machine communication.

Hedberg and Mumford made the point that the human effects of computer systems did not arise through chance. They argued that the human consequences of computer systems were a result of human choices made by those responsible for the system design process. They pleaded for the setting of human goals when computer systems are being formulated and for more consideration to be given to the human consequences of different design alternatives.

Dallinger examined the impact of automation on the jobs of workers. He appealed vigorously for a socio-technical approach to systems design, but maintained that the responsibility for a humanistic organization of work must be assumed by the workers themselves. It could not be left to management, computer scientists, or social scientists.

Lastly, Sackman took a wide-ranging look at many facets of human choice and computers, examining international, economic, environmental, educational, political, and individualistic problems. He stressed the moral implications of the long-range potential of universal computer services for uplifting effective human intelligence for the entire human species. All of these theme issues aroused a great deal of interest in the seminar groups although each group tended to identify a number of particular problems for concentrated discussion. The plenary speakers who were interposed between each meeting of the seminar groups also introduced new concepts and ideas which led the groups into new discussion areas.

3. Computers and management choice

Six of the eight seminar groups devoted considerable time to discussing the assembly and use of *computer based information*. A number of general questions were considered. For example, do people want more or less structured information – a tighter structure of information being seen as providing more security, a looser one as providing more freedom. It was agreed that the computer led to a better structuring of information, but that this process would only be in the interests of the community as a whole if people could understand and use formalized information of this kind. Therefore, when assembling information it was important to ask for whom is this information required, for what purpose will it be used, and, following on from these two questions, what kind of information should we therefore incorporate into our computer-based information system?

A seminar group led by Briefs and Ekberg concentrated on the role of computers in complex *decision-making processes*. It was stressed that this role must be considered in the context of the structure of particular societies and of the power relationships within these societies. It should also be considered at the "individual" level so that account would be taken of an individual's decision frame of reference, his knowledge, experience, abilities, etc. The group was of the opinion that the computer could assist the taking of complex decisions through:

(1) Providing a safeguard against the tendency of information to become rapidly out of date.

(2) Meeting increasing needs for information.

(3) Assisting in scanning relevant social and environmental factors when taking decisions.

(4) Providing more timely information.

(5) Contributing to building up knowledge and facilitating learning.

(6) Generating a wide number of alternatives for human choice as a consequence of its ability to provide more diversified information.

But it was recognized that a number of factors could inhibit the wide-scale use of the computer in this way. These were:

(1) The development of computers and information systems is largely dependent upon the economic objectives of business firms.

(2) Computer technology is developed by privately-owned firms operating in a market environment.

(3) If computers were to be used as universally as the telephone or the radio, large resources would be required, and these might not be available.

(4) There could be resistance, within organizations, to the introduction of computers, and to the rigidity believed to be associated with this technology. Better education in computer usage than we have at present would be required to overcome this.

This group went on to consider why the computer had, so far, been only of limited value in complex decision processes. It was pointed out that all decision-taking involves the steps shown in Fig. 1.

None of these steps are as neutral and scientific as the classical management theorists have suggested. On the contrary, both the "frame of reference" and the "value systems" of the decision takers exert an influence on every stage of the decision process. Political factors frequently have a stronger

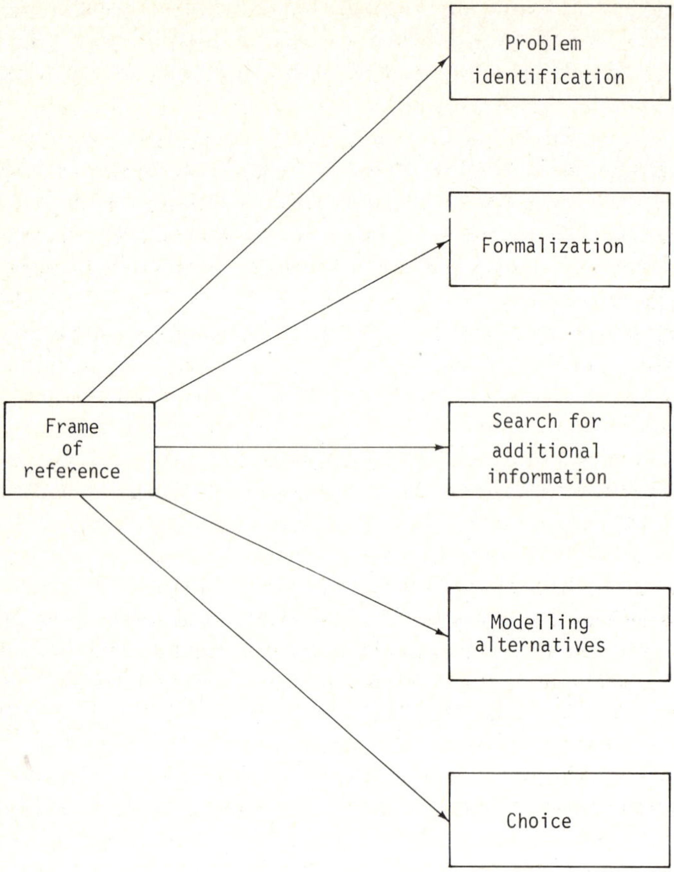

Fig. 1. Steps in Decision-Making

influence on decisions than logical factors and the computer cannot yet deal with these. In addition, the computer has, at present, only a limited ability to generate sensible alternatives for human choice in situations where there are many variables with complex interrelationships between them. Strategic investment decision models are an example of this kind of problem.

A number of the conference working groups examining management information systems devoted considerable time to "public" information systems. That is, to the information concerning the public which government agencies collect and use. Much attention was paid to how the citizen could be safeguarded against some of the possible disadvantages of this kind of information system. It was pointed out that while public service information systems are introduced to assist the centralization of activities and achieve administrative savings, there was a risk that in securing these savings they might impose indirect costs on the citizen through poorer service, inconvenience or even depersonalization. It was suggested that this type of information system should contain a mixture of computers and human agencies; that governments should be aware of the dangers of over-centralization and that they should protect such systems from breakdown through the duplication of equipment and the provision of alternative channels for use. Indirect costs should be examined with great care when costs and benefits of such systems were being estimated.

Much discussion centered on who should have access to public service information systems. "Knowledge is power" and the computer could be a tool for restricting or for furthering democracy. There was a strong feeling that the democratic potential of these systems should be recognized and that all interested individuals and groups should be able to request access to the data held in them, providing that the purpose for which the information was required was stated. Systems should be designed with sufficient flexibility to accommodate such requests and to cope with new data needs as they arose. The public should not only have access to these public systems, it should be involved in their design so that a wide spectrum of information needs could be examined. But it was recognized that the universal availability of data held on files would lead to information overload if the public did not have the necessary skills to make use of this information. There was therefore an educational problem that had to be tackled.

Most groups dealing with this subject felt strongly that ordinary people were able to make informed judgments on matters affecting their own lives. Too much technical data would inhibit this ability to make choices; therefore technical systems designers should take the mystery out of computer technology so that the information contained in any computerized system could be accessible to, and understood by, a majority of people. In this way the decision process would be exposed to public scrutiny. There were a number of specific recommendations on the subject of public and private data banks, and these are set out in suggested principles for a Computer Bill of Rights listed at the end of this chapter.

4. Computers and trade union choice

The trade union position on all subjects discussed by the seminar groups was stated by the trade union members of these groups and is covered in our descriptions of the different subject areas. Nevertheless, some of the groups did discuss a number of specific trade union issues. One group was particularly interested in the points made in the plenary session by Briefs who argued that firms should provide information to meet the needs of workers as well as management. It was agreed that the amount, location, and distribution of computer power in a firm could exert an influence on the relationships between management and the trade unions, and could also affect the ability of the firm to survive in its environment.

One of the most important issues for trade unionists at the conference was the impact of computers on the job security and income of workers. All technological unemployment was seen as socially disadvantageous. Firms should guarantee retraining for displaced workers and provide income security while this training was undertaken. It was stressed that research into the effects of computers should take account of the problems of those displaced by technology and the impact of this displacement on their dependents. Too much attention was being paid to the designers and users of computer systems, and not enough to the victims of computer technology.

The trade unions must defend their members against a loss of employment and a reduction in income as a result of the use of computers. They should also try and influence the design and consequences of computer systems by providing management with information on probable consequences and by representing the interests of their members. If displacement could not be avoided, then they should persuade governments to create new jobs and new forms of industrial activity.

One seminar group felt strongly that workers and their representatives should seek complete involvement in the control and design of computer systems in all sectors of society and should initiate their own research programs into the effect of computers in areas of social concern. Such opinions varied with the political goals of the various types of trade unions.

5. Computers and democratic choice

In this section we need to consider the recommendations of the seminar groups on two subjects. First, how people can be helped to make an informed and democratic choice on the way society should use computers. Second, how computer technology can itself aid democracy by providing the means for rapid surveys of community opinion.

There was much discussion on how computers were affecting the ordinary citizen and would affect him in the future. Could computers be harnessed in such a way that they benefited the community as a whole and not just technocrats and administrators? In most countries there are weak interest groups such as the young, the old, and the technically unsophisticated who might be threatened by the development of computer technology. It was thought that governments should be aware of this danger and take action to see that computers were of benefit to all the community. Public information systems such as the "people's computer" described by Caroll and Tague could be of great assistance in this respect.

Groups discussing computers and democracy all emphasized the need for people affected by computer systems to play a part in their development and to evaluate and choose the use to which these systems were put. The problem was how to help people to participate in this way and to give them the competence to play an informed and meaningful role. It was felt that the present education of computer specialists did not take sufficient account of social factors, such as the way society works, the political process, and the behavior of users. Yet all these provide the context in which computers operate.

One group stressed the fact that systems designers were often required to make decisions which should not be their responsibility, but that of system users and other interested bodies. This situation was beginning to alter with management who were intervening much more in the systems design process, and it was hoped that the conference would stimulate more intervention on the part of trade unions. The progress made by the Norwegian trade unions in this respect was much admired – it was agreed that the Norwegian approach of developing the knowledge and ability of workers at plant level to analyze system plans and identify the likely effects on themselves, was an excellent one. This group suggested that a two-tiered decision and design structure was required to assist participation and democracy when computer systems were introduced. This should take the following form*:

Higher Level: This should consider objectives, strategy and values and should consist of representatives of users and other interested parties. Conflicts of interest should be resolved by this body and not by the technical system designers.

Lower Level: The technical systems designer should provide a service to the higher level body by indicating technical feasibility, technical tradeoffs and cost.

* This suggestion was first made by Professor Bo Hedberg in his paper "Computer systems to support industrial democracy" see pages 211–230.

The role of the higher level body is to provide a specification within which the systems designers can work, although users must also be involved at the operational level.

Most groups perceived dangers in an unwillingness or inability to associate computers with democratic processes. It was stressed that computerized information systems amplify knowledge, enhance thinking and shape world views. Therefore, those who control such systems can gain formidable power, and can alter traditional power balances by widening the gap between the information rich and the information poor. This could affect the relations between management and unions, citizens and their government, and between developed countries and the third world. Those who at present come into the information poor category should develop institutions, procedures and knowledge to understand and evaluate the impact of computers. They should help shape new systems and apply sanctions and controls when necessary. They should also influence design objectives and design processes before and during implementation. There was a feeling in many groups that up to now computers had been used in the interests of management, whereas worker interests had been ignored. Systems design in the future should ensure that more of the benefits of computerization should be for the worker in the form of improved working conditions or an increase in job satisfaction.

A number of groups were interested in how computer technology could be used to assist democracy and there was considerable discussion of the points made in Sveistrup's paper in which he describes a new form of society that he calls "coinocracy". This is a society based on relatively autonomous groups utilizing computer-based information systems to produce a pluralistic society capable of many different life styles. This was perceived as a challenging objective, but it was thought that there might be a conflict between the autonomous group concept and a technocratic infra-structure based on computers. Nevertheless, it was recognized that information technology might encourage the development of intimate, decentralized communities that would enable people to identify with today's complex society. It was also pointed out that although the computer could never replace face-to-face communication, it could facilitate data transfer for television communication links between groups and individuals who were too far apart to communicate on a face-to-face basis.

The remaining areas covered in this chapter span many aspècts of computers and social choice broadly considered. These include education, work, privacy, humanistic system design, international issues, a Computer Bill of Rights, and IFIP recommendations.

6. Educational choice

Education as a means of preparing the public for a sensible use of computers and the form this should take, was discussed by most of the seminar groups. One group pointed out that computer technology and the education schemes associated with computers had been largely developed in a market economy and by privately owned computer firms. But this need not be the pattern of computer education everywhere. In all countries the public sector has a significant influence over the development of computer technology and could make a substantial contribution in the field of education. The role and approach of the computer science community could also influence educational programs.

Education for a computerized world should begin at school. Children over the age of ten should receive instruction in the use and possibilities of computers, but care should be taken in using computer-aided instruction for imparting knowledge. Sackman suggested that CAI should be used only after being tested out in terms of social needs, with social experimentation as a safeguard. Children should be taught about the future, since in the future they will be surrounded by many more computers.

It was suggested that it might be dangerous to replace the teacher with a computer as this could hinder the development of communication skills and the use of intuition. Children should be taught not only how to think more effectively, but also how to enjoy life, and computer education should be related to these and other socially acceptable purposes. Computer literacy will be essential for informed human choice in the future, therefore the universal right to this kind of literacy should be included in any contemplated Bill of Rights. Today most people can drive a car; tomorrow most people will require a minimal knowledge of computers if they are to develop themselves and the societies in which they live. The community of the future would have a number of computer-associated benefits such as program libraries, data registers and archives, terminal access available to all citizens, a public data communication system and a computer communication framework similar to that now provided for the telephone, radio, TV, and postal services.

7. Humanization of work

A number of groups pursued the idea set out in the Hedberg and Mumford theme paper that the design of computer systems should incorporate positive human objectives such as the creation of jobs which provide *more* and not less job satisfaction. The problem of how to humanize work was discussed both from the point of view of workers' needs and the effect of computer technology on jobs. Questions were asked, although not satisfactorily answered, about the meaning of concepts such as "job satisfaction", the ability to use "initiative", and the attainment of "self development" in a computer environment. Whose job satisfaction should we be primarily concerned with? The job satisfaction of computer technologists, of user management, or of clients, customers or employees? How could we find out whether these groups had the same or different job satisfaction needs? It was also emphasized that computers might have different effects on the work of white and blue collar workers. It might not be possible to resolve problems associated with the humanization of work at the corporate level, and agreements would have to be reached at a higher level by trade unions, corporations and even governments.

One group made the point that we must be aware not only of the computer's effect on job structure, but also of its effect on interpersonal relationships in the work situation. The social contact that takes place between individuals greatly assists an organization to work effectively, yet, because this contact is largely of an informal nature, it is not usually taken into account when computer systems are designed. Adverse effects can then result which were totally unforeseen by the designers of the systems. Informal social relationships and other informal practices that assist the effective functioning of the enterprise should be taken account of when design alternatives were being examined. Systems designers are becoming more willing to do this as they become increasingly aware of the social consequences of their work.

8. Privacy choice

The privacy issue was given a great deal of attention at the conference and a number of plenary papers discussed this subject, notably those of Ware, Mallet, Marks, and Gallouédec-Genuys. Some difficulty was experienced in defining what the term "privacy" meant, and it was recognized that it could have many different meanings according to who was using it, and in what kind of situation. There could be a conflict between society's need for information and the individual's need to withhold information concerning himself. Some conference participants were in favor of a general code of fair information practice with detailed rules for particular kinds of information, for example, medical data. It was recognized that the formulation of such a code could only be realized on the basis of a great deal of social trial and error and considerable experience. The Swedish government had already taken some steps in this direction. Safeguards that could prove useful were (a) the licensing of data banks; (b) professional standards for computer practitioners and for data banks; these would include codes of conduct and codes of fair information practice; (c) an increase in relevant computer education; and (d) legal protection to limit extreme forms of abuse.

Although steps were required to protect privacy, the privacy debate itself should be watched if we were not to find ourselves moving into an extreme position in which we either had closed societies with tightly controlled information channels, or alternatively, we had wide-open societies with virtually nonexistent restrictions on information flow. There are many possibilities between these two extremes and we need continually to make careful choices amongst alternatives to find solutions best fitted to our needs.

9. International choice

The Nanus paper on multinational computers also provoked considerable discussion within the seminar groups. It was recognized that we knew very little about the effects of multinational computers or how to control and influence these kinds of large-scale systems. There was a lack of appropriate international institutions to cope with multinational computer systems, and because of this, there might be undesirable consequences for weak groups such as non-unionized workers, poor citizens of less developed countries, and others who could be exploited by the "information rich". Governments in the future might have to develop multinational computer systems in order to deal with powerful multinational corporations. It was suggested that computerized multinational labor unions would provide a logical and desirable set of checks and balances against the power of computerized multinational corporations.

Alternatively, it might be possible to set up an international "watchdog" of some kind with responsibility for investigating and publicizing abuses of multinational computer systems, or it might be necessary to formulate international laws to provide sanctions against abuse. This problem was seen as already urgent, for many international corporations had set up sophisticated computer systems that crossed national boundaries. A group of world economic experts appointed by Secretary-General Kurt Waldheim has made majority recommendations to the United Nations Economic and Security Council (ECOSOC). Amid strong minority views warning against the dangers of excessive national controls, the majority report of "The Group of 20" recommended that a 35-member permanent commission be set up within ECOSOC to keep a global eye on multinational corporations.

The general conclusion on such topics related to social choice was the need to establish social priorities and to devise methods for allocating various types of resources among these. More research would help. In particular, there was an urgent need for an assessment of the impact of computer technology on world society and on existing institutions in order to enable us to identify and choose feasible and desirable futures. All countries, their trade unions, computer experts and professional societies should participate in this research, together with those groups not represented at the conference such as large corporations, government officials, the less developed countries and the public at large. Nations would have to decide if computers should be used to aid growth in the traditional sense or if they should be used to stretch scarce resources and to improve the system of allocation. But, the choice of problems for computer solution should be on the basis of human need and not on the computer's ability to solve a particular kind of problem. A sound policy for human choice requires (a) an assessment of what needs to be accomplished if computer technology is to be of benefit to mankind, and, (b) a knowledge of what has to be prevented if the adverse consequences of computer development are to be avoided. In working toward such a worldwide policy, the conference working groups particularly stressed the long-range social goal of equitable distribution of computer-catalyzed information at a global level to minimize the gap between the information rich and the information poor.

10. Social acceptability of systems

One seminar group which had two of the plenary speakers as its chairmen, Hedberg and Stamper, set out some of the characteristics of unacceptable and acceptable computer systems.

10.1. Unacceptable systems

These are likely to be characterized by:
- difficult man-computer dialogue,
- ambiguity of logic,
- diminished individual discretion,
- lack of flexibility,
- human task area adversely affected,
- undue stress imposed on individuals,

lack of responsiveness to human requirements,
inadequate timing or access to information,
lack of documentation,
cause of isolation or alienation,
lack of appropriate security of information.

These indicators illustrate that designs may fail due to neglect of *human* and *organizational* factors. It was agreed that these factors should play a more prominant part in the design process.

10.2. Acceptable systems

In the group's view, systems would be more likely to prove acceptable if the design process was supported in three essential ways.

(1) The *competence* of those participating in the system design process should be improved. These include not only the system professionals but also managers, administrators, employees, politicians, and the general public.

(2) *Tools and procedures* should be available to facilitate the solving of human and social problems encountered during design work. These include suitable *procedures* for involving those affected by the system, *technical* methods for explaining and studying the problem (e.g., a simulation of the man-computer interface) and a *methodology* of systems design that will ensure the timely identification of these problems.

(3) The *sanctions* of professional standards and of legislation will be required both nationally and internationally to ensure that human and social problems are tackled properly.

This group was responsible for many of the recommendations for action by IFIP which are set out in the last section of this chapter.

11. Toward a Computer Bill of Rights

Conference participants urged that IFIP should encourage the development of an international *Computer Bill of Rights*. This could be a law, code of practice or international agreement constructed to foster the benefits of computers, and protect the individual from any misuse of computer based information systems. It should cover the manner in which information is used to influence individuals and groups, working conditions, other aspects of life, and personal information needs. Such a Computer Bill of Rights could include the following principles:

(a) Individual citizens or groups should have a right of access to public information in order to use it for research, planning, public debate, etc.

(b) Every citizen should have the right of protection against the misuse of information which any organization has about him.

(c) Every citizen should have a right of access to information held about him, and the right to query and correct it.

(d) Individuals and groups should have the right of feasible access to information; information should be presented to them in a readily usable form, and should not be prohibitively expensive to obtain.

(e) There should be controls over the way in which private bodies collect and use information.

(f) Information should not be withheld from, or distorted in, the originating data base.

(g) It should be recognized that each man and woman has a fundamental right to an interesting and challenging job. Any emotional stress caused through an approach to job design which does not take account of human psychological needs should permit compensation through legal processes in the same way as physical injury now does.

(h) Every citizen has a right to become computer literate, if he so wishes, as part of his general and continuing education.

In addition to these major rights there are another set of issues which should be considered. For example:

(i) the assignment of personal numbers to individuals

(ii) the right of the individual to have information about himself deleted or updated

(iii) the option for an individual to include his own commentary

(iv) the ability to protect the privacy of groups as well as individuals

(v) the Bill of Rights should also protect the citizen against the misuse of multinational information systems (e.g., the transfer of information from one country to another or access to information about individuals in another country).

It should be strongly emphasized that the above guidelines are only suggestive rudiments of a Computer Bill of Rights. Many participants indicated that preparation of such a document would entail a major international and interdisciplinary effort in its own right beyond the scope of this conference, an effort that might fall within the purview, for example, of the United Nations.

12. Recommendations for IFIP

All groups saw IFIP as having an important role in furthering the ideas and recommendations discussed and formulated at the conference. It was hoped that IFIP would advance the concept of a Computer Bill of Rights by setting up a committee to consider how some of the principles and related issues listed above could be developed and implemented. As a beginning it would be useful if a "code of fair information practice" could be prepared and published for discussion, building upon the work of such individuals as Ware.

IFIP could also assist the dissemination of information about problems of human choice and computer systems through the documentation and publication of case studies illustrating the impact of computers on jobs, working conditions and the social environment. These case studies should be compiled by interdisciplinary groups of scientists.

Finally the group chaired by Hedberg and Stamper produced the following set of specific recommendations for action by IFIP.

(1) To improve the competence of systems professionals, steps should be taken to ensure that they become well qualified, not only in the technical aspects of their work, but also in the *human and organizational disciplines* involved.

(2) IFIP should try to stimulate the development of design procedures so that, to an increasing extent, technology is considered as a tool by means of which *social, organizational, individual and economic goals* can be accomplished.

(3) There should be an explicit acceptance by systems professionals that they have a duty to *assist non-professionals to understand* computer techniques as they relate to human and social issues.

(4) IFIP should keep technological innovations under review so that likely *problems* in the field of *computers and human choice* can be identified in good time, discussed, clarified, and adequately publicized with recommendations, where any are appropriate.

(5) IFIP should help to identify *areas of research* which would contribute to the understanding of human and organizational aspects of systems design. The dissemination of existing knowledge in this area should also be encouraged.

(6) As the existence of multinational information systems may make it easier to circumvent national sanction, IFIP should encourage the *harmonization of codes of practice* relating both to individuals and organizations, and pursue with UNESCO the possibility of drafting a convention that would harmonize actions by governments in this field.

This group proposed that IFIP should form a committee to follow up and develop the recommendations from this conference. Among the tasks of this committee should be an endeavour to make IFIP publications and meetings reflect the insights embodied in the above recommendations. The conference ended with a motion of agreement that such a committee should be formed.

INDEX